THE DEMISE OF THE AMERICAN EVANGELICAL

An Overview of the History of Racism and White Supremacy in the Church

Copyright © 2022 by Adrianne L. Watson

All rights reserved.

No part of this book may be reproduced in any form or by any means, electronic or mechanical, including photocopying, recording, video, or by any information or retrieval system, without prior written permission from the publisher except for the use of brief quotations in a book review.

Scripture quotations are from the ESV® Bible (The Holy Bible, English Standard Version®), copyright © 2001 by Crossway, a publishing ministry of Good News Publishers. Used by permission.

Published in the United States by Uriel Press
P.O. Box 436987, Chicago, IL 60643
www.urielpress.com

ISBN 978-0-9601047-5-8 (paperback)
ISBN 978-0-9601047-6-5 (eBook)

Cover design by Laura Duffy
Book design by Amit Dey

Printed in the United States of America

THE DEMISE OF THE AMERICAN EVANGELICAL

An Overview of the History of
Racism and White Supremacy
in the Church

MINISTER ADRIANNE WATSON

URIEL PRESS

TERMINOLOGY

LORD is the Hebrew word for the name of God; YWYH (Yahweh)

Lord is the Hebrew word for Adoni which literally means "my lords" and attributed to God

lord in all lowercase letters means "master"

Lord God in Hebrew is YWYH Elohiym translated as Lord God

ACKNOWLEDGMENTS

Editors:

Mrs. Gail Clayworth, theological edits, evangelical perspective.

Pastor E.L. Branch, theological insight.

Mr. Courtlandt Perkins, general editor.

Mrs. Anita Battista, proofreading.

This book would not be possible without my family, friends, and mentors' support. Thanks to my spiritual and theological mentor, Mrs. Gail Clayworth, for giving me sound counsel and a White evangelical perspective to challenge me throughout this book. Thanks to Courtlandt Perkins and Anita Battista for editing this book and for their perspectives. Thanks to Pastor E.L. Branch for checking my theology and challenging me to think outside the box regarding both a racial and biblical perspective. Thanks to Pastor Kenneth West Sr. for writing the foreword.

Thanks to my spiritual team of prayer warriors who held me accountable to the work of the Lord and sharpened me like iron: Lupe Arnold, Rhonda Boston, Carrie Bork, Brenda Calhoun, Norma Duran, Priscilla Haley, Jackie Massey, Anita Murphy, Mollie Watkins, Terresia Williams, and Ashli Young. Finally, I am thankful for the support from my family: Mom, Mary (Mimi), Gladi, Yvette, Vanessa, Willie Jr., Tyrone, both of my fathers-in-law Arthur Watson Sr. and Johnny Green, and to the love of my life, my husband Pastor Arthur L. Watson Jr.

*This book is dedicated to all the pioneers
who have died to fight for equality
and all the allies who have joined the fight.*

TABLE OF CONTENTS

xiii **Foreword**
by Pastor Kenneth West, Berean Bible Fellowship Church

xv **Introduction**

1 **Chapter 1**
Slavery, Racism, The Bible & The Rise of the American Evangelical

29 **Chapter 2**
The History of American Evangelical Christianity

53 **Chapter 3**
Conservative Evangelicals & The Religious Right

67 **Chapter 4**
Civil Rights & The Resurgence of White Supremacy

83 **Chapter 5**
Justice & The American Evangelical

111 **Chapter 6**
The Demise of Evangelicalism through Politics and Presidents

141 **Chapter 7**
President Trump & the Modern-Day Evangelical

183 **Chapter 8**
Where Do Evangelicals Go from Here?

205 **Conclusion**

215 **Appendix**

221 **Works Cited List**

FOREWORD

Terms such as "courageous conversation," "Unity Table," and "Racial reconciliation" — which is more accurately expressed as ethnic reconciliation—have become prevalent in church circles. But how can there possibly be reconciliation without first recognition and the repentance of past grievances and hurts? In *The Demise of the American Evangelical*, Adrianne Watson puts feet to the faith required to truly engage in the courageous conversation concerning the evangelical Christian in America. Minister Watson does a masterful job of handling the delicate topic of how White supremacy infiltrated and took root in American Evangelicalism. And how the effects of White supremacy affect the witness of the faithful Evangelical Christian. The author tackles the task with grace, passion, compassion, and mercy that is not devoid of accountability. Watson does not ask you to take a leap of faith concerning her premise that there is a remaining White supremacy framework in American Evangelicalism. Instead, she leads you on a journey to explore the origination and propagation of the worldview and system that has hijacked true Evangelicalism. But *The Demise of the American Evangelical* doesn't leave you there. Mirroring the Apostle Paul's meticulousness, Watson also provides a prescription and a path forward for the Evangelical Church to reclaim her damaged reputation in the world.

I have known Minister Watson for nearly a decade, and the same passion that she has for ministry, missions — local and global—serving, and teaching is evident in the pages of this book. Reading this book will require you to check your biases, unconscious or otherwise, on the first page and allow your mind to be a blank tapestry able to consume the book's material. In the Introduction, the author warns that the material in the book may make you angry, and you may be tempted to put the book down; but allow me to encourage you as the churches in the region of Galatia were strengthened — "Let us not lose heart in doing good, for in due time we will reap if we do not grow weary." (Gal. 6.9 NASB)

You may ask yourself, "Why should I read such a challenging book?"

The answer is, "The stakes are much too high not to!"

Pastor Kenneth T. West, Sr.
Founding Pastor
Berean Bible Fellowship Church
Plano, TX

INTRODUCTION

"For this is the message that you have heard from the beginning, that we should love one another" (1 John 3.11).

Suppose you are thinking about skipping the Introduction. In that case, this is an introduction that you want to read to help you understand this book. In full transparency, this will not be an easy read for most American evangelicals who have not begun the work of identifying racism or biased behaviors in their hearts. Although this book will target mostly White evangelicals, People of Color play a pivotal role in the necessary changes to heal to the church. This book will be an equal opportunity offender as I will unapologetically reveal racist policies supported by our political system in the Republican and Democratic parties and the church. I will give examples of racist pastors, politicians, and presidents as additional evidence to uncover racism and White supremacy patterns. My goal is not to be politically correct or express preferences but to be brutally honest and biblically correct. I must make it known that I do not hate America or American evangelicals. There are times that I am proud of my country, and there are other times that I am embarrassed or enraged by the actions of our Christian leaders. Moreover, what I hate the most is how the world views American evangelicals.

I will define several words throughout this book to address the sins that plague American evangelicals beginning with the Antebellum years through the present day. The defined words are evangelical, moderate, conservative, progressive, liberal, biblical justice, patriotism, nationalism, systemic or foundational racism, racist, antiracism, White supremacy, White Nationalism, and Christian Identity. In addition to defining the previously mentioned words, this book will also give a historical overview of American history and address these additional topics: slavery, the Confederacy, the Constitution, oppression of the poor and People of Color, and politics. I will explain how biases and discrimination twist the evangelical's worldview and what evangelicals need to do to overcome their stained reputation. My goal is to provide clear distinctions between biblical Christianity and today's twenty-first-century version of evangelicalism. At the end of the book, I will offer a practical application for evangelicals to identify their biases and implement changes where it is necessary.

Dear evangelical brothers and sisters, you have forgotten your purpose. Your purpose as a Christ-follower is to serve the poor and the oppressed, live a holy and righteous life and spread the good news of Jesus. Unfortunately, the focus for numerous evangelicals has shifted to the consumption of politics and power. My heart is grieved at the state of the American evangelical as evangelicalism has become an elitist and exclusive religion based on White supremacy undertones and divisive political rhetoric. Too many evangelicals have aligned themselves with people and conspiracy theory groups that are overtly evil. There is an ever-increasing absence of empathy and love for those people that evangelicals disagree with politically. As countless evangelicals focus on picking a political side and alienating the opposition, the result is a lack of resolve for biblical justice and truth, especially for the poor and People of Color.

The increasing divide in American evangelicalism is no longer about theological or denominational differences. The divide is more about the Christian's role in politics and supporting a particular political party. America's mistreatment of slaves in the past is something that most evangelicals would agree is an egregious sin on our nation. The evangelical's neglect of the poor, the oppressed, their lack of love for the LGBTQ community, their stance surrounding systemic racism, and the support for evil politicians have also hurt the reputation of Christianity. Evangelicals have shamefully given public support for leaders, worship pastors, celebrities, politicians, and vigilantes whose mouths are "filled with cursing and deceit and oppression; under [their] tongue[s] are mischief and iniquity . . . The helpless are crushed, sink down, and fall by his might" (Psa. 10.7-10). Worst of all, too many evangelicals think supporting this kind of behavior is amusing instead of heartbreaking. By no means does their behavior exemplify the gospel message of Jesus' moral standards or represent all evangelicals. I plan to expose the lies and false indoctrination that too many American evangelicals have come to believe. My prayer is that this book will challenge you to see the truth. This book might make you angry, but hopefully, it convicts your heart. I hope you will be inspired to become an ally who will expose all forms of racism and White supremacy and be a bridge to the communities of the poor, the oppressed, and People of Color without compromise.

The Bible says, "The righteous hates falsehood, but the wicked brings shame and disgrace" (Pro. 13.5). To the American evangelicals reading this book, it is time to course-correct and move back to the gospel message of Christ. I can no longer sit by and watch prominent evangelicals wink at sin and embarrass the name of Christ. I cannot continue to watch the church become a place of ridicule instead of a place of refuge. Change must start with you as you are reading this book. If your heart is willing, you can do the necessary work to change the narrative so that the gospel message of love and salvation does not become eradicated. Furthermore, suppose you are a White pastor reading this book. In that case, I pray that you will embrace increasing your racial intelligence and learn how to identify implicit biases in your sermons and your thoughts about politics. After you have identified these areas, you must be brave enough to increase your congregation's awareness of the social responsibilities that God's church has to the poor and the marginalized to achieve true multiculturalism, which celebrates the beauty of ethnicity in the gospel.

The most important lessons you should learn from this book are not the historical facts but what you discover about yourself. Will you retreat or get angry at my words? Will you stop reading halfway through the book? Or will you do the demanding work to let the words in this book challenge your thinking? I am asking that, as you read the pages of this book,

Introduction

do a self-examination of your implicit biases and racial views you grew up believing, no matter your racial identity. Even if it gets uncomfortable, I challenge you to continue reading this book in its entirety and pray when you feel convicted or even angry. If you have already begun doing the arduous work of being an ally for the poor and People of Color, then I ask that you challenge any other areas of bias that you may still need to focus on and help others do the same.

Racism is not a sin that is exclusive to White people because everyone has biases. If you are a Person of Color reading this book, you are not exempt from racist thoughts or actions. Therefore, I ask that you allow the Holy Spirit to heal your hurt, so you are willing to collaborate with our White brothers and sisters who want to be allies for change and not be a part of the problem. I challenge my fellow Christians of Color to work together and not sabotage the activism of other groups. As you witness our White brothers and sisters doing the work, I also ask that you give them the grace to make mistakes, get frustrated, and ask you questions as they work things out in their hearts. I plead for all readers to have a heart change for the evangelical witness, no matter your race or your gender, and to be leaders of light and truth amid these dark and polarized times. I also want to remind you that the enemy of this world wants nothing but to destroy the church's reputation and, therefore, diminish the beautiful message of the gospel. However, let us remember the Apostle Paul's words.

> "Finally, be strong in the Lord and in the strength of his might. Put on the whole armor of God, that you may be able to stand against the schemes of

the devil. For we do not wrestle against flesh and blood, but against the rulers, against the authorities, against the cosmic powers over this present darkness, against the spiritual forces of evil in the heavenly places. Therefore, take up the whole armor of God, that you may be able to withstand in the evil day, and having done all, to stand firm. Stand therefore, having fastened on the belt of truth, and having put on the breastplate of righteousness, and, as shoes for your feet, having put on the readiness given by the gospel of peace. In all circumstances take up the shield of faith, with which you can extinguish all the flaming darts of the evil one; and take the helmet of salvation, the sword of the Spirit, which is the word of God, praying at all times in the Spirit, with all prayer and supplication" (Eph. 6.10-18).

To my readers, I want you to know that this is spiritual warfare and American evangelicals are on the front line. Evangelicals, you cannot win this fight without putting on God's spiritual armor, which requires self-reflection, humility, lamenting, repentance, passion, and a desire for sustained change.

Sincerely,
Minister Adrianne Watson

CHAPTER 1
SLAVERY, RACISM, THE BIBLE & THE AMERICAN EVANGELICAL

"If anyone says, 'I love God,' and hates his brother, he is a liar; for he who does not love his brother whom he has seen cannot love God whom he has not seen" (1 John 4.20).

What is more important to you, politics, or your relationship with Jesus? American evangelicals would argue that politics should never come before a personal relationship with Jesus. However, the actions of numerous evangelicals indicate that they believe politics is as equally as important as their "religion." I would even go as far as to say that today, many American evangelicals prefer to support the actions of racist narcissistic politicians than support biblical truth. More precisely, evangelicals who worship the America of White capitalism, power, and privilege replace biblical truth for their political preferences. The importance of "loving thy neighbor as thyself" has been substituted with worshipping politicians and political preferences. There has been an elevation of the American flag, the National Anthem, a resurgence of the Confederate flag, and fighting to maintain Confederate statues and legacies. However, to the Christ-follower, God said, "You shall have no other gods before Me" (Exo. 20.3).

In the eyes of non-Christians today, evangelicals are synonymous with racists. A racist believes that their race is superior and is usually intolerant of other races. A racist is not necessarily an extremist or a violent person who burns crosses, lynches African Americans, or kills Jews. On the contrary, a racist is someone who believes that his race is superior and uses financial and political means as an advantage to elevate his race. In contrast, antiracism is more than not being a racist. Antiracism is an overt action against racism. For example, an antiracist actively seeks opportunities to expose, contradict, and speak out against racism, oppression, and social injustices. An antiracist acts as an ally for those individuals oppressed by racism and unjust social and judicial systems.

In contrast, White supremacy is a form of racism and a belief in the superiority of the White race above all other racial groups. Misinformation and divisive rhetoric coming from White governing officials, Christian talk-show hosts, and evangelical pastors who repeat White supremacist assertions contribute to the elevation and normalization of White supremacy today. Unfortunately, many evangelicals contribute to the normalization of White supremacy because they do not believe that policies or politics can be racist. In addition, the evangelical's denial of racism as a social construct is causing disunity and a divide in the church (Kendi 4). The disunity in evangelicalism is also separating White evangelical circles from People of Color. Evangelicals who remain in denial of racism that still exists in our country remain disconnected from the harsh realities and suffering of the poor and People of Color. Both racism and greed have had an influential impact on America's foundations, beginning with the justification of slavery, the neglect of the poor, and silence from the church. To fully understand today's polarization, we must go back in history and look at the Bible, slavery, and the American evangelical.

Racist and discriminatory behavior is not something new but has existed for centuries. For example, God commanded the Prophet, Jonah, "Arise, go to Nineveh, that great city, and call out against it, for their evil has come up before me. But Jonah rose to flee to Tarshish from the presence of the LORD" (Jon. 1.2-3). Nineveh, mentioned several times in the Bible, was the sixty-mile-wide capital of Assyria and home of the Assyrian empire. A Black man named Nimrod founded Nineveh (Gen. 10.11). Nineveh was known for prosperity, fertile ground, and agricultural and economic prosperity from exporting various metals. The people of Nineveh were notorious for their absolute rule of terror and cruelty. Nineveh was also famous for the worship of the fertility goddess Ishtar ("Brakeman 1"). Jonah fled to Tarshish, which is modern-day Lebanon, instead of obeying God's command to preach repentance to the people of Nineveh. Jonah was indignant because the LORD wanted to give the people of Nineveh an opportunity to repent from their sins. For whatever reason, Jonah, a Jew, did not want the Nineveh people to repent or receive God's grace. The Jews were known for their exclusivity, acting as if they were better than all other races of people because they were the chosen people of God.

Sadly, many American evangelicals' actions resemble Jonah because they have moved away from the message of love and repentance and instead have adopted a message of exclusivity, hate, and destructive rhetoric. After spending three days inside the belly of a giant whale, Jonah obeyed God's command. Jonah went to Nineveh and proclaimed the destruction coming in the next forty days if they did not repent. The Bible tells us, "The people of Nineveh believed God" (Jon. 3.5). After hearing the message of repentance, the people of Nineveh turned away from their sins. Jesus even mentions the people of Nineveh's repentance while he condemns the Jewish leaders of his day (Matt. 12.41[1]). Several years later, Nineveh and the Assyrian Empire fell siege to the Babylonians in 612 AD. After Jesus' crucifixion, the Assyrian people became some of the early church's first converts, and the *Assyrian Church* continues to exist today ("Ancient Nineveh"). I fear that too many American evangelicals have become Jonah-like, buying into the self-serving political agendas of racism, exclusivity, hate, and entitlement. As a result, they are operating from a place of rebellion, just like Jonah. The version of evangelicalism we are witnessing today no longer hints at America's racist past but has exposed and embraced its links to racism and White supremacy. Unfortunately, various evangelicals are duped by a religious subculture that has long since left the gospel message.

---

[1] "The men of Nineveh will rise up at the judgment with this generation and condemn it, for they repented at the preaching of Jonah, and behold something greater than Jonah is here." Matt. 12.41.

There are several other examples of discrimination mentioned in the Bible besides Jonah's story. The Jews were often discriminatory toward the Gentiles and Samaritans. You may think that racism began in America with the arrival of slave ships in 1619, but that is not entirely true, as these examples show us. As a social construct, race was invented to justify slavery and White supremacy in the West by the first European settlers. In the 1600s, the Europeans began classifying human beings into distinct categories based on skin color and used the term "race" for these classifications. America's racist ideology emerged when the Puritan settlers saw their presence and dominance in the Northern Colonies as "God-ordained." These Puritans misinterpreted God's promises to the Israelites and instead claimed America as their own "promised land." Indentured English and Dutch immigrants who came to the Americas physically worked with Africans in the Virginia Colonies. Taking advantage of the free labor class, the Planter Class[2] became wealthy from the transatlantic slave trade. In the seventeenth century, King Charles II gave land to the English settlers in Virginia and the Carolinas, and the Planters began to see themselves as an upper-class society. The English workers, or indentured servants, were the foundation of the White working class. After years of harsh treatment, the English indentured servants revolted and fled to the Carolinas, resulting in a labor force decline. As a result, the Planters

---

[2] The Planter Class was made up of Southern Aristocrats who dominated the seventeenth- and eighteenth-century agricultural markets through the transatlantic slave trade. They were known for planting crops like tobacco, cotton, and coffee.

chose the economic gain of slave ownership to offset the labor shortage from English workers who fled. This decision would prove to be much more profitable, so more slaves were trafficked for labor ("African Americans: Overview").

In 1664, the colonial government provided slave traffickers sixty acres of land for every slave laborer they added to work the land (Harper). Virginia declared a law in 1667 that Christian baptism no longer took away an African's slave status, nor would they have the same rights and privileges as European workers. In 1668, New Jersey implemented fugitive slave laws[3] to ensure that slaves who fled from their masters could not gain freedom. The distinction drawn between the social classes, the European working class, Africans, and Christians, set the foundations for laws that would lay the groundwork for privileges for the White working class. In 1704, New Jersey passed a slave code preventing African Americans from owning property. This social class structure initiated what we understand today as foundational racism against Africans and other minorities. In the eighteenth century, slave laws shifted from the status of the father's freed state to the mother's status. This shift allowed hundreds of thousands of children to be born as slaves and slave owners to inherit slaves, including those they fathered by rape. At this time, Europeans began calling themselves "White" and referred to Africans as "Black." In 1768, a court system was created solely to punish crimes by slaves. By 1829, half of the States had abolished slavery, but ninety

---

[3] Not to be confused with the Fugitive Slave Act passed by Congress on September 18, 1850, requiring all escaped slaves to be returned to their masters.

percent of African Americans remained enslaved ("African Americans: Overview). White superiority and advantages were subsequently passed down from generation to generation. Knowing this, I do not understand why it is so difficult for many American evangelicals to believe that racism and White supremacy never ended when slavery was abolished.

In addition to passing laws, Christian pastors embraced slavery and taught their congregations to believe in White superiority and view their slaves as personal property. Americans have been misled to believe that only Southerners and Confederates owned slaves, but most of the Christian institutions in Virginia owned slaves (Watson). For example, in 1685, a minister named James Blair introduced owning slaves to colleges. Churches had sold child slaves by the time the child was eight years old. Churches enticed ministers in England to relocate to Virginia so that those who owned slaves could use them to care for the orphans and the elderly (Watson). Pastors preached the gospel of Jesus from their pulpits but simultaneously owned slaves, often in the harshest of conditions. In 2006, Virginia Theological Seminary reported that eighty-two percent of the Virginia Episcopal clergy in the 1860 census owned at least one slave, and many owned dozens (Oast 87). Churches like the Anglican Church, Catholics, Lutherans, Presbyterians, and the Church of England established by the Virginia Colony owned and sold adult and child slaves (Watson). For example, Princeton University's third President, Jonathan Edwards, Sr., was influential in American religious and intellectual thought. Edwards considered slaves his spiritual equal, but he owned slaves his entire career (Anderson).

Some preachers arrogantly believed that without slavery, Africans would have never been introduced to Christ, which is a lie. While Christianity was sweeping its way across the colonies, Native Americans and Mexicans were murdered by groups like the Texas Rangers near the border (Lenthang). There is too much evidence of White supremacy in the church's history for evangelicals to ignore the negative impact it has had on generations of People of Color (Williams, Y. "Most"). Therefore, rewriting history to make slavery palatable and downplay the murders of several ethnic groups will only allow for more decades of injustices.

Christians who opposed slavery were known as abolitionists. In the 1830s and 1840s, abolitionists convinced many Northerners that slavery was inhumane. White Southerners were enraged because the abolitionist movement threatened their financial stability (African Americans: Overview). Other Christian groups like the Quakers, also known as Levelers, initially participated in slavery in the colonial days. Eventually, the Quakers became abolitionists, advocating for equality and liberal reforms for African slaves. The Quakers resisted racial enslavement and, in 1783, submitted a petition to Parliament speaking out against the slave trade. Unfortunately, Parliament denied the Quaker's petition and created laws that made racism against Africans more prevalent. For example, shortly before the Civil War in 1857, the Supreme Court ruled that a slave was his master's property and not a U.S. citizen. This ruling was known as the Dred Scott decision. Dred Scott was a slave who sought his freedom because he lived in a "free" territory with his slave owner. The Supreme Court also declared that the Missouri Compromise, which prohibited slavery in certain areas, was unconstitutional because it deprived slave owners of their "property" ("Dred Scott Decision"). Shamefully, the Supreme Court's decisions in the Dred Scott and Missouri Compromise cases are just examples of how slavery and colonization were justified. Some evangelicals viewed this time when Native Americans were removed from their homeland, slaughtering Mexicans, and enslaving Africans as necessary evils. Others take this view further by claiming that slavery was humane, Africans did not mind being slaves, and chattel slavery was similar to the laws that protected the Jews' slaves (Exo. 21.1–32).

Although the Bible mentions slavery, Christians used these passages to condone or justify slavery. In the Old Testament, the Jews took slaves for themselves, but Moses wrote various laws explaining how the Jews were to treat their slaves. The Jews were forbidden to mistreat their slaves. The children of Israel remembered when the Egyptian slave masters treated them harshly and cried out to God to free them from the Egyptians' cruelty (Exo. 6.5). The Lord granted the Israelites requests and delivered them (14.1–30). After the Israelites became free, Moses constructed laws concerning slavery that prohibited murder, mistreatment, kidnapping, and chattel slavery. For example, Moses said, "Whoever steals a man and sells him, and anyone found in possession of him, shall be put to death" (21.16). Moses also included stipulations in the law providing a Year of Jubilee so that slavery did not continue from generation to generation. The Year of Jubilee occurred after seven sets of seven years or completion of forty-nine years. In the book of Leviticus, Moses recorded how the children of Israel observed the Year of Jubilee. He said, "On the Day of Atonement you shall sound the trumpet throughout all your land. And you shall consecrate the fiftieth year and proclaim liberty throughout the land to all its inhabitants. It shall be a jubilee for you, when each of you shall return to his property and each of you shall return to his clan" (Lev. 25.9–10). Moses also instructed the Jews how to free their slaves during the Year of Jubilee. He said, "If your brother becomes poor beside you and sells himself to you, you shall not make him serve as a slave: he shall be with you as a hired worker and as a sojourner. He shall serve with you until the year of the jubilee. Then he shall go out from you, he, and his children with him, and go back to his own clan and return to the possession of his fathers" (Lev. 25.39–40).

Slavery in ancient Israel was voluntary servitude similar to the indentured servitude of Dutch and European immigrants in America. The poor often sold themselves into slavery to pay off debts or to find a better way of life. Many of the poor and widows lived without shelter or provisions, so the only means of survival was to sell themselves as indentured servants. Moses gave strict instructions never to sell fellow Israelites into slavery (Lev. 25.43). Even the Gentile slaves were given provisions and protected by Mosaic Law (Exo. 20.10, 21.20–21; Deu. 5.14, 23.15–16). In contrast, Christians who used the Bible to justify chattel slavery knew exactly what they were doing. Interestingly, the words slaves and slavery are not found in the U.S. Constitution, but our forefathers willfully ignored the humanity of African slaves in favor of economic self-interest ("African Americans: Overview"). African slavery in America was neither indentured servitude nor was it voluntary. Slaves in America were property, and there were no laws preventing slave owners from abusing, beating, raping, or killing slaves. There is absolutely no comparison between slavery in the Bible and America's history of chattel slavery.

The Apostle Paul also explained slave treatment in the book of Timothy in addition to warnings about false teachers and several kinds of sins. He said, "For the sexually immoral, men who practice homosexuality, *enslavers*, liars, perjurers, and whatever else is contrary to sound doctrine" (1 Tim. 1.10, emphasis added). Let us focus on the *enslavers*. The Greek word for enslavers is *andrapodistais*, translated as "slave traders" or "man stealers." Andrapodistais is used once in the entire Greek New Testament. Both "slave traders" and "man stealers" can also be defined as those who kidnap or steal to make someone a slave for profit (Clarke). The Apostle Paul condemned slave traders, enslavers, and human traf-fickers. If the first Christians who set foot in the "New World" embraced Paul's teaching, chattel slavery would have never existed in America.

The Bible is clear that all of humanity is created in the *imago dei*, that is, the image of God. "God created man in His own image, in the image of God he created him; male and female he created them" (Gen. 1.27). God said, "Let us make man in our image, after our likeness" (Gen. 1.26). Unfortunately, in America, People of Color are not always treated as image-bearers of God. The Apostle Paul also declared, "There is neither Jew nor Greek, there is neither slave nor free, there is no male and female, for you are all one in Christ Jesus" (Gal. 3.28). I previously mentioned that the Jews believed they were superior to all non-Jews because of God's covenants with them. However, Paul's statement, "There is neither Jew nor Greek," meant that the Jews were not superior to the Gentiles (the Greeks); instead, Jews and Greeks are equal in Christ. Secondly, Paul declared that slaves and free men are equal. Therefore, even the universal existence of slavery did not exclude slaves from access to salvation. In Christ, the slave and the master are equal. Finally, Paul declared that men and women are also equal. This statement would have been highly controversial in ancient days. Society viewed women as inferior beings, but Paul said that women are equal to men in Christ. Knowing Paul's teachings, it is difficult to understand how racism and sexism exist in evangelical circles today. Paul understood the biblical principle that all people are equal in Christ, no matter their age, gender, race, or socioeconomic status. We are all saved in the same manner, by grace through faith. Baptism in the Holy Spirit occurs at the point of conversion, and He seals us as a guarantee (Eph. 1.14), and we all have the same privileges in Christ with the promise of eternal life (John 3.16). Therefore, Christians should treat everyone as equals because we are all made in the image of God, and as Christ-followers, we are all saved by the blood of Jesus Christ.

The Declaration of Independence states, "We hold these truths to be self-evident, that all men are created equal, that they are endowed by their Creator with certain unalienable Rights, that among these are Life, Liberty and the pursuit of Happiness." At least on paper, our forefathers understood this premise even if they were only referring to White men who owned property. President Abraham Lincoln, whom most American evangelicals consider the most excellent American Christian President of all time, also did not believe that African slaves were equal to European settlers. The question remains if Lincoln was really a professing Christian or just a free thinker, but either way, evangelicals claim Lincoln as one of their own. In the Lincoln-Douglas Debates on August 21, 1858, Abraham Lincoln said, "I have no purpose to introduce political and social equality between the white and black races. There is a physical difference between the two, which, in my judgment, will probably forever forbid their living together upon the footing of perfect equality, and inasmuch as it becomes a necessity that there must be a difference, I, as well as Judge Douglas, am in favor of the race to which I belong having the superior position" (Abraham Lincoln Speech). Lincoln's statement affirms the racism that is threaded throughout America's history, laws, and churches.

Unfortunately, racism and White supremacy are learned behaviors passed down from generation to generation. Throughout American evangelical history, racism is perpetuated through education, textbooks, entertainment, media, and especially American evangelical preachers. These evangelicals intentionally diminished the contributions of People of Color throughout the Scriptures by glossing over their stories. Although some pastors did not overtly teach racist rhetoric to their congregations, they were complicit in their silence of slave treatment and the oppression of People of Color. The children of Israel were guilty of these same sins and more. For example, the prophet Amos rebuked the Israelites for living in sin, oppressing the poor, and swindling the helpless, which only tarnished God's name (Amos 5.21–24). The children of Israel were not following the Ten Commandments, or more importantly, the commandment to love thy neighbor as thyself. Instead, the Israelites took advantage of their neighbors and were only concerned about themselves. Amos' rebuke expressed God's disdain for the Israelites lack of justice and held them accountable for their actions (Swindoll). The sins that beckoned Amos' rebuke of the children of Israel are the same sins that plague many American evangelicals today. Amos rebuked the children of Israel for looking out for their self-interests. In the same manner, this is a warning to evangelicals who continue to abuse the name of Christ in quest of their personal, financial, or political gain.

The Apostle Paul publicly rebuked the Apostle Peter, also known as Cephas, for racism and discrimination. "When Cephas came to Antioch, I opposed him to his face, because he stood condemned. For before certain men came from James, he was eating with the Gentiles; but when they came, he drew back and separated himself, fearing the circumcision party. And the rest of the Jews acted hypocritically along with him, so that even Barnabas was led astray by their hypocrisy. But when I saw that their conduct was not in step with the truth of the gospel, I said to Cephas before them all, 'If you though a Jew, live like a Gentile and not like a Jew, how can you force the Gentiles to live like Jews?'" (Gal. 2.11–14). Antioch was a multicultural church filled with Gentile (non-Jew) converts. Peter was eating and drinking with the Gentiles, having an exciting time until the Jews from Jerusalem arrived. In front of the Jews, Peter acted like he was not associated with the Gentile converts, and he completely ignored his friends. Paul was so enraged with Peter's behavior that he got in Peter's face in front of the entire congregation and called Peter out. Paul gave us a clear example of our responsibility as Christ-followers to call out racism and discrimination, especially when it is occurring in the church.

Today, you can witness examples of evangelicals laughing at racist comments spewed from "Christian" politicians' mouths and evangelical megachurch pastors. Other pastors turn their backs on the poor and the oppressed, citing "minorities were not raised to value hard work or education" (Smietana). Fortunately, there are prominent evangelicals who are calling out the complicity of the White evangelical community. For example, Dr. Robert P. Jones, CEO, and Founder of Public Religion Research Institute (PRRI) and a leading scholar and commentator of religion and politics, said that White evangelicals are "perpetuating White supremacy" (Jones). In other words, the framework of American evangelicalism is deeply rooted in White supremacy and not just extremist groups like the Ku Klux Klan, Skinheads, or White Nationalists but in the shared beliefs of typical White American evangelicals. America's forefathers never intended for this country to be a country of equality for all races. America was always supposed to be dominated and led by the White race, more importantly, White men. For centuries, American evangelicalism has played an integral part in perpetuating these sins and, unfortunately, continues to do so. Fortunately, God loves humanity so much that He sent His son Jesus to die on the cross to save us from all sins (John 3.16). As Christ-followers, we must remember we are all one in Christ (Gal. 3.23). Heaven will represent every nation, every tongue, every tribe, and every skin color (Rev. 7.9). As Christians, we must err on the side of love and grace instead of hateful rhetoric. We must uphold justice and righteousness and denounce injustice and unrighteousness. For "to do righteousness and justice is more acceptable to the LORD than sacrifice" (Pro. 21.3).

When American evangelicals operate from racism or hate, the beauty of multiculturalism displayed throughout the Scriptures becomes diminished. For centuries, slave owners and White evangelical pastors downplayed the importance of People of Color in the Bible. They intentionally removed and twisted portions of the Scriptures to manipulate and line their pockets. During the slave trades, kidnapped and enslaved Africans in Haiti staged a revolt and overthrew their slave owners. When the rest of the Western world heard about the Haitian slave revolt, slave owners in the Americas and Caribbean began manipulating the Bible so their slaves would not get any ideas. Slave owners removed the majority of Old Testament scriptures like the story of the Israelites fleeing Egypt and portions of the New Testament. The primary factor for removing portions of the Bible was the fear that slaves worldwide could potentially revolt. Passages that included stories of slavery were twisted to reinforce the treatment of slaves and to own them as property (Little "Why"). For example, one of the lies that continue to be elevated in White supremacy circles today is most commonly known as the "Curse of Ham." The Curse of Ham propaganda, most commonly perpetrated by Christian slave owners, the Klan, and Mormons, was used to justify slavery. The leader of Mormonism, Joseph Smith, believed the entire Black race descended from the Canaanites and therefore deserved slavery. Both the Klan and Mormons gave too much credence to Ham's cursed lineage as a justification for the enslavement of Africans. Even today, Mormons and the Ku Klux Klan teach that all Black people are cursed, slavery was justified, Black people deserve enslavement, and Black people are inferior to all other races.

I seriously doubt slave owners read the book of Philemon to their slaves. Paul wrote to a fellow Christian named Philemon to command him to treat his slave Onesimus like an equal. Paul said, "I am bold enough in Christ to command you to do what is required, yet for love's sake I prefer to appeal to you—I, Paul, an old man now a prisoner also for Christ Jesus—I appeal to you for my child, Onesimus, whose father I became in my imprisonment. (Formerly he was useless to you, but now he is indeed useful to you and to me.) I am sending him back to you, sending my very heart. I would have been glad to keep him with me, in order that he might serve me on your behalf during my imprisonment for the gospel, but I preferred to do nothing without your consent in order that your goodness might not be by compulsion but of your own accord. For this perhaps is why he was parted from you for a while, that you might have him back forever, no longer as a bondservant but more than a bondservant, as a beloved brother- especially to me, but how much more to you, both in the flesh and in the Lord. So, if you consider me your partner, receive him as you would receive me" (Philem. 1.8–18).

Instead of talking about Paul's message to treat slaves as equals, slave owners used Scripture to support the racist ideologies of the Curse of Ham. Before Genesis 9, there is no mention of Noah's racial identity or his sons. American historians began linking Ham to the African race in the nineteenth century to justify American slavery. Prominent Christian, Islamic, and Jewish scholars believed Ham was a man of either Black or African descent and a cursed lineage. "And the sons of Noah, that went forth of the ark, were Shem, and Ham, and Japheth. (Ham was the father of Canaan.)

These three were the sons of Noah, and from these the people of the whole earth dispersed. Noah began to be a man of the soil, and he planted a vineyard. He drank of the wine and became drunk and lay uncovered in his tent. And Ham, the father of Canaan, saw the nakedness of his father, and told his two brothers outside. Then Shem and Japheth took a garment, and laid it on both their shoulders, and walked backward and covered the nakedness of their father. Their faces were backward, and they did not see father's nakedness. When Noah awoke from his wine and knew what his youngest son had done to him, he said, 'Cursed be Canaan; a servant of servants shall he be unto his brothers.' And he said, 'Blessed be the Lord the God of Shem; and let Canaan be his servant'" (Gen. 9.18–27).

Verse twenty-seven is the central verse emphasized by slaveowners and racists because it says, "Let Canaan be his servant." One might wonder why Noah cursed Ham's son Canaan but did not curse Ham? Some theologians think Noah cursed Ham's son because he was humiliated. In this theory, Ham saw Noah's nakedness, so Noah retaliated and cursed Ham's son Canaan (Ross 41). Other scholars believe this passage refers to some same-sex act while Noah was in a drunken stupor. However, two verses of scripture affirm this view as a strict instruction against incest (Lev. 18.6, 20.17). However, my theological assessment is that Noah cursed Ham's son out of his embarrassment from drunkenness. In that society, shame was a big deal. Ham laughed about Noah's nakedness, and if the incident were revealed in the community, it would have brought Noah shame. Honestly, who has the power to curse anyone but God himself? Noah's words were merely his own words, and they were not God's words. God did not curse Ham's son Canaan; Noah did. The Curse of Ham, relating to the enslavement of the African race, was derived from a lie by White supremacists to justify racism and slavery.

What contradicts the Curse of Ham lie is, if Ham were a Black man, wouldn't that mean that Noah or his wife might also be Black or at least biracial? Wouldn't he be of the same ethnicity as his brothers Shem and Japheth if Ham were Black? However, according to the Curse of Ham claims, only the Black race was cursed by God (which it was not), and White men should enslave African descendants. Noah's grandsons were Cush, Egypt, Put, and Canaan (Gen. 10.6). The Curse of Ham lie stems from the name Cush, which means Black or Ethiopian in Hebrew. However, Noah did not curse Cush or Ham but Canaan. Despite these facts, most scholars continue to perpetuate the lie that Ham was a Black man of African descent cursed by God. The so-called cursing of the African race has resulted in the oppression of African nations, as was seen in the Transatlantic slave trade and in Apartheid in South Africa (La Feuvre).

Contradictory to this lie is the deductive reasoning about the origins of the other descendants of Ham; the Egyptians, Libyans, and Canaanites (7–20). Since the Egyptians, Libyans, and Canaanites all descended from Ham, they must be of African or of Middle Eastern descent. Many scholars continue to argue that Egyptians were Caucasian. Do scholars believe this argument because the Egyptians educated Moses? How can some of Ham's descendants be Black people of African descent and not all the others? How are Nimrod's advancements reconciled? Not only was Nimrod a Black man who was the son of Cush, but he was also and from the lineage of Ham. Nimrod "was the first on earth to be a mighty man. He was a mighty hunter before the LORD" (8–9). The Bible gives credit to Nimrod for building the kingdoms "Babel, Erech, Accad, and Calneh, in the land of Shinar. From that land he went into Assyria and built Nineveh, Rehoboth-Ir, Calah, and Resen between Nineveh and Calah" (10–12). Nimrod was significant in the Bible for all of his outstanding accomplishments. If all African people are cursed, why did Moses marry an Ethiopian woman named Zipporah and have two sons? (Num. 12.1). Zipporah's Black father, Jethro, was a priest of Midian and advised Moses to delegate responsibility to help judge the people of Israel (Exo. 18.1–27). If all African people were cursed, why did Moses ask Hobab, the son of a Midianite, to scout out the promised land (Num. 10.29)?

As you can see, the argument of the enslavement of the African race due to the Curse of Ham contradicts logic and whitewashes the essential roles of the People of Color mentioned in the Bible. There are other examples of biblical characters who were People of Color that are often underrepresented or understated. The Ethiopian Queen of Sheba was the richest of her time (1 Kings 10; 2 Chr. 9). In the Song of Solomon, King Solomon's lover is a dark-skinned woman (Song of Sol. 1.5), and his wife is the daughter of Pharaoh (1 Kings 3.1). The Prophet Zephaniah, who has a book of the Bible named after him, was a Black man from the lineage of Cush (Zep. 1.1). Abraham's slave Hagar was an Egyptian woman, and his son Ishmael was biracial (Gen. 21.8–21). Jacob sojourned in the land of Ham in Egypt's region (Gen. 46.6; Psa. 105.23), and the Egyptians were the most advanced people of their time (Gen. 46.6; Psa. 105.23).

Judah had sons from two Canaanite women, Tamar and Shuah. Shuah's three sons were named Er, Onan, and Shelah (Gen. 38.2–5). Tamar's two sons were named Pharez and Zerah (1 Chr. 2.4; Gen. 38.29-30). Joseph married an Egyptian woman, the daughter of a priest named Asenath, and they had two sons, Ephraim and Manasseh (Gen. 41.50-52, 48.5). A Canaanite woman believed in Jesus when he withdrew to Tyre and Sidon (Matt. 15.21–22). Simon of Cyrene, present-day Libya, who carried Jesus' cross because he was too weak from being whipped, was also a Black man (Luke 23.26–27; Mark 15.21; Matt. 27.32). In Scripture, Simon of Cyrene's sons, Rufus and Alexander are also mentioned (Rom. 16:13). Simon the Canaanite, also known as Simon the Zealot or Niger, was an apostle, a prophet, and a teacher who was also a descendent of Ham (Acts 13.1; Luke 6.15; Matt. 10.4; Mark 3.18). Lucious of Cyrene was a prophet and teacher alongside Simon, also known as Niger (Acts 13.1). Apollos was born in Alexandria, Egypt, and was a great preacher of the gospel and church leader (Acts 18.24–25). The individuals mentioned above are People of Color who have historically been assumed to be White or deemed unimportant. These individuals were influential figures of African descent whose stories should not be devalued.

Ephesians 6 is another passage that was frequently used to support the Curse of Ham lie. Paul said, "*Bondservants*, obey your earthly masters with fear and trembling, with a sincere heart, as you would Christ, not by the way of eye-service, as people-pleasers, but as *bondservants* of Christ, doing the will of God from the heart, rendering service with a good will as to the Lord and not the man" (Eph. 6.5–8; emphasis added). The word *bondservant* in Greek is *doulos* defined as a "worker" or an "employee" who frequently came from the working class. The bondservant is not a reference to a slave, or someone owned as property but implies a servant bound by a limited time or even for life. Often, indentured servants came from the working class because they were refugees or immigrants displaced due to conquest and wars. Even indentured servitude in Rome was nothing like American slavery as we understand it today. ("δουλος (doulos)") In part, the English translations "slave" and "bondservant" are too narrow for a full emphasis and meaning behind the traditional usage of the word *doulos,* which is also found 127 times in the New Testament (Clarke; Eph. 6). Therefore, using the scripture to justify the Curse of Ham lie is a gross misrepresentation of the Scriptures.

The entire lie of enslaving Africans based on the Curse of Ham breaks down for several other reasons. In Acts chapter 2, the disciples were together, distraught, and discouraged because Jesus was crucified right before their very eyes. Their hopes and dreams died with Jesus, and they were terrified. However, when the Holy Spirit came upon them, they all began to speak in other tongues (languages), of which three—Egyptian, Libyan, and Cyrene—were African (Acts 2.10). If the African race were cursed, would God have allowed the Holy Spirit to enable the disciples to speak three "cursed" languages? A second reason for the lie's breakdown is the significance of the Church of Antioch, located in Syria. The Church of Antioch was a multiracial church with multicultural leadership, and it was central to the expansion of the early church. Paul and Barnabas spent over a year in Antioch preaching and teaching Antioch Christians (Acts 11.19–30). A third reason for the lie's breakdown is that Paul and Barnabas built Christianity's foundation in a multiracial community. More importantly, why did they allow Apollos, a Black man, to lead that community? Paul said, "There is neither Jew nor Greek, there is neither slave nor free, there is no male and female, for you are all one in Christ Jesus" (Gal. 3.28). These words defy the lies of the Curse of Ham and White supremacist claims of superiority over People of Color.

Where the Curse of Ham theory completely loses its credibility is the denial of the salvific work of Jesus. For argument's sake, if the Curse of Ham theory were true, and the entire African race was cursed through Ham, the curse became invalid when Jesus died on the cross. The Bible says, "There is therefore now no condemnation for those who are in Christ Jesus. For the law of the Spirit of life has set you free in Christ Jesus from the law of sin and death" (Rom. 8.1–2). Christ's death on the cross would have reversed the curse of the Ham from his descendants, but American Christians continued to use this curse to justify the enslavement of Africans. As male slaves were ripped away from their families and used for hard labor, female slaves were used as sex objects to procreate and produce children to work as young as eight years old in the fields (Watson). As a result of slavery and the disparities against African Americans, generations of families have suffered. Single mothers still raise a significant percentage of children in the Black community due to generations of separated families that could never bond from the beginning.

Our country is experiencing a cultural shift, and it is interesting to see the changes implemented by companies, institutions, and states. Churches are finally having honest conversations about racism, equity, diversity, and inclusion. Organizations are beginning to inspect their practices of self-evaluation for racist and discriminatory policies and procedures. For decades, organizations remained silent on social issues. However, since the summer of 2020, these organizations have come out in public solidarity with Black Lives Matter and Asian American Pacific Islander (AAPI) organizations.[4] I know some of you are reading this book are opposed to Black Lives Matter. I am not going to speak for or against the organization. I just want you to think about it like this, would the Black Lives Matter organization need to exist if Black and Brown lives genuinely mattered in the eyes of *all* Americans? Would there be a need for such organizations if Black and Brown people were not killed in the streets by police? Would there be a need for AAPI organizations if President Trump did not call Covid-19 the "China virus," inciting anti-Asian hate across America (Ellis)? Would there be a need for any of these organizations if the judicial system and many police officers were not inherently biased against People of Color? More importantly, Black Lives Matter and Stop AAPI Hate would not be big headliners if the church consistently led the way of justice and antiracism.

Since 2020, major organizations have started removing federal monuments with known racist individuals, Confederate traitors, flags, and other racist symbols from military bases. Private institutions, schools, buildings, and churches started removing pictures of the "White Jesus" and other

---

[4] Black Lives Matter is an organization formed to protest against systemic racism and injustices against Black and Brown People of color. AAPI stands for Asian American Pacific Islanders.

offensive items from their walls. As the evil truth of our country's history toward People of Color is revealed, more of America's dark history is exposed. American evangelicals must confront the hidden evils of this nation's history, so it does not continue to repeat in future generations. Evangelicals, especially those in authority with a platform, must speak out against racism and oppression, not downplay it. Evangelicals cannot afford to continue to overlook racial injustice or hide behind secular arguments as they only stain the church. For example, six Southern Baptist Seminaries declared systemic racism, White privilege, and Critical Race Theory[5] incompatible with being a Baptist. The Southern Baptist Convention (SBC) received so much backlash that African American churches have begun leaving the denomination because of the racial inequality, lack of diversity in leadership, and the seminary president's comments on race (Hopfensperger). The statement from the SBC is just another way for evangelical leaders to put justice and inequities into a political or sociological box instead of viewing racism as a humanitarian crisis and biblical issue in the church.

I often think about what it would be like today if Jesus were walking the streets of America after yet another shooting of a Person of Color. Can you imagine Jesus outside protesting with the protestors? Would you find him with the outcast, the poor, and the oppressed? There is no question in my mind that Jesus would be standing in solidarity, providing empathy and justice to the poor and oppressed.

---

[5] Critical Race Theory (CRT), not to be confused with Critical Theory or Marxism, examines society as it relates to race, law, and power. It also affirms that the laws and legal institutions are inherently racist.

Jesus had the unique ability to assess the day's information, see the truth, and pursue justice because he always focused on the most vulnerable in society: the poor, the widow, the immigrant, the refugee, and the outcast. For "He executes justice for the fatherless and the widow, and loves the sojourner, giving him food and clothing" (Deu. 10.18).

Jesus took the spotlight off the influential and elite leaders like the Pharisees and Sadducees and magnified the oppressed and outcasts living life on the margins. Jesus warned the disciples saying, "Watch and beware of the leaven of the Pharisees and Sadducees" (Matt. 16.6; Mark 8.15). Leaven was a form of yeast used to help make the dough rise, and it only takes a small amount of leaven to transform dough. In this example, Jesus warned the disciples against harmful and religious teachings from the Pharisees and Sadducees, which lacked love and empathy for the poor and oppressed. The Pharisees and Sadducees created numerous laws and restrictions with endless regulations that often dominated the lives of the Jewish community. Therefore, Jesus' reference to the leaven of the Pharisees and Sadducees concealed their real motives for power and elitism. Similarly, Christ-followers must beware of the teachings from salacious evangelical pastors who mix evil and politics with Christianity. They, like the Pharisees, lack love and empathy for the poor and oppressed and have embraced a celebrity status to achieve money and power.

Unlike the Jewish elites, Jesus displayed empathy to the vulnerable and those overlooked by society and forced to survive without help. For example, there was a woman caught in the act of adultery (John 8.1-22). The Pharisees brought the woman to Jesus and insisted that Jesus stone her to death.

Jesus responded, "Let him who is without sin among you be the first to throw a stone at her" (7). Since every man knew that he was guilty of sin, they put down their stones and left. In the infamous line in the story, Jesus said, "Woman, where are they? Has no one condemned you?" She said, "No one Lord." Moreover, Jesus said, "Neither do I condemn you; go, and from now on sin no more" (11). Jesus did not shame the woman for her sin. He did not stone her, which was the punishment of adultery according to the law. On the contrary, Jesus showed empathy and mercy when the woman did not deserve either and it changed her life forever.

Other examples of Jesus' empathy are a blind man named Bartimaeus, a woman with a bleeding disorder, and the Samaritan woman. Bartimaeus sat on the roadside daily begging for money for food. With empathy and compassion, Jesus healed Bartimaeus so that he received his sight. The woman with the bleeding disorder had been suffering for over twelve years and it was a complete disruption to her life. The woman was required to yell "unclean" any time she encountered someone in public, as was per Jewish law (Lev. 15.19–33). When the woman heard that Jesus was passing by, she rushed into the crowd in spite of the laws and touched Jesus' garment. Jesus realized the level of courage and faith that it took for her to do what she did. So, Jesus said to the woman, "Daughter, your faith has made you well; go in peace and be healed of your disease" (Mark 5.34).

One day while traveling with his disciples, Jesus met a Samaritan woman at a well. In this story, the unidentified woman was drawing water from the well in the middle of the day. Drawing water at the hottest time of the day was an indication that she was likely an outcast amongst the other women in the village. I mentioned earlier that the Jews considered themselves superior to non-Jews, but this was especially the case with Samaritans.[6] Well, in that day, you would never find a Jewish man talking to a Samaritan, much less alone with a Samaritan woman. Nevertheless, Jesus approached the woman, began a conversation with her, and even told her about her sexual history. Once the woman realized she was talking to the Savior, she evangelized many people in her village. In each of these scenarios, Jesus acted upon his empathy, and these individuals' lives were changed forever. So how can we follow Jesus's examples? Whatever you do from this day forward can change the lives of those around you by simply showing empathy. Imitate Jesus by caring for people in a way that addresses their natural and physical needs. Do not be like the Pharisees and Sadducees, who were only concerned about their self-interests. Choose to love unconditionally by showing empathy.

---

[6] Samaritans were biracial, half Jewish and half Gentile, so they were deemed as inferior to the Jews.

CHAPTER 2
THE HISTORY OF AMERICAN EVANGELICAL CHRISTIANITY

"They did not obey or incline their ear, but everyone walked in the stubbornness of his evil heart" (Jer. 11.7).

I am a Christ-follower who believes in the inerrancy of Scripture.[7] The Word of God is the final authority in my life. I believe we are all sinners, and Jesus died on the cross for our sins so that we could accept his gift of salvation by grace through faith. I believe that Christians should strive daily to abstain from sin. We should take care of the poor, bring justice to the oppressed, unconditionally love the LGBTQ community, and pursue a life that represents Jesus Christ. I believe all Christ-followers should desire to share the good news of the gospel message and display the love of God in our lives. By definition, my beliefs would technically classify me as an evangelical Christian. If you are a Christ-follower reading this book and share these same beliefs, you

---

[7] Inerrancy means infallible, without error, without fault in its original translation.

too are classified as an evangelical Christian. Unfortunately, the evangelical Christianity that exists in today's America is in opposition to these biblical principles. Evangelical seems to function more like a political identifier than a Christian religious group (Robbins, 93). Our society often equates the word evangelical with judgmentalism, condemnation, White supremacy, and hypocrisy. What is being exposed in the hearts of many evangelicals today is White supremacy expressed through racial rhetoric and social inequities. These inequities continue to influence the framework of our country's systems, organizations, churches, and politics. For these reasons, as well as many others I address throughout this book, I cannot consider myself an American evangelical.

This chapter looks extensively at the unsettling themes present in American evangelicalism today and how it diminishes the validity of Christianity in the eyes of non-Christians. Evangelicals represent all age groups, races, ethnicities, and cultures. However, the majority of American evangelicals are primarily Caucasian. Therefore, when I use the word evangelical, I am referring to White American evangelicals. Today, society defines *evangelicals* as those who traditionally vote Republican, have conservative family values, and place a high value on patriotism. American evangelicals have specific beliefs that often guide selecting schools and neighborhoods, giving to charities, and choosing their political candidates. For People of Color and the poor, these beliefs are often problematic, oppressive, and hypocritical. As a result, many non-Christians believe that evangelicals are hypocrites for supporting sinful and evil politicians. Another unsettling theme is the evangelical's ever-growing lack of empathy for the poor and People of

Color. For example, evangelical leaders in the past and many evangelical leaders today still believe the effects of slavery stopped at the end of the Civil Rights era. Throughout the years, many evangelicals believed and embraced stereotypes like "all Black people are lazy," or "Black people only want to live off tax-payers' money." Nevertheless, one of the most unsettling themes is how these same evangelicals believe that systemic racism is created to blame White people for the disparities of People of Color. Even worse, some evangelicals completely deny the mistreatment of slaves but maintain support for policies centered on White supremacy and oppression.

The history of evangelicalism began in the European exploitation of the Americas led by Christians George Whitfield and Jonathan Edwards. In 1740, there was a push for revivalism and conversions from the gospel message of Christ. The Anglican and Puritan churches expanded in America, while racist ideology, idealistic patriotism, White supremacy, and the belief in American exceptionalism as the savior nation expanded with them. From the very beginning, when the first Christians came to America, the Bible was used to establish superiority, justify slavery, segregation, and a social class system with a White hierarchy. As a result, there are several issues with the Protestant movement of the past and the evangelical political movement today. Both movements have shaped American Evangelical Christianity into a religion that is not operating according to the love and inclusion that presents itself in the pages of Scripture. For example, the Declaration of Independence's original document supported anti-slavery laws that would have provided equality for People of Color (Williams, Y. "Why"). Although

Thomas Jefferson crafted the Declaration of Independence, the statements that afforded African slaves their rights were removed from the Constitution's final document. The Founding Fathers refused to stand up for liberty and justice for African slaves and women. Some of the Founding Fathers rejected the notion that African slaves were equal to White Americans. However, people still believe that America is a Christian nation or at least a nation with Christian principles.

White evangelicals believed that their skin color made them superior to African slaves because it was taught from the pulpits of Christian churches. The Protestant Reformation or mass dissent from Rome's total control of Catholicism began in the sixteenth century. Reformers rejected the Roman Catholic doctrines that elevated the papacy and corrupt traditions, but it did not change their views of the African race. A major highlight in the Reformation period was in 1517 when the famous theologian Martin Luther wrote the infamous Ninety-Five Theses. He boldly stood up against the sin and corruption that was occurring in the Catholic Church. Martin Luther and many others believed that the papacy was corrupt and no longer adhered to the Scriptures but was moving further from the message of Christ. Therefore, Martin Luther's rejection of the Roman Catholic Church's liturgical and politically corrupt traditions eventually led to the developments of the Baptist, Lutheran, and Presbyterian denominations.

In the eighteenth-century Great Awakening, the Baptist church emerged as a prominent group leading the charge in how religion was viewed in the colonies while putting a stamp on Protestant Christianity. Initially, many American immigrants were Catholics, but that changed due to the U.S. Constitution's provision for the separation of church and state. This newly found freedom of religion released Catholic immigrants from the Roman Catholic Church's control. Historically, Protestant Christians in America were Christians who did not align with the traditions of the Anglican Church, Roman Catholicism, or Eastern Christianity. Instead, Protestants believed in a literal interpretation of the Scriptures, and the Bible was the absolute final authority. Traditional Protestants tend to be progressive in their views of social justice and the oppression of African Americans but are less conservative than their evangelical counterparts. The Fundamentalist movement grew in the nineteenth century out of the Protestant movement due to theological modernism. Theological modernism taught that the Bible had errors and that it was not to be interpreted literally. Theological modernism also supported evolution, more specifically Darwinism. Fundamentalists also believed in a literal interpretation of Scripture, but they also had a strict adherence to the Bible, often legalistic. Fundamentalism was an extreme to the Protestant movement in that it split churches and denominations and opened the door for a sub-movement called Evangelicalism. Evangelicalism grew in opposition to Fundamentalism with an emphasis on evangelizing the gospel.

The word evangelical can be defined traditionally as "Christian churches that emphasize the authority of the Scriptures, and stress that salvation is achieved by a personal conversion" ("Evangelical"). In contrast, American evangelical Christianity today is a religion shaped through the eyes and values of White Christians who profess love and concern for the poor and the oppressed while also perpetuating hate and division in their pursuit of power, prestige, and financial gain. The gospel does not condone hatred, divisiveness, or selfishness. However, it promotes ethnic unity as stated so eloquently by the Apostle Paul when he said, "I am not ashamed of the gospel, for it is the power of God for salvation to everyone who believes, to the Jew first and also to the Greek" (Rom. 1.16).

Its Greek interpretation might better explain the word evangelical. Derived from the Greek word *evangelion,* evangelical means evangelizing the gospel message of salvation (Bloesch 7). Since the 1600s, the Scriptures have been primarily interpreted from a White evangelical bias that is often culturally insensitive and self-centered. The Scriptures are often interpreted absent of a higher ethic of love, community, unity, equality, and a global multi-ethnic worldview. I do not believe that all American evangelicals are inherently racist, nor intentionally or purposefully interpret Scripture from a White perspective to the detriment of others. Nor do I believe that all evangelicals realize that silence and a lack of support for biblical justice speaks volumes to the oppressed and People of Color. I remember when I was a seminary student where, although the school admitted women and People of Color, it often seemed like we were an afterthought or the fulfillment of a quota. Sometimes my White male colleagues let me know that, as a Black woman, I was not welcomed in our male-dominated theological tract or the preaching classes we were required to take. My professors and male counterparts' interpretation of Scripture often lacked a well-rounded perspective of ethnicity, gender inclusion, acceptance, and love in the classroom.

The constant denial of implicit biases and learned behaviors makes it almost impossible to have an authentic conversation about racism. For evangelicals, the consideration of prejudice is often viewed as an assault on their character and integrity. The refusal to acknowledge pride and implicit biases means there is no motivation for introspection or acknowledgment of sin. Evangelicals who refuse to recognize that White supremacy remains in the church are reinforcing it through their denial. Racism conversations are also difficult with White American evangelicals, not just because White supremacy is in the framework of evangelicalism, but because many White evangelicals do not believe these issues continue to exist. For example, race conversations are challenging to have in predominately White churches. White evangelicals prefer to listen to other White evangelicals talk about racism. Frequently, when People of Color, especially Black people, bring up the subject of racism, we are dismissed as being angry. Alternatively, we are accused of calling White evangelicals racist when the topics of White supremacy, racism, or discrimination are discussed. Even when a White evangelical offends a Person of Color, the offender often becomes hysterical so that the offended Person of Color is left comforting the offender.

Evangelicals who believe they know everything there is to know about America's history of slavery and racism are usually closed off to the topics of systemic racism, advantages, and White supremacy. What makes things even more problematic are the evangelicals who believe the issues of White supremacy and racism could never personally apply to them. They usually say something like, "My closest friends are Black." "I don't see color because I look at everyone the same way." "I'm not a racist, I love Black people," or "I love minorities." To help you better understand these misconceptions, let us discuss the history and definition of White supremacy in more detail.

White supremacy is not just a term that refers to slave owners and the Ku Klux Klan of the past or the tiki torch-carrying White nationalists today. White supremacy is a view that the White race is superior to all other races, and there is an intrinsic value to being white-skinned. The hierarchy begins with the Caucasian race, next lighter-skinned People of Color, and finally, at the bottom are the Black/African people. I stated previously that White supremacy exists in the core of the foundations of America, but it also exists in American evangelicalism. For example, when White pastors try to talk to their predominately White congregations about racism and injustice, their congregants become uneasy or outraged. Some congregants leave the church, while others get so worked up that they eventually get the pastor fired. Why are White evangelicals angry when topics like social justice and White supremacy are discussed from the pulpit? If we cannot openly talk about the sin of racism and White supremacy in the church, and the church is supposed to be the hospital for sin and sickness, then where else do we go to expose it? If we cannot expose the sins of White supremacy, then the church continues to be complicit in defending it.

In the book of Colossians, Paul said, "He is the image of the invisible God, the firstborn of all creation. For by him all things were created, in heaven and on earth, visible and invisible, whether thrones or dominions or rulers or authorities—all things were created through him and for him. And he is before all things, and in him all things hold together.

And he is the head of the body, the church. He is the beginning, the firstborn from the dead, that in everything he might be preeminent" (Col. 1.15–23). In other words, White supremacy is an adversary to Christianity and one of Christianity's biggest threats. It is an assault against God's order for humanity created in His image. Therefore, Christ-followers must expose the lies and sins of White supremacy that have been protected too long by silence. Suppose evangelicals can acknowledge that White supremacy continues to exist in extreme groups like the Ku Klux Klan. Why then is it so difficult to accept that White supremacy continues to remain present in the church today? You would have to deny our nation's history and a legacy of church silence in social issues, racism, and discrimination of the poor and People of Color not to believe this is a real issue. Racial reconciliation will continue to be hindered when evangelicals feel attacked by minorities sharing their experiences and pain. White supremacy is a sin, not a political or social justice issue that exists outside the church. White supremacy is a sin that stifles unconditional love and inclusion, erodes empathy, and pushes non-Christians away from the gospel message of Christ.

For example, traditionally, "White Jesus" images have historically upheld Christianity's White supremacy and dominance. Purity is often associated with whiteness, and evil is often associated with darkness or the color black. White supremacists easily associated whiteness with the White race and darkness with darker-skinned races. The images of a "White Jesus" displayed on the church's stained glass windows only infer that all other ethnicities are inferior to the White symbolism. Today, churches that display

"White Jesus" images are more likely to have historical ties to White supremacy groups. Pictures depicting Jesus as a White savior only preserve the inequality of races and further perpetuate a White supremacy hierarchy. Despite the biblical references and Jesus' historical ancestry from Jewish descent, the White American church has rejected an ethnic or darker-skinned Jesus to favor the supremacy of the White race. Slave owners who used the Scriptures to manipulate their slaves also used "White Jesus" images to pursue the narrative of a White God and the supremacy of the Caucasian race. The Emancipation Proclamation allowed slaves their freedom, but racism continued to be propagated through the pulpit, often inciting acts of violence through lynch mobs in the name of protecting White women from the perceived danger of African Americans. Fortunately, slaves gained the courage to secretly learn to read, write, fight back, escape to freedom, and eventually protest for equal rights.

Many evangelicals and prominent leaders in our country opposed slaves who sought freedom and escaped to the North. For example, America's first president, President George Washington, was a slave owner. In 1796, George Washington relentlessly hunted his slave, Ona Judge, after she escaped to freedom (Pruitt). Slaves who got caught were severely beaten, killed or re-enslaved. Sometimes their entire families were enslaved even if they were previously free. Slavery was affirmed by Christians and non-Christians, both reinforcing and twisting the Scriptures to proliferate a free labor force providing wealth and inheritance of slaves to their children. Today, these facts have contributed to generations of Christians lacking empathy towards the poor and People of Color. Sadly, many American evangelicals continue to display a lack of empathy and compassion for the poor and People of Color, and it is dividing our nation both politically and racially. It is no secret that American evangelicals have not always handled police brutality, racism, oppression of People of Color, and the acceptance and treatment of the LBGTQ community in the most Christ-honoring way. The evangelical's lack of empathy is an obstacle to non-Christians, resulting in all evangelicals being viewed as unloving, insincere, and lacking credibility.

One of the most famous evangelicals of our time, Evangelist Billy Graham, said, "In my view racism is the biggest social problem we face in the world today, and I believe it still is" (BGEA). I agree with Billy Graham's sentiment. Too many American evangelicals believe in a political version of Christianity, corrupted over time, without questioning its validity or inherent biases. Most evangelicals are God-fearing and God-loving people, but many, unfortunately, are misguided. In my experience of surveying global perceptions of American evangelicalism, I found that people in other countries perceive American evangelicals as racists, bigots, arrogant, hypocritical, corrupt, and an exclusive rather than an inclusive religion. I do not believe that American evangelicals realize their religious beliefs are integrated into a White supremacist culture. The gospel message of love, empathy, and acceptance cannot coexist with a White supremacist belief of dominance, superiority, and exclusivity. **American Evangelicalism embraces a dangerous, loveless pharisaical mindset—which blends conservative political values with biblical interpretation.** Today's American evangelicalism has moved away from the centralized message of the gospel. Provided is a list of issues considered most important to evangelicals. The list is not exhaustive, nor are these issues listed in order of importance. I will not make a personal argument for or against these issues. However, I will list what defines the principles and motivations of the White American evangelical and let you decide from there. The words conservative, moderate, progressive, and liberal in the context of Christianity and politics will be defined to help you understand these viewpoints.

The *conservative* focuses on preserving existing conditions and traditions ("Conservative"). Conservative American evangelicals tend to be resistant to what they believe are extreme changes that may infringe on their religious rights. They primarily vote for policies that restore or uphold traditional laws or conditions that resemble that of a 1950s Christianity and may resist embracing societal changes like climate change, LGBTQ issues, and social justice. The *moderate* is "a person who is opposed to extreme views of politics or religion" ("Moderate"). At one point, the moderate was viewed as a liberal thinker. However, in today's society, the moderate is neither a conservative nor a liberal in the way they vote, their views of social justice, or how they interpret the Bible. The moderate is usually more willing to compromise for unity and at times may have both conservative and liberal viewpoints depending on the issue. The *progressive* is "a person who favors political progress or reforms instead of keeping things the same" ("Progressive"). Progressives in today's political scope tend to have more of an aggressive political agenda, especially in climate change, equality, LGBTQ rights, social justice, free trade, and gender equality. A *liberal* is a person who pursues liberalism, freedoms, rights and liberties, and the protection of civil liberties ("Liberal"). Liberalism has had several meanings over the years, depending on the political party. In the twenty-first-century, the word liberal is used interchangeably with the word progressive, oftentimes democrat, and at times, some moderates are referred to as liberals. These definitions are essential to understanding the viewpoints of evangelicals in the past as well as modern-day evangelical Christians.

One of the most significant priorities of the American evangelical is support for the Pro-Life Movement. Opposition to abortion is the most critical issue that shapes how most White American evangelicals view all other social and spiritual issues. Most evangelicals believe that outlawing abortion in America is the essential moral responsibility of the Christian faith. Some churches have sanctity of life services where they educate their congregations on the effects of abortion and how life begins at conception. Although there is nothing new about the abortion issue, there is no direct mention of it in the Bible. Opposition to abortion for the American evangelical typically supersedes all of the other voting issues and it is the perceived duty of the evangelical to support candidates who profess to be Pro-Life. American evangelicals usually do not have the same level of commitment towards social issues that non-Christians view as pro-life issues, such as hunger, healthcare, infant and maternal mortality, gun violence, and police brutality. This lack of commitment to the other social issues often makes People of Color feel that their lives or their children's lives after birth are not a priority to the White evangelical community.

American evangelicals quote statistics that abortions are the modern-day genocide of Black and Brown communities by the hands of Planned Parenthood. While evangelicals often blame Planned Parenthood or the abortion industry in general, the way they quote these statistics seems to infer that People of Color value their babies less than White women. Evangelicals are usually very outspoken about abortions but remain silent about anti-abortion extremists who bomb abortion clinics and kill doctors and nurses (Schenck). For example, in 1984, there was a clinic that an anti-abortion activist bombed. In 1998, a remote-controlled nail bomb exploded outside an abortion clinic, killing off-duty police officer Robert Sanderson and injuring Emily Lyons, leaving her half-blind (Stack). Ironically, many American evangelicals oppose sex education in schools, social programs, and funding that would reduce the number of pregnancies and abortions in poor communities. In the eyes of non-Christians, the opposition to these programs is hypocrisy, and it turns away many who might be otherwise attracted to Christianity. However, not all evangelicals believe that opposition to sex education and social programs is the right course of action.

The next issue important to American evangelicals is the sanctity of the conventional nuclear family, including traditional gender roles. Customarily, the family structure aligns with their interpretation of the Bible, whereas the husband is the family's provider, leader, and head. The wife typically is the primary caretaker and homemaker who manages the children and the home. The family may decide to homeschool the children or send them to a private Christian school. The literal interpretation of the creation story in Genesis explains the evangelical's understanding of humanity's responsibility to populate the earth through marriage and childbirth (Gen. 1.28). American evangelicals may oppose contraceptives, but if a female becomes pregnant from premarital sex, rape, or incest, evangelicals believe she should carry the child to term and consider placing the baby for adoption if they cannot parent the child. We see a present-day example of this with the Texas abortion ban after six weeks of pregnancy, with no exceptions for rape or incest.

The American evangelical's promotion of the traditional family becomes problematic when it alienates low-income families with working single mothers and ostracizes the LGBTQ community. Evangelicals portray the LGBTQ community as an immoral affront to God's creation and design for humanity. Some American evangelicals believe it is an oxymoron to consider oneself as homosexual, same-sex attracted, or actively a part of the LGBTQ community and believe oneself a Christian. Ironically, evangelicals do not believe that one cannot be a Christian as an adulterer or a thief, but gay people cannot possibly be saved. Historically, the universal church has maligned the LGBTQ community instead of loving them as Christ loves us all. Some evangelical Christians believe it is immoral to support the LGBTQ community, and many believe that in no uncertain terms should American evangelicals support same-sex marriages (Rom. 1.26–27).

One example of how American evangelicals used religion to ostracize the LGBTQ community is the Christian bakery shop owner, Jack Phillips, who refused to bake a cake for a gay couple's wedding. Jack Phillips cited an affront to his freedom of expression that contradicted his religious views (Williams, P.). Evangelical groups flocked toward Jack Phillips, supporting him on social media while at the same time ostracizing the LGBTQ community, leaving them to feel unloved and ridiculed by Christians. Another example is when Rowan County Clerk, Kim Davis, refused to give a marriage license to a gay couple. The 2015 United States Supreme Court decision, *Obergefell v. Hodges*, legalized same-sex marriages. Kim Davis refused to issue the license because she felt that the law did not apply to her due to a legal doctrine known as qualified immunity. Kim Davis felt that the plaintiffs could go somewhere else to obtain their marriage license (Reuters). These examples display how American evangelicals make it difficult for the LGBTQ communities to feel loved and embraced by Christians.

American evangelical Christians today tend to view life through a highly personalized lens. They seem ambivalent to systemic social issues, and often lack love and empathy. Evangelicals may tie their faith to religious pride and the love of "God and country." Evangelicals believe that the United States is called to police the world as the savior nation who will eventually usher in the eternal reign of Christ. American evangelicals believe the United States is one of the ten kings mentioned in the Book of Daniel and America is represented in the book of Revelation in the end times (Dan. 10, 11, 12; Rev. 17.16). The American evangelical's elevated sense of patriotism, with the view of the United States as a righteous savior nation, is perceived as arrogant, racist, and anti-gospel to Christians in other countries.

To support the literal interpretation of end times prophecy, the United States must remain an ally to the nation-state of Israel, a vital subject for American evangelicals. Since the Romans destroyed the Jewish temple in 70 A.D., evangelicals believe they must support Jewish control of Jerusalem for the reconstruction of the temple, thus ushering in the return of Christ (Dan. 9.26–27; Rev. 11, 13; 2 Thess. 2). According to evangelicals, America's backing of Israel will result in thousands of Jews converting to Christianity and Jesus' one-thousand-year reign. America's support of Israel over Palestine is cited as both a traditional evangelical and Republican value. Evangelicals support Israeli sovereignty over a two-state option with a Palestinian capital. This theological perspective disregards the ancestral claims of Palestinian Christians living in Palestine. According to the 2017 Palestinian census, approximately 47,000 Palestinian Christians live in Palestinian territories (Casper) and 115,000 live in the predominantly Arab areas of Bethlehem, Jerusalem, Gaza, and the cities of Nazareth ("Christians in Gaza"). Republican evangelicals are often pro-Israel, but ironically, many American Jews tend to vote for Democratic candidates. Since 1968, seventy-one percent of American Jews have favored voting for Democratic candidates, and only about twenty-five percent vote for Republicans (Maisel). Interestingly, like evangelical preachers and Christian radio hosts, American evangelicals seem to be more concerned about Israel's future in prophecy than the Jews who live in the United States. As a result, American evangelicals have lost the respect of many eastern and orthodox Christians worldwide.

Another critical issue for American evangelicals is voting for the Republican Party. Most evangelicals believe that Republicans promote conservative moral Christian values, and the Democratic Party does not. I must note that not all Republicans consider themselves evangelical Christians and, not all evangelicals vote Republican. Are moral values only limited to values favored by White American evangelicals?

Evangelicals would have to assume that anyone who does not vote Republican can't possess moral Christian values. Conservative Republican evangelicals desire to preserve the existing conditions and limit change, which is often problematic because many conservative laws continue to oppress the poor and People of Color.

The word "conservative" calls into question which time in our history has conservative politics positively influenced the poor or People of Color? I will discuss the abortion issue in more detail in a later chapter. However, the perspective of the Republican Party as the only Christian option for evangelicals began in the late 1970s and early 1980s when many stopped supporting Democratic politicians over the abortion issue. Most evangelicals began supporting the Republican Party after the U.S. Supreme Court decision of *Roe v. Wade* in 1973. This decision allowed for legal abortions nationwide under the Republican President Richard Nixon. However, by the time Jimmy Carter became President, abortion was seen as an unforgivable sin in the eyes of many evangelicals. Some evangelicals believe that if you do not vote Republican, you cannot possibly be a Christian. (I must remind them that they are not the Holy Spirit Jr.). To say Democrats are not Christians assumes that all Republicans are Christians, and it also assumes those who make this declaration are qualified to judge the heart. Thankfully, Christianity is not based on what we believe about a person's eternal state, but it is solely on God's grace.

Many evangelicals who will only vote for Republican candidates have no problems disregarding the moral character of that candidate. For example, in both the 2016 and 2020 elections, American evangelicals gave unwavering support for the Republican Party candidate Donald Trump. President Trump's immoral and unethical character cannot be justified or overlooked just because he supports evangelical policies. Prior to Donald Trump's presidency, character mattered to evangelicals. Character mattered and forced the resignation of President Richard Nixon. Character mattered when President Bill Clinton committed adultery with Monica Lewinski and lied about it. However, for some reason, evangelicals are willing to completely overlook President Trump's bad character because it served their political interest.

When Trump's character came into question, evangelicals claimed that they did not vote for him based on his character but based on the policy issues that are important to them. I have a tough time understanding this hypocritical and dangerous logic. How can the character of our leaders not be an essential standard for Christians anymore? There are too many examples in the books of First and Second Kings and First and Second Chronicles where the last reference about the king said, "he did what was evil in the sight of the LORD" (2 Kings 23.32). As long as evangelicals perceived President Trump was upholding conservative values and policies, many were willing to overlook his immoral behavior and character issues. The tragedy of evangelicals willingly putting morality on the shelf to elect a Republican leader is that Christianity is considered a laughingstock in the eyes of non-Christians.

For example, in 2017, many evangelicals endorsed the Alabama Republican Senate special election nominee Roy Moore, although several women accused him of sexual molestation and pedophilia. As uncomfortable as it was to watch evangelicals quote Scripture on camera and tout Roy

Moore's "conservative Christian values," they justified this as a reason to elect him to office despite of the numerous allegations. The same evangelicals who were quick to overlook his evil character did not challenge or investigate the allegations. They blindly supported Roy Moore in the name of supporting a fellow evangelical Republican on the ticket. Evangelical Christianity is in trouble when White evangelicals publicly scorn a gay couple for wanting to purchase a wedding cake from a Christian bakery but run to support an alleged pedophile (Robbins and Crockett 41). Presidential candidate Donald Trump was accused of sexual misconduct and assault by several women. Instead of supporting the victims, evangelicals freely ridiculed and maligned them. The misogynist, xenophobic and racist comments that consistently came out of President Trump's mouth make atheists and non-Christians have a challenging time trusting anything that comes out of the mouths of evangelicals. Many non-Christians reject Christianity because it is seen as inconsistent with the message that Jesus preached. The acceptance of immoral character in the name of supporting the Republican agenda is flawed thinking. I must note that evangelical support for immoral candidates did not start with the election of President Trump. White rage emerged from President Barack Obama's election, the first biracial Black man elected as President of the United States of America.

The final issue important to the American evangelical is the desire to appoint conservative judges to the Supreme Court. When President Trump nominated Judge Brett Kavanaugh to the Supreme Court to replace retiring Justice Anthony Kennedy in 2018, evangelicals overwhelmingly supported Kavanaugh despite several sexual assault allegations. They also dehumanized and ridiculed Christine Blasey-Ford for daring to come forward and publicly accuse Kavanaugh of sexually assaulting her in college. Although Kavanaugh vehemently denied the allegations, evangelicals believed there was too much at stake. Evangelicals assumed Kavanaugh's appointment could change decades of legal rulings in their favor (Sweetland Edwards). At the end of President Obama's second term, Senate Majority Leader Mitch McConnell and Senator Lindsey Graham made sure that President Obama's Supreme Court nomination of Judge Merrick Garland did not get an opportunity for a Senate hearing.

This display of hypocrisy became even more apparent after Supreme Court Justice Ruth Bader Ginsburg died and Senator McConnell rushed the nomination of Judge Amy Barrett two weeks before the Presidential election. Judge Amy Barrett received raving remarks and support from the White evangelical community touting her "conservative Christian values." Many White evangelicals fail to understand that conservative White judges have continued to perpetuate racism and racist policies that hurt Black and Hispanic men disproportionately to White men. For example, Black men are imprisoned at six times the rate of White male inmates (Carson and Sabol 11). The Bible says, "Do not judge by appearances, but judge with right judgement" (John 7.24), not tainted judgment. Although prosecutors have discretion for the kinds of charges they can bring, if any, more often than naught, conservative White male judges pronounce harsher and longer sentences against Blacks and Hispanics than White defendants.

The problem with many American evangelical conservative values is that they perpetuate an already existing problem in a climate more concerned with winning at all costs rather than losing for the sake of Christ. For communities of Color, American evangelical values are perceived to lack empathy and inclusion and miss the essentials of loving the poor and the oppressed taught throughout Scripture. Conservative American evangelicals today have fallen into the trap of rejecting anyone who disagrees with their beliefs or refuses to take their side. This aggressive conservatism often erodes the Christian's commitment to the gospel because it is selfish and self-seeking. At times, conservatism abandons the foundations of the gospel message of Christ. It aligns Jesus to the conservative's agenda rather than the conservative evangelical aligning to Jesus' agenda of unconditional love and sacrifice. American evangelicals have reconstructed a version of Jesus that simply does not exist. Jesus did not come to adhere to what the Jews understood as the role of the Messiah. The Jews thought the Messiah would overthrow the Romans and re-establish an earthly government and rulership. Jesus rejected this notion and refused to take sides with the Pharisees or Sadducees. Jesus came to reverse the order of all things by not winning but losing at all costs. That is, Jesus came to lose his life so that we all might inherit eternal life.

The second chapter of Philippians explains an authentic first-century version of Christianity that unfortunately is scarcely seen today in American evangelicalism. Part of which is to "Do nothing from selfish ambition or conceit, but in humility count others more significant than yourselves. Let each of you look not only to his own interests, but also to the interests of others" (Phi. 2.3–4). Paul understood the difference between unity and uniformity. He appealed to the Church of Philippi to have the highest of spiritual motives because they were selfishly looking out for their interests instead of looking out for the interest of others. Rather than hunkering down taking sides with polarized Republican or Democratic Party extremes, the evangelical Christian who aligns himself with Christ must find ways to love people according to Jesus' agenda. Jesus' agenda is not a self-aggrandizing one, but it puts your neighbor before yourself. As Christ-followers, we must portray the true principles of Christ's love, which starts with a posture of humility and a willingness to love our neighbors as ourselves. Otherwise, in the words of the famous poet and author James Baldwin, "If the concept of God has any validity or any use, it can only be to make us larger, freer, and more loving. If God cannot do this, then it is time we got rid of Him" (Baldwin).

CHAPTER 3
CONSERVATIVE EVANGELICALS & THE RELIGIOUS RIGHT

"I do not sit with men of falsehood, nor do I consort with hypocrites" (Psa. 26.4).

One can easily trace the origins of divisiveness polarizing America's religious footprint in the world today, and this is troubling. American evangelicalism is transforming into a self-centered, self-serving, entitled, and racist political subclass as high-profile evangelical leaders focus on conspiracy theories and lobby for partisan political ideals. The evangelical is so self-focused that racism is seen as an individual issue, not a communal issue (Hackett). When non-Christians witness overwhelming evangelical support for immoral and corrupt leaders, Christianity becomes an impotent and worthless religion to them. While the first American evangelical settlers used the Bible to justify slavery, today, American evangelicals use the Bible to defend Christian leaders and politicians' unethical and immoral behavior. Sadly, this has weakened Christianity's appeal to non-Christians, and it elevates American ideals over social concerns and marginalized communities. Many non-Christians and People of Color also perceive that White supremacy and politics are the motivations behind American evangelical Christianity. Consequently, many conservative evangelical values are disconnected from the reality of what marginalized communities experience in their daily lives. In response to the evangelical's public support of immoral candidates and leaders, Billy Graham's granddaughter, Jerushah Duford, equated the word "evangelical" with hypocrisy and disingenuousness in a recent article posted by *USAToday.com*.

A political version of evangelicalism, commonly known as the Religious Right, has been the most dominating voice of the evangelical community. The Religious Right is an outspoken group of evangelicals consisting of Segregationists and Fundamentalists.[8] They believe in traditional family values, support anti-abortion laws, and are extreme loyalists to the Republican Party. The Religious Right became a powerful political pact that continues to affect voting and elections today (McVicar). The Religious Right, led by influential, highly politicized evangelicals, twisted Christianity to serve their purposes. They prioritize what they see as traditional family values, unconditional political support for Israel, and an elevated view of the United States as a savior nation. The Religious Right often looks down on the poor and disregards their needs as laziness. Due to widespread ignorance of the Religious Right's history, many American evangelicals believe that racism ended after the Civil Rights Era, and evangelicals have consistently opposed abortion.

---

[8] A Segregationist believes in support of segregation of races. A Fundamentalist is a person who has a strict belief in the literal interpretation of a religious text like the Bible or the Quran.

However, these assumptions cannot be further from the truth.

The Religious Right, who also calls themselves "The Moral Majority," claims that they began opposing abortion after the passing of *Roe v. Wade*. President Nixon resigned because of the Watergate scandal in 1974, and Vice President Gerald Ford finished Nixon's term. Jimmy Carter was elected President in 1977. Ironically, Carter is the one who is blamed for the passing of *Roe v. Wade* even though it passed under President Nixon's administration. *Roe v. Wade* went into law four years before evangelicals began prioritizing it and turning it into a political issue. The truth behind the history of the Religious Right is quite different than one might think. The first misconception pushed by the Religious Right is that overturning *Roe v. Wade* would outlaw abortions throughout the country. However, before *Roe v. Wade*, abortions were consistently practiced on U.S. soil from the 1600s to the 1900s (Acevedo). In 1776, abortions were legal in the entire country, and by 1972, there were over 600,000 legal abortions before *Roe v. Wade* was ever passed (Foley). Many states passed anti-abortion laws in the 1860s resulting in women participating in illegal underground abortions, which continue to occur today, even after the passing of *Roe v. Wade* (Acevedo). States determined their positions on abortion, as was the case before *Roe v. Wade*, which allowed any woman who could afford to travel from one state to another to obtain a legal abortion. Most people are misled to believe that evangelicals have always supported anti-abortion issues, but prior to *Roe v. Wade*, American evangelicals were both pro-life and pro-choice. Evangelicals were also equally

Republicans and Democrats. For a long time, abortion was viewed as a Catholic issue or just "socially unacceptable." Abortion was never the evangelical's issue, that is, not until the Religious Right made it one.

Another lie that seeped into American evangelicalism is how a Southern Baptist Pastor, the late Jerry Falwell Sr., created the Moral Majority. Falwell would have you believe he helped create the Moral Majority because of *Roe v. Wade*. However, the truth is, Falwell was enraged by the Supreme Court's decisions of *Green v. Kennedy* and *Brown v. Board of Education*. The 1954 passing of *Brown v. Board of Education* forced the desegregation of all-White public schools. In response to this decision, evangelicals created private but segregated "Christian schools" to remove their children from the integrated public school system. Falwell Sr. attempted to skirt the law by keeping his "Whites only" school segregated under the guise of Christian education (Rogue Fundegelical). Another prominent evangelical, Bob Jones Sr., created Bob Jones University, a Christian "Whites only" institution. The University lost its tax-exempt status in 1974 because it continued to remain segregated. The institution's loss of tax exemption infuriated many prominent evangelical leaders (Robinson, B.A.).

The 1970 *Green v. Kennedy* decision ruled in favor of the Internal Revenue Service's removal of an institution's tax-exempt status if they remained segregated. The forced desegregation of public schools brought out White evangelical grievance and outrage. Abortion was the issue that galvanized the "Moral Majority," and the Religious Right gained political power. Evangelical leaders like Jerry Falwell Sr., the

Heritage Foundation's[9] co-founder Paul Weyrich, and the Christian Coalition's founder Ralph Reed blamed President Carter for the IRS's removal of the tax-exempt status for religious organizations. They vowed to keep President Carter from winning reelection and would only back a presidential candidate who would protect their religious preferences and freedoms. President Carter, a devout Baptist, found himself abandoned and despised by the Religious Right's evangelicals. Both Falwell Sr. and Weyrich saw that moment as crucial to court evangelicals who were uncomfortable with *Roe v. Wade*.

Falwell Sr. and Weyrich turned abortion into a conservative religious issue to derail President Carter and catapult Republican candidate Ronald Reagan. With the abortion issue front and center, Falwell Sr. was able to cover up his real agenda, that is, to keep his schools segregated and preserve White Christianity (Robbins and Crockett 42). Jerry Falwell Sr. sued to keep his schools segregated and that is problematic by itself, but what is worse is it is anti-Christian in every notion of the word. Ralph Reed, another leader of the Religious Right, admitted that firing up evangelicals to participate in politics had nothing to do with the abortion issue. In the opinion of the Religious Right, the IRS stepped over the line of separation of church and state, so someone had to be blamed (Yancey 248). Unfortunately, President Carter took the blame from the evangelical community.

Although Falwell Sr. lost his lawsuit against the IRS, he got his wish, and Reagan was elected President. President Carter

---

[9] Heritage Foundation is a conservative organization geared towards public policy in Washington, DC.

was defeated in 1981, leaving him as a one-term President. The Religious Right now had President Reagan to rally behind because he would uphold their segregationist views. Reagan promised to appoint pro-life conservative Justices to the Supreme Court, and his administration supported Falwell Sr.'s lawsuit to keep his religious institutions racially segregated. Instead of enforcing desegregation, Reagan's Department of Justice began a battle with the IRS to maintain segregation in religious schools and institutions. Once Reagan realized this position might hurt his reelection chances, he had his Justice Department drop the issue. Falwell Sr. lost his lawsuit in the Supreme Court by a decision of 8–1. Justice Rehnquist was the only Justice who voted against desegregation in that decision. Afterward, President Reagan elevated Justice Rehnquist to Chief Justice. Jerry Falwell had no choice but to pivot to the abortion issue to keep his political lobbying power. The Moral Majority became a "pro-life," "pro-traditional family," "pro-moral," and "pro-American" political lobbying group established for political power and prestige (Falwell 388). So, the abortion issue was just a ruse to stir up American evangelicals to provide Falwell Sr. with a political base and financial backing for his lobbying efforts against desegregation. Falwell Sr.'s political pact pushed the abortion issue front and center and changed the course of evangelicalism in America, turning most evangelicals into single-issue voters from that point forward.

The idea of voting for Republican candidates to reverse *Roe v. Wade* continues to be the driving force behind the evangelical community's political platform. American evangelicals still believe that Republican presidents will appoint conservative judges to the Supreme Court who will reverse *Roe v. Wade*. One of the problems with this premise is believing that abortions can only decrease under Republican presidential administrations. It has been fifty years since the passing of *Roe v. Wade*. The Supreme Court has primarily consisted of conservative Republican judges, yet *Roe v. Wade* is still the law of the land (Hammer). The Religious Right's strategy is not working, and it is their only strategy to address abortion. Evangelicals consistently oppose public policies like affordable health care, including contraceptives, and the federal Special Supplemental Nutrition Program for Women, Infants, and Children (WIC). They also oppose the federal and state partnerships with Children's Health Insurance Program (CHIP), and others that could reduce the demand for abortions. Simply appointing conservative Judges to the court will not reduce or eliminate abortions (Putterman). Even if the Supreme Court overturned *Roe v. Wade* and abortions became illegal in the U.S., this does not necessarily mean that abortions will decline. In actuality, abortions have been declining equally under Republican and Democratic Presidents without any changes to *Roe v. Wade* (Siemaszko). President George W. Bush signed a partial-birth abortion ban, while President Trump did not sign any essential pro-life legislation (French). Under President Obama's administration, America saw a decrease in abortions because of his administration's approach to make abortions unnecessary rather than illegal.

    The Religious Right also overwhelmingly supported candidate Donald Trump and his reelection. Many evangelicals claim they support traditional family values, yet they openly embraced candidate Trump even though he bragged about sexually assaulting women and supported White supremacist groups (Kobes 2). Donald Trump portrayed himself as the candidate who would rescue White America from the fallacy that a Black man like Barack Obama could be elected and reelected as President. To many Trump supporters, the election of Barack Obama proved that White America was no longer significant, even though President Obama lived the traditional family values that evangelicals claim to uphold. Trump promised to protect evangelicals from the religious persecution they imagined they were suffering as well as from People of Color, immigrants, and Muslims. Of course, Trump also promised to appoint pro-life conservative judges to the courts. He also promised to reinforce other issues like law and order, unrestricted gun rights, a strong military, overturn the Affordable Care Act (Obamacare) and eliminate gay rights and social programs for the poor. Trump knew that White evangelicals were more likely to support a "law and order" President, the death penalty, harsher sentences for criminals, and justify police brutality against People of Color. Conservative evangelicals happily support war efforts but vehemently oppose all forms of gun control, even after school children and church attendees were victims of mass shootings. Finally, Trump exploited the evangelical's opposition to Brown refugees and asylum seekers admitted into the country with chants of "build that wall" on America's border with Mexico. As a result of the evangelicals unwavering support of Donald Trump, evangelicals are labeled Islamophobic (exaggerated fear or hatred of Muslims), homophobic (exaggerated fear of people who are gay, lesbian, bisexual, or transgender), and xenophobic (the exaggerated fear or hatred of foreigners).

Many evangelical leaders were outspoken Trump supporters despite his character, racist rhetoric, and morality issues. Let us talk about Franklin Graham, the eldest son of the late evangelist Billy Graham and Chief Executive Officer of the Billy Graham Evangelistic Association and the Samaritan's Purse. On October 26, 2020, Franklin Graham wrote a lengthy Facebook post bragging and praising President Trump. Graham mentioned the appointment of two hundred federal judges, and the U.S. Embassy move to Jerusalem, peace treaties in Israel, tax cuts to Americans, and defending religious freedoms during the pandemic. Graham ended the Facebook post by saying that he was not telling people whom to vote for but was encouraging people to pray for the President (Franklin). Graham's post was so partisan that many people, including non-Christians, were upset. Faithful America, a grassroots Christian organization, spoke out against Graham's post because they were tired of politics and people like Franklin Graham giving Christianity a bad reputation. Faithful America issued a statement in response to President Trump's handling and response of the COVID-19 pandemic. They advocated for Trump's removal (Lemon). Franklin Graham's niece Jerushah Duford also expressed her disdain. Jerushah said she felt like "a homeless evangelical" due to the broad support in the Christian community for Trump, whom she sees as opposed to Christian values (Kuruvilla). Graham ultimately removed the Facebook post as a result of all the backlash.

To address Franklin Graham's post, I begin with the two hundred constitutionalist federal judges appointed by Trump. I previously said that evangelicals think the appointment of conservative judges will change *Roe v. Wade* forever

(Lindevaldsen). However, emphasizing a constitutionalist approach to law is problematic since the Constitution did not give equity to women, the poor, or People of Color. Graham failed to mention that most of the Trump-appointed judges were primarily White men, and not one was a Person of Color (Nelson).[10] A constitutionalist approach only highlights the problems that People of Color have experienced for decades by conservative White male judges who historically sentence People of Color with longer prison sentences. Graham also failed to acknowledge that the only reason why President Trump was able to appoint so many conservative judges is that the Republican Senate blocked President Obama's judicial candidates during his second term in office. An unprecedented number of judicial vacancies were left open for the incoming President Trump to fill.

Franklin Graham mentioned President Trump's order to move the U.S. Embassy to Jerusalem. As I previously stated, the Religious Right believes America must do everything to remain an ally to Israel. President Trump's decision to move the U.S. Embassy to Jerusalem pleased evangelicals. Additionally, Graham claimed President Trump "stood up to Russia," but this would be a joke to any serious American who kept up with the facts during Trump's presidency. President Trump's failure to stand up to Vladimir Putin alarmed many American security experts. Trump also failed to stand up to Turkey. In 2019, without consulting military experts, Trump abruptly withdrew a small contingent of American special forces from Northern Syria. Trump's order to

---

[10] *Note since this article was written, the Trump Administration appointed a total of 222 conservative judges

withdraw allowed Turkey to slaughter the Kurds, who had been long-time allies of the U.S. in fighting Isis (Lamothe). Trump's supporters had no concern that many of the slaughtered Syrian Kurds were Christians.

Concerning Graham's statement about the Israeli peace agreements, Israel was not in armed conflicts with the United Arab Emirates (UAE) and Bahrain. The agreements opened Arab markets to Israel, but it angered the Palestinians and made peace between Palestine and Israel less likely. Trump's peace agreement pales compared to former President Jimmy Carter's Camp David Accords, which brokered lasting peace between Israel and Egypt. Graham's suggestion that President Trump should win a Nobel Peace Prize reflects Trump's jealousy and the evangelical community's resentment of former Presidents Carter and Obama, both of whom did win the Nobel Peace Prize. Lastly, Graham mentioned that President Trump lowered taxes. Graham failed to mention that President Trump's tax cuts went to corporations that only redistributed wealth to the wealthy, not the poor. I mentioned previously that Religious Right evangelicals have the tendency to look down upon the poor, and this is another example. Graham's disregard of the poor is antithetical to the teachings of Scripture that speak about the Christian's responsibility to the poor, like Proverbs 22.22, which says, "Do not exploit the poor because they are poor and do not crush the needy in court." Furthermore, Psalm 14.6 says, "You would shame the plans of the poor, but the LORD is his refuge."

Pastor Robert Jeffress is another influential evangelical pastor who was very outspoken in his support for President Trump. Pastor Jeffress is the Senior Pastor of First Baptist

Dallas, a megachurch of approximately 13,000 members in Dallas, Texas. On one of Pastor Jeffress' appearances on The Todd Starnes Show, a three-hour daily syndicated radio program, Jeffress referred to 'Never Trump' evangelicals as morons (Young, S.). Jeffress' statement insulted evangelicals who choose to vote based on a candidate's character. In the past, Pastor Jeffress was considered a conservative evangelical pastor who taught conservative values. Today, Pastor Jeffress is more like a politician who spends most of his time appearing on FOX News (Maples) and lobbying in Washington, D.C. than he does in his pulpit. However, you should not be surprised as Pastor Jeffress has always been a controversial pastor. After Pastor Jeffress' public support for Trump, he lost respect from many in the evangelical community. In a FOX News interview with Lou Dobbs, Pastor Jeffress praised the evangelical's overwhelming support of Donald Trump ("Dr. Robert"). How can Pastor Jeffress overlook the hateful and racist statements spewed from President Trump's mouth? Trump called Haiti and El Salvador "Shit-hole countries,"[11] and National Football League players "Sons of Bitches."[12] He referred to Mexicans as "rapists"[13] and infamously, White supremacists in Charlottesville "very fine people."[14] If we are all equals in

---

[11] January 11, 2018, meeting with lawmakers in the White House
[12] September 22, 2017, Huntsville, Alabama address for Senator Luther Strange, Trump's reference to NFL players kneeling during the National Anthem
[13] June 15, 2015, Trump kicks off his presidential campaign with this statement
[14] April 25, 2019, press conference about the violence in Charlottesville, VA White supremacist march

Christ, there is no distinction of race or one's social-economic status (Wiersbe 136–137). Our forefathers refused to provide equality for Native Americans, African slaves, and Mexican Americans, choosing instead to ignore the teachings of Paul, and it's still occurring with evangelicals today. Why did evangelicals justify President Trump's behavior? They hardened their hearts against their brothers and sisters of Color. They could not empathize with them as human beings created in God's image.

Interestingly, The Freedom From Religion Foundation, an atheist group, filed a complaint with the IRS against Pastor Jeffress. The lawsuit stated that Pastor Jeffress was conducting political activity in the church, which violates IRS rules. They alleged that Pastor Jeffress was campaigning for President Trump and Vice President Pence. The complaint says Pastor Jeffress invited Vice President Pence to speak at his church on Sunday, June 28, 2020. The service was during the height of the COVID-19 spike and gathering restrictions in Dallas, Texas. While introducing Vice President Pence to his congregation, Pastor Jeffress praised President Trump saying how great it would be to reelect Trump and Pence. The complaint also stated that the church displayed American flags and played patriotic music during the service. Other Republican politicians in attendance that day were Texas Lieutenant Governor Ken Paxton, Texas Senator John Cornyn, Texas Governor Greg Abbott, and Housing Secretary Ben Carson ("FFRF Asks IRS").

The actions of Jerry Falwell Sr., Franklin Graham, and Pastor Robert Jeffress reflect why many non-Christians, Millennials, and zoomers do not take evangelical Christians seriously. More importantly, because of these men, racism,

White supremacy, homophobia, and Islamophobia are often equated with Christianity (Rogue Fundagelical). America's forefathers and the evangelical Religious Right allowed the sins of superiority and racism to flourish in their hearts. The conquering of People of Color in the past has shifted to upholding White supremacy today through divisive and racist rhetoric and damaging laws and policies. While many twenty-first-century evangelical leaders will not overtly make racist comments or publicly support segregation, their silence supports systems that perpetuate racism in America. If you think that racism no longer exists in the church, you are mistaken. The politics of present-day evangelical leaders of the Religious Right are evidence that racism has not ceased to exist but remains to be a problem.

CHAPTER 4
CIVIL RIGHTS & THE RESURGENCE OF WHITE SUPREMACY

"But if you show partiality, you are committing sin and are convicted by the law as transgressors" (James 2.9).

On August 28, 1955, a fourteen-year-old Black boy named Emmett Till was lynched in Mississippi by a mob of White men after being accused of whistling at a White woman. Emmett Till's murder was the spark that ignited the civil rights movement. Sixty-five years later, on May 25, 2020, my generation watched with horror the infamous video of an unarmed Black man named George Floyd lying face down on the concrete over an "alleged" counterfeit twenty-dollar bill. We witnessed the now-convicted Minneapolis police officer Derek Chauvin on video kneeling on Mr. Floyd's neck for eight minutes and forty-six seconds. Officer Chauvin suffocated the life out of Mr. Floyd while he cried out for his dead mama. George Floyd's murder spurred months of national and international protests. These protests catapulted conversations about systemic racism, police brutality against People of Color, and discrimination worldwide. I was devastated watching Mr. Floyd plead for his life. The video reminded me of too many Black and Brown deaths before Mr. Floyd, but the scenario was different this time. So many emotions flooded my mind after watching Officer Chauvin with what looked like an arrogant posture and a stone-cold look on his face, his left hand in his pocket, showing absolutely no remorse. I will never forget the emotions I felt that weekend. It began with Mr. Floyd's murder, followed by peaceful protests during the day, and then it escalated to rioting, violence, vandalism, burning buildings, and parked cars the first night. Over the next few days, the vandalism, looting, and rioting continued. The police and national guard sprayed the peaceful and violent protestors with pepper spray, tear gas, and rubber bullets.

While the government should not solely be held accountable for the actions of rogue police officers, these offenders usually have a trail of overlooked complaints from the poor and minority communities. For example, Officer Chauvin had seventeen complaints of aggressive force before the day he fatally killed George Floyd (Nashrulla). Where else can you have seventeen infractions at work and still be willfully employed, except on the police force? Police departments are aware of these "bad actors" fired and rehired in multiple precincts and protected by the law and police unions. Unruly behavior is often encouraged by supervisors, while nothing is done to stop rogue officers. The absence of accountability violates the Fourteenth Amendment, which guarantees all Americans equal protection (Rothstein 142–143). The actions of Officer Chauvin confirm that there is a system in place that supports criminal and inhumane behavior by bad police officers. Officer Chauvin became the symbol that represents little to no accountability for officers who use deadly force. The police system is rooted in a long history of racist White supremacists who have infiltrated the law enforcement and criminal justice systems to gain influential positions.

After watching the video of Mr. Floyd's death, the subsequent vandalism, and looting that extended for days, it was difficult to go back to "business as usual." As the tears and emotions of anger, fear, anxiety, and confusion gripped our country, I was too emotional to continue as if the entire world had not witnessed this atrocity. When I did go back to work, it was hard to find a reason to care about jumping on our Monday morning sales call pretending that one of my Black brothers was not murdered in front of the world. At least for the Black community, our world was turned completely upside down. Here was the death of another Black man at the hands of the police. It was just too much to bear after so many before George Floyd like Sandra Bland, Freddie Gray, Michael Brown, Tamir Rice, and Eric Garner, to name a few (Meier). Two weeks before the George Floyd video went viral, I was still reeling from the murder of another Black man, Ahmaud Arbery. Now-convicted Travis and Gregory McMichael, a retired police officer and his son, and William "Roddie" Bryan pursued Ahmaud Arbery. They killed Mr. Arbery while he was jogging in a neighborhood near his home. On the heels of Mr. Arbery's death, the public was made aware of the incomprehensible shooting of Breonna Taylor. Ms. Taylor was shot and killed inside her own home because of a no-knock warrant for the wrong suspect. The no-knock warrant included multiple addresses, permitting the police to knock down the doors of several homes. Breonna's address was included in the warrant because the police claimed her ex-boyfriend had packages of drugs delivered there. The post office later denied those claims. The real suspect was apprehended earlier that night before Breonna's door was broken down. All I could think was, *here we go again,* and I cried out, "Come, Lord Jesus. Come!"

The Covid-19 pandemic combined with the viral video of George Floyd's death created a perfect storm in our society, enabling months of nationwide protests, violence, and vigilante shooters. Everything happening that weekend displayed the ever-present lack of leadership from the church and our government. Hundreds of thousands of people were out of work due to the Covid-19 stay-at-home orders. The absence of basketball and other sports meant typical distractions were not there. Many people had nothing else to do and nowhere else to go, so they went to the streets to protest as emotions ran high and tensions rose. As the protests grew and continued day after day, I was surprised to see so many White people protesting side by side with the Black Lives Matter protesters. White people were not just protesting. Some became activists and allies who spoke out against police brutality. For too long, the voices of People of Color have been muted, so it was time for the protesters' voices to be heard finally. All the looting and property damage began to overshadow the protesters' message; sadly, many White evangelicals chose to focus on the violence rather than the cries for justice. Conservative media like FOX News was quick to slander even the peaceful protesters as rioters and looters, primarily because most protesters were People of Color.

The events of that weekend brought back my painful memories and experiences of racism. My mother's family had deep roots in rural Alabama, and my father's family came from the inner city of Cleveland, Ohio. My parents lived through Jim Crow laws, with segregation that never lived up to the description as separate but equal, and overt racism. It upsets me to know that my almost-eighty-year-old mother had to witness this familiar scene all over again. My mother grew up on a farm with her parents and four sisters in Camp Hill, Alabama, in the 1940s. With roots steeped in Southern Baptist Christianity, the "Morgan Sisters," as they were called, led worship at their church, and during the week, they picked cotton on the farm. I remember one summer we drove from Cleveland, Ohio, to Camp Hill, Alabama, to visit my grandmother. On the way to my grandma's house, we stopped by to see my mom's childhood home. After a significant walk on the large farm through the horse patties and thick weeds, we approached what still stood as an aged, small wooden house. I remember my mom telling stories about them living on the farm of a White family. Although my mom's family was highly active in their small country church, two of the Morgan Sisters left Alabama for Ohio to get away from the disparities of the South. Shortly after moving to Ohio, my mom and my aunt left their roots of Christianity and converted to a Black version of Islam known as the Nation of Islam.

My father grew up in Cleveland, Ohio. I am not sure about his family's religious history because he never talked about it. My paternal grandparents were deceased by the time I was born, and my dad never talked about going to church as a child. All my dad ever talked about was the Nation of

Islam and Minister Louis Farrakhan. At the age of eighteen, dad was introduced to the Nation of Islam. According to my father, the Nation of Islam saved his life from the streets of inner-city Cleveland. Segregation was the norm where my father grew up, and Blacks were not welcome in certain parts of town. Unfortunately, many of those areas in Cleveland remain segregated today. After joining the Nation of Islam, my dad met my mother at the "Mooslim" temple and after ten years of marriage, I was born.

My dad always talked about Minister Farrakhan and his distaste for White people, especially White men. After years of experiencing racism as a foreman at General Electric and as a business owner denied loans and credit, dad always had deep pain and resentment for White men. My parents lived through the murders and assassinations of Emmett Till, Medgar Evans, Dr. Martin Luther King Jr., and Malcolm X. My father personally experienced different forms of racism, like being called "boy" or "nigger" even by Christian White men. I remember one family vacation as we took the long drive from Ohio to Alabama to visit my grandmother, we stopped at a park to eat. My mom, dad, youngest sister and two cousins who were traveling with us jumped out of the car, and we sat on the park bench to eat. I was about eight or nine years old at the time, but I can remember the experience as if it were yesterday. A group of young White men drove by the park in a dark blue rusted pickup truck with a giant Confederate flag on the back. A man sitting in the back of the truck bed screamed out "Nigga" as they peeled off on the dirt and gravel road. So, it is not surprising that while I was growing up, my dad often referred to White people as "the blue-eyed devil" or believed that Christianity was the

"White man's God." Why is this so? I can think of many reasons from my dad's witness of systemic racism in the poor Black communities, like Jim Crow laws, unfair housing practices and banking policies, deceptive and discriminatory practices in healthcare, and the murders of too many Black men from his community.

When I think about it, it is astonishing that Black people in America still want to believe in an American version of Christianity after so many years of dealing with slavery, Jim Crow, lynchings, domestic terrorism, and police brutality. Alternatively, in the words of the Los Angeles Clippers coach Doc Rivers, "It's amazing why we keep loving this country, and this country does not love us back" (Helin). Years of racism and implicit bias against Black people perpetrated in the church pushed many African Americans like my father to embrace Islam during the civil rights era. Today, many African Americans who are not wooed by the Nation of Islam are often won over by the Black Hebrew Israelite movement.[15] Black Christians are perceived as weak and gullible for believing in the White man's religion and for worshipping images of a White Jesus. The perception arises from the assumption that Christianity is a European White man's religion, and that Africans had no exposure to it until they were brought to America as slaves. Segregationists like Pastor Bob Jones, President of the Bob Jones University, perpetrated this lie. In one of Bob Jones' sermons, he said the only reason Africans had access to salvation was because of slavery (Taylor). Pastor Jones must have forgotten about Acts

---

[15] Hebrew Israelites are Black African Americans who believe they are descendants of the children of Israel in the Bible.

8.27-28, where the Ethiopian Eunuch, an official of Candace, Queen of the Ethiopians, was returning from worshipping in Jerusalem when he met Philip on the road. Why would the Eunuch be returning from worshipping in Jerusalem if he did not believe in the Messiah? After hearing the gospel message, the Eunuch knew Jesus as the Messiah, and Philip baptized him. The Eunuch went back to his country, spreading the gospel message of Jesus. Even more important to note is that it was not until Acts chapter nine that Paul took the gospel to the European nations. In other words, the African nations received the gospel before the European nations received it based on the chronology of the stories in the book of Acts. Europeans who claimed the African race would not have known the gospel message unless slaves were brought to America fed into the lies perpetrated by White supremacy and racism.

As today's increasingly charged society, racially and politically, moves farther away from the gospel, I am forced as an African American Christ-follower to re-evaluate evangelicalism. I attended a predominately White seminary, and what I learned about evangelical Christianity never felt right to me. I started questioning the motives of evangelicalism while I was in seminary by exposing undertones of racism. I began studying the Scriptures with different lenses, not colored solely by a White American evangelical perspective but from a historically ethnic background of contextual Christianity. I remember one of my adjunct professors, a Black doctoral student, was writing his dissertation on Dr. Martin Luther King, Jr.'s letters. The doctoral student's challenge was that many of the seminary's professors did not believe Dr. King was a Christian. I was appalled by the White evangelical professors questioning Dr. King's salvation based on his writings. Dallas Theological Seminary had a history of not allowing Black students admittance to the seminary until the 1970s. I experienced racism and sexism firsthand from seminary professors and male classmates. There is no question in my mind that Dr. King was a follower of Christ, based on his writings and his life. Just like all Christians have doubts, discouragements, and even fall into sin and temptation, this does not disqualify our salvation. Dr. King was by no means perfect, but he understood the message of the love of Jesus Christ even though he based his view of non-violence on the teachings of Gandhi.

Many people are unaware that Dr. King did not start out embracing non-violence to pursue civil rights. The fact is, Dr. King had a deep resentment towards White people after several personal encounters of racial discrimination while in college. However, after reading the teachings of American Protestant theologian Reinhold Niebuhr *and* Mahatma Gandhi, Dr. King realized that a non-violent approach to civil rights would be more potent than one of violence and retaliation. He also recognized the complexities of race and the Christian religion for the African American as one that identifies with oppression and how it affects People of Color (Williams 128). Unfortunately, on April 4, 1968, Dr. Martin Luther King, Jr. was assassinated while standing on the balcony of his hotel in Memphis, Tennessee. He died striving for the equity of People of Color in this country. Prior to his death, Dr. King was the essential voice of the civil rights era. The march to Selma on March 21-25, 1965, directly impacted the passing of the Voting Rights Act of 1965. The Voting Rights Act passed during President Lyndon B. Johnson's administration incited more violence from hate groups like the Ku Klux Klan.

Under the leadership of Elijah Muhammad and spokesman Malcolm X, the Nation of Islam was also an important influencer to the African American community. Unfortunately, the media portrayed Malcolm X and Dr. King as adversaries to bring disunity to the African American community. Dr. King and Malcolm X agreed on many aspects of racism and freedom for African Americans, even if they disagreed on the method. Thousands of years ago, the prophet Habakkuk said, "The wicked surround the righteous; so justice goes forth perverted" (Hab. 1.4). That was held true during the civil rights era. Dr. King and Malcolm X's enemies drove a wedge between them to block their common objectives of justice, equality, and absolute freedom for African Americans (Cone 192). As both Malcolm X and Dr. Martin Luther King, Jr. began gaining ground in the African American communities with organized marches and boycotts, the Ku Klux Klan terrorized African American communities, bombing Black schools and churches to deter unity.

By the twentieth century, the resurgence of the Klan's violent terrorism included their old tactics of lynching, cross burnings, mob rallies, and marches executed against White activists and Black protesters alike. The Klan continued to denounce African Americans, Jews, immigrants, and Catholics, which fueled more hate and violence during the civil rights era. Terror and ridicule were used in movies to help perpetuate racial biases and unfounded stereotypes about People of Color. For example, Black men historically were portrayed as violent and dangerous men deserving of harsh treatment. Black women were often portrayed as "auntie" or

"Mamie" in subservient roles or mere sex objects. On February 8, 1915, the movie *The Birth of a Nation* was released that exploited these stereotypes. The film was explicitly racist, initially titled *The Clansman*, and featured White men beating a White man dressed in black face ("Birth of a Nation").

White Klansmen were not the only ones who pushed a racist agenda of White supremacy. A group formed in 1894 after the Reconstruction Era called the United Daughters of the Confederacy (UDC). The UDC are wealthy White women who used their social influence to pressure local governments to erect Confederate monuments all over the country, rewrite history about the Civil War, and glorify the Ku Klux Klan (Speegle). White children grew up believing that slavery was acceptable, and they also were told that the Confederate soldiers were not traitors but honorable Americans. The UDC promoted a revised version of the history of the Civil War, saying the war was over "States rights," not Southern states' "rights" to maintain their slaves. Tell me, in what other country can a defector and loser of war be allowed to erect monuments to its leaders who committed treason? According to Article III Section 3 of the United States Constitution, treason is "the betrayal of one's own country by waging war against it or by consciously or purposely acting to aid its enemies" ("Treason"). Erecting monuments and statues of Confederate Generals and flying the Confederate flag, in my observation, is a betrayal of allegiance to the United States, not just mere expressions of Southern heritage.

Like the UDC, many Southern Christians believe that the Confederacy was only about state's rights. A little education is needed here. The Confederacy was a collection of eleven states that broke away from the United States in 1860 after the Presidential election of Abraham Lincoln. The eleven southern states were angry and fearful of losing their right to own slaves under Lincoln's administration. You might think that the UDC is a relic of the past, but the organization still exists today. The nostalgia of antebellum dresses and slavery is still celebrated at the UDC headquarters in Richmond, Virginia (Holloway). On Sunday, May 31, 2020, protestors set the UDC's headquarters on fire because of George Floyd's death. Evangelicals are seen as unsympathetic when they defend and celebrate the Confederate symbols. These symbols represent intimidation, oppression, racism, and violence to their brothers and sisters of Color. Many evangelicals fight for the unborn, the right to bear arms, the freedom of speech and religion, and the right to display Confederate symbols and monuments. However, many of these same evangelicals show no passion for fighting for the rights of equity and justice for People of Color. Numerous evangelicals grew up learning Revisionist history (intentional misstatements of history). So, do these same evangelicals value their patriotism over their faith in Christ? Or is it simply that these evangelicals lack empathy, compassion, and kindness that makes it easy to ignore the oppression of People of Color?

Although many evangelicals only view the Confederate flag as Southern heritage, it is an attempt to preserve the memory of those who died to continue slavery and keep White supremacy alive. The President of the Confederacy, Jefferson Davis, was a former United States Senator and pro-slavery enthusiast who owned more than a hundred slaves. He said, "African slavery, as it exists in the United States, is a moral, a social, and a political blessing" (Jefferson Davis Quotes). Jefferson also believed that owning slaves was not sinful because God sanctioned it, and White men founded America for White men (Jefferson Davis Quotes). To further confirm the origins of White supremacy in the Confederate flag and monuments as symbols of racism and hate, I refer you to Alexander H. Stephens' own words. Alexander was the Vice President of the Confederacy. Stephens gave a famous speech in Savannah, Georgia, after President Abraham Lincoln was elected on March 21, 1864, in which he said, "The negro is not equal to the white man; that slavery subordination to the superior race is his natural and normal condition" (Alexander Stephens Cornerstone Speech).

The racist symbolism of the Confederate flag to Black people is what the Swastika is to Jewish people. However, many evangelicals continue to hold onto these White supremacist beliefs. These same Confederate flag-loving evangelicals are more likely to align their political beliefs with groups like Christian Identity, QAnon,[16] and the Alt-Right. The Alt-Right, also known as the "alternative right," is a White supremacist organization that promotes White nationalist ideology. Although the Ku Klux Klan and The United Daughters of the Confederacy may not have the same power today as they did in the past, new White supremacist groups, including White supremacist Christian groups, are on the rise. For example, Christian Identity, which sounds like an innocent term, is a violent, conspiracy-theorist, White supremacist religious movement with Klan and Nazi roots. Christian Identity

---

[16] QAnon is a cult-like organization based on conspiracy theories. The organization believes there is a secret cabal of pedophiles and Satan worshippers who are trying to take down former President Donald Trump. They also believe that pedophiles are running an international sex-trafficking ring within the government.

views are rooted in racism and a White superiority hierarchy (White Nationalism). According to Christian Identity, they believe that Jews are half-devils and are the greatest enemy to the White race because they are taking over the government. Christian Identity believes their followers are the true descendants of Adam and the chosen seed of Abraham from the lost tribes of Israel. Christian Identity is also linked to the views and opinions of Adolph Hitler. Some extreme versions of Christian Identity believe that Satan had sex with Eve, producing the "evil-breed" of Jews. The African/Black race are considered aliens and are conspiring with Satan. They also believe Jesus was not a Jew but an Aryan from the lost ten tribes of Israel. Unfortunately, immature evangelicals are easily duped into extremist ideas like Christian Identity because conservatives are devoted to abortion and the economy.

After reading this chapter, my prayer for you is that your eyes have been opened and that you will become sensitive to the symbols that are racist and offensive to People of Color. I also pray that you will open your eyes to the truths about organizations like QAnon, the Alt-Right, White Nationalism, and Christian Identity. For years, minorities have protested racist symbols, statues, and national monuments, and they are finally being removed or placed in a museum. For years, Native Americans have protested the racist and offensive logos of many American sports teams. The aftermath of the George Floyd protest prompted teams like the National Football League Washington Redskins, and the Major League Baseball team, the Cleveland Indians, to remove the Native American imagery from their logo and name. As we continue to witness states remove Confederate symbolism from their flags, statues, and monuments, this gives us pause to celebrate this progress with all People of Color. Although these symbols of oppression and racism are being removed from our American culture, unfortunately, a celebration might be premature. As soon as these symbols were removed, sales of Confederate flags skyrocketed. Nonetheless, the Bible says, "The Lord works righteousness and justice for all who are oppressed" (Psa. 103.6). I am thankful for the progress, although there is still a long way to go. Therefore, I long for the day that American evangelicals will completely turn from this darkness and become leaders in righteousness and love. I pray that all evangelicals will denounce racism, Confederate flags, White supremacy, and anyone associated with these things.

CHAPTER 5
JUSTICE &
THE AMERICAN EVANGELICAL

---

*"He has told you, O man, what is good;
and what does the Lord require of you
but to do justice, and to love kindness,
and to walk humbly with your God"
(Mic. 6.8)?*

To help you understand the American evangelical's historical and present-day position toward justice, but more specifically social justice, examples will be given to show how prominent evangelical leaders continue to operate in rebellion to the gospel message of Christ regarding this issue. This chapter will define ideas and groups that many evangelicals align with, such as Christian conservatism, Christian nationalism, patriotism, Christian democracy, and White nationalism. Foundational systems that continue to bring injustice to the poor and People of Color will also be addressed as we uncover the American evangelical's responsibility in supporting those systems. Beginning with *Christian conservatism*, it is associated with attempts to turn the clock back to when the poor, women, and People of Color had no justice. Christian conservatism is similar to the Religious Right's conservatism.

It too has a laser-focused view of politics that only supports the Republican Party's political agenda, supports opposition to abortion and promotes traditional "family values." Not all evangelicals who align with Christian conservatism consider themselves aligned with the Religious Right or the Moral Majority. What differentiates the Religious Right from Christian conservatism are issues like social justice, the poor, minorities, immigrants, affordable healthcare, and affordable housing because they are disputed or completely disregarded. While the Religious Right is more concerned with maintaining White supremacy and political power, Christian conservatism focuses on one major social justice issue, and that is abortion. Christian conservatism views abortion as an assault on human life and an intrinsic evil. All other social injustices take a back seat to the abortion issue for Christian conservatism or are disregarded altogether. Unfortunately, evangelicals who fall under Christian conservatism are often obstacles to the progress of social justice, freedom, and equality for the poor and the People of Color.

One example of Christian conservatism on display is a Twitter post from a megachurch pastor in Plano, Texas, Pastor Jack Graham. On July 24, 2020, Pastor Graham criticized then-candidate Joe Biden for promoting health and safety but being a pro-choice advocate (@JackGraham). Pastor Graham's statement about abortion is one of the quintessential arguments made in Christian conservativism circles. The main question we should be asking is, where is your care for children's rights after they are born? More specifically, where is your care for the rights of children of low-income families and People of Color after they are born into underprivileged socioeconomic environments? It is hypocrisy that evangelicals can ignore gun violence, the lack of healthcare for the poor, police brutality against People of Color, food insecurity, and the inequities in administering the death penalty to People of Color. All I can say is, "Let justice roll down like waters, and righteousness like an ever-flowing stream" (Amos 5.24). Like the Religious Right, Christian conservatism has morphed into a political doctrine, not a religious movement, because they believe that the Republican Party represents morality and the Democrat Party represents immorality (Walker, A.). Frankly, it is not easy to believe that either party truly represents morality. Alternatively, in the words of Paul, "None is righteous, no not one; no one understands; no one seeks for God. All have turned aside; together they have become worthless; no one does good, not even one. Their throat is an open grave; they use their tongues to deceive. The venom of asps is under their lips. Their mouth is full of curses and bitterness" (Rom. 3.10-14). Christian conservatism connects politics and patriotism to American exceptionalism, a political ideology that places America above all other nations to receive the favor of God. Lastly, Christian conservatism has completely disregarded justice for the poor and oppressed to embrace the power and political agendas like the Religious Right ("Conservatism") by opposing social programs and social justice, labeling these programs too progressive or liberal. This behavior contradicts what the Bible teaches, for it says, "Evil men do not understand justice, but those who seek the LORD understand it completely" (Pro. 28.5).

 Christian conservativism can sometimes be confused with Christian nationalism. *Christian nationalism* is a dangerous religiopolitical movement that also has an elevated view of America. Christian nationalists believe that the Bible set the foundation of America, our Founding Fathers were Christians, America is the most elite country in the world, and God ordained White supremacy (Seidel 112). You can find numerous examples of our country's Founders and Presidents who quoted the Bible, but this does not necessarily mean that these men were Christians. Although most of the Founding Fathers were indeed Christians, many of them were deists. Deists believe in a Higher Power or Supreme Being, similar to an agnostic, but trust in reason and observation. A deist does not necessarily refer to a Higher Power or Supreme Being as "God," and most have no devotion to a religious group. Christian nationalist theology also misconstrues eschatology (the end times) by giving America a Messianic identity as the savior nation that has a pivotal role in ushering in the millennial reign of Christ. Christian nationalism links Christianity with Republicanism (Ross, Jr.) and like the Religious Right, Christian conservatism unconditionally endorses Republican candidates based on their "faith."

Many Christian nationalists fear their values are being threatened by liberals, immigrants, and People of Color. Because they believe that America has a biblical foundation, they have an extreme focus on America's national defense, their religious freedom, capitalism, and economic growth. Instead of focusing on essential issues to Jesus like justice, taking care of the poor, and racial equality, these issues take a back seat for the Christian nationalist. I mentioned that Christian nationalists believe America is an elitist country, but that elitism is at the expense of other countries (Hamm).

You may think that Christian nationalism started with President Trump's administration, but the American evangelical elites have displayed it for centuries. Christian nationalists are also known for their distrust of science and scientific experts. Many consider themselves antivaxxers.[17] For example, many in the Religious Right and Christian nationalist groups refuse to accept the science of public health threats like the COVID-19 pandemic. Instead, Christian nationalist groups turned mask-wearing and social distancing during the COVID-19 pandemic into an issue of religious rights violations. According to the 2020 Public Religion Research Institute survey, seventy-one percent of Republicans believed the coronavirus was an intentional virus made in a lab. Only thirty-nine percent of Republicans believed that COVID-19 was a critical issue, and they were less likely to wear a mask in public or get vaccinated (O'Leary).

If you think I am picking on the Republicans, let me acknowledge that neither Democrats nor Republicans in and of themselves are holy nor outright evil. However, neither party truly represents the kingdom of God. God's kingdom is relevant regardless of who is the President or which party has the majority in the House and Senate. The kingdom of God stands on its own because it is its standard. Remember, "God will judge the righteous and the wicked, for there is a time for every matter and for every work" (Ecc. 3.17). Therefore, if you try to cherry-pick a perfect political party or a politician based on God's standards, you will find that your expectations will be left unmet. Believing that your political

---

[17] Antivaxxers are people who refuse to take vaccines and also refuse to vaccinate their children.

party is more moral or righteous is a slippery slope that can lead you down a dangerous path of idol worship. Politics or your favorite political party will never replace your relationship with Christ and loving your neighbors as yourselves.

Patriotism is the love of country. A true patriot follows the country's laws and is an excellent tax-paying citizen who contributes to society ("Patriotism"). Patriotism in and of itself is not inherently wrong, but for many evangelical Christians, patriotism is placed above one's devotion to Christ. More often than naught, patriotism for the evangelical is the love of country, power, and position. For example, Matthew 5.14 is typically quoted by evangelicals and Presidents like Kennedy, Reagan, and Obama (Kristian). The verse says, "You are the light of the world. A city set on a hill cannot be hidden" (5.14). Too often, the evangelical places an elevated view of patriotism, which can turn into Christian nationalism or jingoism, which is nationalism in the form of aggressive policy or extreme chauvinism. As Christ-followers, we must beware that our patriotism remains in the right place. Our allegiance should always be to Christ and not tied to a group, political party, ideology, persona, patriotism, nationalism, or the President.

Both Christian nationalism and Christian conservativism are different from Christian democracy. *Christian democracy* is a political movement based on Roman Catholic philosophy that supports welfare and traditional family values, the dignity of humanness, equal power given to governing authorities, and opposition to socialism ("Christian Democracy"). Christian democracy is an attempt to reconcile Christianity with modern-day democracy. Christian democracy views social justice issues through the eyes of social capitalism and the government's role in religious education so that the Christian promotes democracy (Pinkoski). Christian democracy also sees politics through a Christian worldview believing their religious views inform their politics and political decisions. I understand why good Christians try to input morality into politics through Christian democracy. However, in my opinion, Christian democracy is an ill attempt to combine Christianity with politics, especially democratic politics. Christianity and politics are not co-equals. So many evangelicals have fallen into the trap of claiming religious politics when it just does not exist. While Christian nationalism has an elevated religious view of America, patriotism is the love of country, Christian democracy is a political movement; none should be confused with White nationalism.

White nationalism is a racist White supremacist ideology rooted in Klan, Nazi, skinhead, neo-Confederate, and Christian Identity ideology. While the U.S. is positively changing some racist policies, White nationalism tries to maintain them. White nationalism believes in a White racial identity and White purity similar to neo-Nazism ("White Nationalist"). White nationalists fear they are losing their power and privilege to minorities. This belief is called the "great replacement," wherein White nationalists think immigration will eventually wipe out the "pure" White race. These individuals are often violent extremists or home-grown terrorist groups who reject the idea of equality. Evangelicals who affirm the theology of White nationalism often believe that social justice discussions should be reserved for politicians, not the church. White nationalism is a hate-driven extremist group that is dangerously attracting evangelicals into their fold. What is even crazier is how white supremacy has returned to mainstream politics (Clark). For example, in 2017, hundreds of White nationalists marched through the University of Virginia's campus in Charlottesville, Virginia, with tiki torches screaming, "Jews will not replace us." President Trump aided in making extremist groups mainstream by affirming them when he said, "There were good people on both sides." He also gave a shout-out to another extremist hate group called the Proud Boys by saying, "stand back and stand by." The worst thing about these extremist groups is that many followers call themselves "Christians," hence associating Christianity with White supremacy.

In contrast to White supremacy, the word *justice* occurs over two hundred times in the Bible and is often used in conjunction with righteousness. The Bible teaches us that justice and righteousness go hand in hand, because without righteousness, there is no justice. Justice means to make right the unfair things in our society's systems so that everyone experiences equity. Righteousness means to do right by the oppressed and to adhere to moral principles. Christians are biblically responsible for bringing justice and righteousness to the poor and oppressed groups like women, People of Color, and the LGBTQ community. Our obligation is not to live like the Pharisees of the past and the hypocrite evangelicals of our day. We must work hard to eliminate unfair systems in our country that continue to infringe on the rights of the poor and the oppressed. Understanding the importance of biblical justice and righteousness is an essential responsibility for all Christ-followers because our racial attitude determines our view of justice. Biblical justice is treating people with equity and loving one another just as Christ loves us. Biblical justice is upholding Jesus' words, "You shall love the LORD your God with all your heart, with all your soul, and with all your mind. This is the first and great commandment. And the second is like it: You shall love your neighbor as yourself" (Matt. 22.37–40).

We each have a moral responsibility to respond to injustices like racism, oppression of minority groups, and police brutality. Therefore, in the words of the prophet Isaiah, Christians must "learn to do good; seek justice, correct oppression" (1.17). Furthermore, our responsibility is, as the prophet Jeremiah said, to "Do justice and righteousness, and deliver from the hand of the oppressor him who has been robbed" (22.3). However, it is a conscious or unconscious belief in the dominance of the dominant race, which has always been the Caucasian race in America. The problem accelerates when evangelicals continue to believe that oppression and racial injustice ended at the cessation of the civil rights movement. America's long history of oppressing the poor, immigrants, Native Americans, Mexicans, Asians, and African Americans still impact these communities today, just as it did when slaves were brought to America.

In Jesus' day, it was not uncommon to find him eating with the "sinners," like the outcasts and the tax collectors who were often discriminated against and oppressed by the Jewish leaders. In his Gospel, Luke tells the story of a noticeably short man named Zacchaeus, whom the Jews despised because he was a chief tax collector (19.1-7). Tax collectors were called "traitors" because they collaborated with the Romans to impose harsh penalties and taxes on the Jews. The tax collector was also considered the worst kind of "sinner" in the Jewish community. When Zacchaeus heard that

Jesus was passing through Jericho, he climbed onto a tree to see Jesus over the crowd. "And when Jesus came to the place, he looked up and said to him, 'Zacchaeus, hurry and come down, for I must stay at your house today.' So he hurried and came down and received him joyfully. And when they saw it, they all grumbled, 'He has gone in to be the guest of a man who is a sinner'" (4–7). Jesus singled out Zacchaeus and asked to stay at his house that night, and this enraged the Jewish leaders. They believed that good religious people should always shun "sinners" and outcasts. Despite the response of the Jewish leaders, Jesus displayed love and empathy toward Zacchaeus, and it changed Zacchaeus' life forever. Zacchaeus is an example of loving those who may not fit the norm regardless of their history, background, ethnicity, gender, or race. Unfortunately, the church has treated specific groups like the poor, People of Color, and the LGBTQ community as "sinners," like the Jewish leaders treated the tax collector. As a result, these communities feel ostracized by evangelical Christians instead of loved. Zacchaeus' story is a referendum for all Christians to love as Jesus loves, and at the core, this requires empathy.

As Zacchaeus was an outcast in his day, today, the poor, People of Color and the LGBTQ communities are also often viewed as outcasts. Individuals, institutions, and structural systems in our society continue to alienate the poor and People of Color today. These structural entities can be defined as systemic racism. For this book, systemic racism is discriminatory practices that perpetuate power and privilege to the Caucasian race through the financial banking sector, the economy, the government, the church, the family, education, and the housing sector. While many evangelicals do not believe systemic racism exists, it is often a harsh reality for People of Color in many aspects of their lives. Although many laws and policies have been changed over time to correct the wrongs of systemic racism, there is still a lasting effect from those laws, and it continues to hurt People of Color today (Rothstein 194). Undeniably, there were laws that allowed White people to receive favorable resources and privileges, whereas People of Color were either denied or rejected those same privileges (Cole). However, Psalm 89 reminds us that God desires to bring both righteousness and justice to marginalized communities. For it says, "Righteousness and justice are the foundation of Your throne; steadfast love and faithfulness go before You" (Psalm 89.14). God's judgments are ethical righteousness, not a political party, not a dominant race, not one's gender, or one's socioeconomic status. Jesus extended justice and righteousness to all of humanity, placing us in right-standing with God when he went to the cross and died for all our sins.

Therefore, evangelicals should influence change and challenge the unfair systems of injustice like systemic or foundational racism by adhering to the moral principles and guidance that Jesus provided for us. No longer can evangelicals hide behind the Religious Right or Christian conservatism while supporting inequality and injustice and not being seen as complicit. American evangelicals who support racist tactics like voter suppression, gerrymandering, and racist rhetoric, knowingly or unknowingly support foundational racism through bias, public policy, and even by what comes across the pulpit. Unfortunately, many evangelicals are opposed to diverse programs and view them as an affront to their status, or they consider these programs "reverse racism" (Cole). However, as long as evangelicals support the political agendas of the Religious Right and Christian conservatism, they remain active participants who continue to cause harm to the poor and People of Color.

The preamble to the United States Constitution states, "We the People of the United States, in Order to form a more perfect Union establish Justice, ensure domestic Tranquility, provide for the common defense, promote the general Welfare, and secure the Blessings of Liberty to ourselves and our Posterity, do ordain and establish this Constitution for the United States of America" ("Preamble"). If these words written by our Founders included the poor, women, and People of Color, then racism and discrimination would have never been woven into the fabric of our country. Unfortunately, too many evangelicals have excused racism under the guise of "color blindness," and it is risking the reputation of Christianity. The phrase "I don't see color" is often an attempt to say that you are not a racist. Although with good intent, when White evangelicals say, "I don't see color," many People of Color believe this statement diminishes the uniqueness of their ethnicities, race, and culture. The phrase "I don't see color" can also feed into a system of racism that devalues those who are different. "Colorblindness" expands the existing disparities of privilege and social class systems segregate the rich from the poor and minorities by race and color. Sadly, you can still find evangelicals retweeting and reiterating racist rhetoric on their social media feeds from prominent pastors and politicians at the expense of their friends of Color. By doing so, they are reinforcing an already existing narrative that is a deterrent to non-Christians. Specifically, evangelicals who refuse to call out racist posts, or comments from their friends, family, pastors, and leaders, are accomplices to these injustices.

Do you ever wonder why more evangelical pastors do not preach about the sinfulness of hateful rhetoric and injustices to their congregations? The answer might be that most White pastors are uncomfortable with speaking about these issues to their predominately White congregations because they are worried about the backlash. I have personally witnessed White pastors who have spoken about injustices and their members leave the church. Additionally, when members leave the church, tithes and offerings decline. Furthermore, pastors who preach about race are not immune from being blasted on social media by congregants who choose to leave their church. As Christ-followers, who are we to pick and choose who deserves justice and who does not? Our role as Christians is to love despite the offense and offer grace whenever possible. For example, my pastor announced that our church would support the Bail Project[18] and care for AIDS patients. I thought this announcement was a fantastic idea and a beautiful way for evangelicals to show the love of Jesus. However, I overheard several conversations with evangelicals and leaders in our congregation who were uncomfortable with the church's support for these issues. Some members felt like the church should not pay to bail out someone for their crimes, even if they were misdemeanors. My pastor explained the disparities of the poor and People of Color in the justice system, but these same evangelicals refused to display any empathy. I am so glad that the Lord

---

[18] The Bail Project is a non-profit organization aimed at helping to pay the bail for the poor for misdemeanor offenses.

does not treat us the way we treat others. I said it before, and I will repeat it. Seeking justice for the oppressed is our responsibility as Christ-followers.

As we look back at American History and the countless opportunities evangelicals had to influence change, there are several periods in history where the evangelical's voice was non-existent. American politics started with two major parties, which were the Whigs and the Democrats. The Whig Party fell apart due to internal dissension over slavery which opened the door to the Republican Party ("Abraham Lincoln Prairie Years"). During the Reconstruction Era (1863-1877) following the Civil War, a concentrated effort to integrate the Southern states with almost four million slaves as freedmen and women provided an opportunity for African Americans to start a new life. African Americans built hospitals, churches, and communities for independence ("Reconstruction"). However, segregated churches, schools, and Jim Crow[19] laws developed out of the Reconstruction Era only forced hardships on African Americans. White supremacist "Christian" terrorist groups like the Ku Klux Klan emerged and murdered African Americans who rose to power.

The Klan also assassinated White leaders who supported or defended the Black communities. The question remains, where was the church to speak out for the oppressed during the days of Jim Crow and the murderous actions of the Klan? Jim Crow laws were local and state ordinances that legalized segregation based on race. Beginning as early as 1865, when the ratification of the 13th Amendment abolished

---

[19] "Jumping Jim Crow" was a routine performed by author Thomas Dartmouth and actor Joseph Jefferson.

slavery in the United States, these laws disrupted the lives of countless African Americans. Jim Crow laws existed for over one hundred years until 1968, denying African Americans the right to vote, fair housing, equal education, equal pay, and equal employment opportunities. Anyone who chose to defy the Jim Crow laws was often humiliated, beaten, tortured, thrown into prison, forced to pay excessive fines, and many were murdered. Black codes were also initiated in the South as local and state laws that added restrictions on African Americans' jobs and income. Confederate soldiers often infiltrated the judicial system as judges, police officers, and politicians so that African Americans would lose court cases ("Jim Crow Laws").

During the Reconstruction era, the Ku Klux Klan terrorized African Americans, destroying their schools, businesses, and churches. African Americans began migrating to the northern states to escape the South's Jim Crow laws, and White northerners demanded Jim Crow laws in their cities ("Jim Crow Museum"). As a result, segregation increased in all aspects of life, from restaurant counters, bus stations, department stores, phone booths, water fountains, and movie theaters. Public parks and swimming pools were off-limits for African Americans, and any violation could be costly. Interracial marriage was illegal in the South, and segregated housing communities, jails, and hospitals divided the Black communities from the White communities. As lynchings of African Americans by the Ku Klux Kan increased, so did race riots as Black people began to fight back.

The segregationists were racists that opposed giving African Americans equal access to their facilities, services, communities, jobs, and churches. They resisted any progress made by the African American community but opposed any label of being called a racist (Kendi 5). For example, on May 31, 1921, a White mob attacked a thriving Black neighborhood in the Greenwood district in Tulsa, Oklahoma. The mob burned and bombed hundreds of homes and businesses, killing many of the residents. The Greenwood district neighborhood is more commonly known as Black Wall Street because it was a prosperous business district. The African Americans acquired the land in the neighborhood and built a grocery store, barbershop, and schools. The neighborhood also had doctors, realtors, and newspapers ("Reconstruction"). After the bombings, the African Americans who chose to rebuild faced adversity. Once again, where was the church to support those affected by the racist bombings and loss of livelihood?

There are too many inequitable systems that continue to disenfranchise People of Color even today. No matter how much data and statistics are given to support this issue, many evangelicals continue to refuse to believe these systems still exist. Critics reading this book will say I support things like Critical Race Theory (CRT) because I am saying systemic racism exists. Before I explain what CRT *really is*, I will note that the church uses secular terms too often to define social issues instead of using the Bible as our point of reference. Let me start by saying what CRT is not. CRT is not a theory to pin Blacks against Whites or to start a race war. CRT is a *secular* theory that affirms a system of racism that continues to exist through legal institutions such as the police, judges, and the prison system. CRT notes that the legal systems in America are inherently racist, and racism is a socially constructed concept used by White people to further marginalize People of Color to support their personal economic and political interests (Curry). You do not have to agree with CRT to acknowledge the numerous systems in America that emerged from oppressive beginnings that continue to affect People of Color today. For example, in 1896, in the case of *Plessy v. Ferguson*, the U.S. Supreme court ruled that segregated schools were legal as long as the facilities for Black and White children were the same. We all know those facilities were never the same. Even today, rich children are still more likely to receive a better quality education in less crowded schools because they have the taxpayer dollars to provide up-to-date textbooks, computers, and tablets.

On May 17, 1954, the U.S. Supreme Court ruled in the case of *Brown v. the Board of Education* that segregation in the schools was unconstitutional and a violation of the Equal Protection Clause of the Fourteenth Amendment. So, what did evangelicals do to get around *Brown v. the Board of Education*? I already told you; the Religious Right evangelicals erected private Christian schools and institutions to keep their White children segregated. Even today, White children tend to receive better treatment in the classrooms, whereas minority children are seen as aggressive and receive harsher treatment or punishments. Young People of Color are often counseled that they are not "college material" and are encouraged to enter trade schools instead. When a Person of Color excels in school, they are considered an "exception" or "gifted and talented" instead of recognizing that People of Color can be just as smart without it being an anomaly. For example, First Lady Michelle Obama wrote in her best-selling book *Becoming* that her college counselor said she did not have what it took to get accepted into Princeton University (Collman). Not only did Michelle graduate from

Princeton University, but she also graduated from Harvard Law School. Many White children score higher on the SAT and ACT tests mainly because their vocabulary and backgrounds are similar to those of the test maker's background and vocabulary. Additionally, White parents are also more likely to have the financial resources to afford tutors for their children to score with high scores, or as in the college admissions scandal, pay for their children's results ("U.S. Charges Dozens"). Despite affluence and socioeconomic advantages, White students are often assumed to be more intelligent than students of Color. While schools are no longer segregated by race in America, many schools remain segregated based on socioeconomic status.

Voter suppression efforts against minorities, especially those since the 2020 presidential election, are simply a resurgence of racist strategies like redistricting and gerrymandering that are meant to silence the voices of People of Color. American elections are supposed to be free and fair, but more voter suppression laws are signed to suppress the votes of People of Color and keep the rich in power ("Fair Maps"). In 1812, Massachusetts Governor Elbridge Gerry enacted a law to define a state senatorial race. The law strengthened the Federalist Party votes, which provided the Democratic-Republicans an unfair advantage. The term *gerrymandering* is named after the governor. It describes how a party draws geographical boundaries around a city's electoral districts to give their party an unfair advantage over the other political party. Racial gerrymandering is similar but aims to suffocate the voting power of minorities (Duignan). Today, electoral fraud is often equated with Black and Brown "unqualified" voting communities, but it is the same tactic used during the Reconstruction and civil rights eras. Voter suppression was attributed to terrorist groups like the Ku Klux Klan in the past and today's extremist groups, like "poll watchers" and those who stormed the Capitol on January 6, 2021. Certain parties over the years have tried everything from gerrymandering to violence to suppress the votes of the poor and People of Color while many evangelicals continued to sit quietly on the sidelines.

In the late 1830s, the police aimed to keep enslaved Africans inside the borders by inciting fear to discourage slave revolts. For example, vigilante slave catchers began monitoring the U.S.-Mexico border to keep slaves from escaping to Mexico from Texas. Slave catchers relied on the Fugitive Slave Act of 1850,[20] enabling masters to enact harsh punishments for any who interfered with a slave's capture. While the 13th Amendment abolished slavery in 1865, the 14th Amendment allowed slaves to become citizens in 1868, and the 15th Amendment gave all men the right to vote regardless of race in 1870. President Lyndon B. Johnson signed the Voting Rights Act of 1965 in an attempt to help overcome many of the legal voting barriers we are still facing some fifty-six years later ("Voting Rights Act of 1965").

After the Jim Crow era ended, it did not stop unfair and discriminatory practices. For example, People of Color were routinely paid lower wages than their White counterparts for the same job, and they were less likely to be hired or even interviewed if their names sounded too ethnic or hard to pronounce to White employers. Segregationists used

---

[20] Fugitive Slave Acts forced slaves who ran for freedom to be captured and returned to their slave owners.

discrimination in the housing sector to keep minorities from living in their neighborhoods. If African American families dared to move into an all-White area, mobs would show up on their front lawns burning crosses, spray painting racial slurs on their houses, and destroying their property. The Fair Housing Act of 1968 made it a crime to commit violence in neighborhoods to prevent integration. However, the federal government and local law enforcement hardly did anything to stop the White terrorism Black families endured.

Racially segregated laws and regulations were not just confined to the South either. The practice of redlining was happening all over America because the government implemented it to create and separate urban ghettos from White suburbs (Rothstein 111). Redlining is an illegal mortgage lending practice where lenders deny loans to People of Color and restrict them to lower property value areas. People of Color were often charged higher interest rates than White applicants, allowing the property values of Black neighborhoods to drop and increasing White neighborhoods' value. Outright deceptive loan practices with prepayment penalties were underwritten, so the poor and People of Color suffered unjustly. The term redlining came from the red marks used on loans to delineate minority neighborhoods ("Reconstruction"). As a result, People of Color were not allowed to live in nicer neighborhoods. At the same time, White families could purchase homes at nominal prices, gaining equity in their homes and passing down their accumulated wealth to future generations. On the flip side, minorities spent a higher percentage of their income on inadequate housing with higher interest rates. As a result, many minorities and their descendants continued to live paycheck to paycheck or relied on government assistance ("Jim Crow Laws"). Even

African American and Hispanic Vietnam Veterans were denied fair housing. The Fair Housing Act of 1968 was implemented to stop banks from intentionally denying Black and Hispanic patrons business loans or only offering loans with outrageous interest rates ("Fair Housing Act"). After the Civil Rights Act began to take effect, droves of Confederate loyalists and White supremacists began infiltrating high-level government and law enforcement positions to fight the new laws that gave African Americans and other minorities more rights.

Organizations like the Ku Klux Klan were not the only ones who terrorized African Americans and other minorities. Government organizations were responsible for their fair share of violence too. For example, in the 1960s the FBI, led by J. Edgar Hoover, harassed civil rights leaders, specifically Dr. Martin Luther King, Jr. On March 7, 1965, activist John Lewis and over six hundred people of all races marched across the Edmund Pettus Bridge in Selma, Alabama. Did you know that the Edmund Pettus Bridge is named after a former U.S. Senator, Edmund Pettus, who was hell-bent on preserving slavery and segregation? (Whack). The marchers were brutally attacked by the police and police dogs ("Selma Bloody Sunday"). What is outrageous about the violence toward the American citizens on that day is that the police were never held accountable for their brutality.

For one thing, the society as a whole approved of the police's actions, including the church; but secondly, qualified immunity[21] continues to protect the police from being held legally accountable (Qualified Immunity"). For decades,

---

[21] Qualified immunity protects government officials from lawsuits by determining if the defendant's rights were indeed violated.

African Americans and Hispanic minorities have been terrorized by the police, but they have often found ways to fight back. For example, the Black Panther Party began in 1966 in response to the extreme police brutality against African Americans in Oakland, California. Black Panthers dressed in all black and wore black leather jackets. The Black Panthers started a free lunch program for children and had an armed citizen patrol. In 1968, the Federal Bureau of Investigation's counterintelligence activities dismantled the Black Panther Party ("Black Panthers").

Excessive force, the abuse of power in police departments, and not being given the presumption of innocence lead to death or harsher penalties for Black and Brown communities. In New York, African Americans and Hispanics were disproportionately harassed because of controversial policies and pressure by police departments to make criminal arrests. Stop and Frisk policies were introduced in New York City under the leadership of Mayor Michael Bloomberg and continued under Rudy Giuliani's administration (Grimsley). Stop and Frisk violated the Fourth Amendment, which requires police to suspect a crime before pulling over a suspect. People of Color are disproportionately racially profiled, resulting in increased fear and distrust of the police. In New York in 2003 and 2009, a report exposed that more than forty percent of police stops targeted minorities and low-income areas (Aaro). Unfortunately, once People of Color enter the criminal justice system, it is difficult to prove their innocence. Most minorities cannot afford the cost of an attorney, and they are left subject to public defenders, many of whom are overworked and underpaid. Without the benefit of a well-paid attorney, People of Color can be held for hours in an interrogation without proper counsel and are coerced to make confessions that hurt them at trial. Many minorities are forced to take plea deals for crimes they did not commit in front of all-White or predominately White juries (Grimsley). I believe Jesus would have stood in the gap for those treated unjustly like the outcasts and tax collectors of his day. So then, where are the pastors and leaders leading the protests to lobby our congressmen and bring attention to these injustices?

During the Reconstruction Era, the prison system was the primary means of maintaining legalized involuntary servitude of Black men. Although the Thirteenth Amendment abolished slavery in 1865, it left a void of laborers in the South. Freed slaves who were no longer employed by their masters found themselves violating the law because it was illegal to be unemployed. So, states passed discriminatory laws to incarcerate masses of free Black men at the rate of ten times the population. The mass incarceration and free labor force, also known as convict leasing today, enabled private corporations to cut costs by employing convicts (Little "Most"). The conditions in the prisons were harsh, inhumane, and as a result, many Black men died. Black men are imprisoned not by the system of chattel slavery but by a system that would enslave them all over again to be used legally for free labor. Today, the prison systems are still modern-day slave trades led by private contractors and benefited by large corporations. Some companies that benefit from convict labor are Whole Foods, Haystack Mountain Goat Dairy, Quixotic, McDonald's, Wendy's, Walmart, Starbucks, Sprint, Verizon, Victoria's Secret, Fidelity, JC Penney, American Airlines, and Avis (Riley). Additionally, conservative judges and all-White juries used racist stereotypes to impose lengthy jail sentences. Decades of People of Color caught up in the prison system have resulted in America with the highest incarceration rate in the world (Wallis).

African American and Hispanic communities continue to be brutalized by the police through excessive use of deadly force. I already mentioned how George Floyd was suffocated to death by Minneapolis police officer Derek Chauvin in May 2020. In 2014, Eric Garner died after police placed him in a chokehold. In 2019, Javier Ambler died after being tasered three times in police custody. House Bill 7120, the George Floyd Justice in Policing Act of 2020, was introduced in the House of Representatives by Democrats and the Congressional Black Caucus to combat police misconduct, excessive force, racial, religious, and discriminatory profiling. The bill aims to de-escalate interactions between police and civilians, ban chokeholds, and hold police accountable for their actions by creating the National Police Misconduct Registry. However, it has yet to pass the Senate. On June 15, 2017, the Sandra Bland Act was signed into law by Texas Governor Greg Abbott. This law brought changes to bail reform and prisoner safety, including officer training and the collection of racial profile data ("What Is Sandra Bland Act"). Sandra Bland was stopped on July 10, 2015, for failing to signal while changing lanes. After a heated exchange, Trooper Encinia wrestled Sandra Bland to the ground (which was not captured by his dash camera) and arrested Sandra. Sandra was found dead in her jail cell three days after her arrest ("What Is Sandra"). The circumstances surrounding Sandra's death are speculative as there are some reports of an apparent suicide, but her family does not believe that is possible. How is it that Sandra lost her life for a minor traffic infraction? The question arises, if Sandra had not been a Woman of Color, would the traffic infraction have even escalated to the point of an arrest?

In 1865, the Salvation Army was created to provide hope and help the poor and marginalized who were not welcomed into a traditional church. The Salvation Army provided food, medical supplies, lodging, and the gospel to the poor. Access to quality healthcare continues to plague poor, minority communities today. This disparity has multiplied for People of Color in the COVID-19 pandemic as Black and Brown patients died in overwhelmingly more significant numbers than White patients. The profit-driven American healthcare system has always been geared towards those who can afford quality care instead of providing quality healthcare equitably to all social classes. Slaves who were not privy to proper nutrition were often forced to eat the scraps of animals. Decades later, African Americans are more prone to heart attacks, hypertension, strokes, and Diabetes because many cannot afford to eat healthier food choices ("African Americans Heart Disease"). Within these communities is a lack of trust in the medical community due to inhumane and illegal medical practices like intentionally infecting hundreds of Black men with syphilis in the Tuskegee experiment ("U.S. Public Health"). Another example of the mistrust is doctors who operated on Black female slaves concluding that Black women experience less pain than White women (Carlton). This assumption continues to persist in the medical profession today. Statistically, Black women are more likely to die in childbirth than White women and are less likely to get prenatal care or the best medical advice needed to treat an illness. White people are more likely to live longer lives from years of advanced medical treatment and access to better quality healthcare. So should it matter if evangelicals *believe* that systemic racism exists or agree with all the examples I mentioned in this book? There is enough historical data and present-day examples to provide evidence of racial discrimination and oppression in America's past and present. It does not matter if evangelicals choose to believe the truth. Unfortunately, despite all the information in this book, many evangelicals will continue to refuse to believe any of it because it shines an ugly light on their heritage or possibly themselves.

The prophet Micah said, "He has told you, O man, what is good; and what does the Lord require of you but to do justice, and to love kindness, and to walk humbly with your God?" (Micah 6.8). The Lord requires that we "do justice." To do justice means that you do not have to agree or disagree with systemic racism or CRT components intellectually. It does mean, as a Christ-Follower, you have a heart that desires to bring justice to those who are experiencing injustice. Think about how you can leverage your circle of influence to help bring justice. More importantly, figure out ways you can display the love of Jesus Christ to those who are hurting and oppressed. The church's silence has hurt decades of minorities for way too long, but it can stop with you. I challenge you to ask yourself, "Am I personally remaining silent in racism, oppression, and injustices against the poor and People of Color?" If so, tap into those uncomfortable feelings you get when injustices are being brought to light and refuse to remain silent.

If this chapter made you feel uneasy or even angry, is it because the Lord will no longer allow you to ignore these disparities? On the other hand, do you feel threatened, like something is being taken away from you? If the answer is yes, then write down what you feel is being taken away. If you are a follower of Christ, you should believe that God is your provider, and He is in control. God allows you to gain wealth and prosperity. So then, People of Color and the changes happening in society are not taking anything away from you. If you happen to lose anything, it is because God allowed you to lose it. For the evangelical, the obstacle to justice is what you allow to guide your heart. Remember that your neighbors, though they may not look anything like you, are made in the image of God as you are.

However, it is not too late for these evangelical leaders to repent and change course. As Scripture says, "Trust in the Lord with all your heart, and do not lean on your own understanding. In all your ways acknowledge him, and he will make straight your paths. Be not wise in your own eyes; fear the LORD and turn away from evil" (Pro. 3.5–7). Christians must trust God and not in man because man will always fail us, but God never fails. In many cases, evangelicals have trusted pastors and politicians and misinterpreted scripture that supports their political views. I end this chapter by remembering the words of the Psalmist when he said, "Satisfy us in the morning with your steadfast love, that we may rejoice and be glad all our days. Make us glad for as many days as you have afflicted us, and for as many years as we have seen evil. Let your work be shown to your servants, and your glorious power to their children. Let the favor of the Lord our God be upon us, and establish the work of our hands upon us; yes establish the work of our hands" (Psa. 90.14–17). Let us put aside personal feelings that are getting in the way of standing up and fighting for justice for our brothers and sisters. Fighting for justice is not a red or blue thing, a Black or White thing, nor a Democrat or Republican thing. Fighting for justice is a loving-your-neighbor-as-yourself kind of thing.

CHAPTER 6
THE DEMISE OF EVANGELICALISM THROUGH POLITICS AND PRESIDENTS

"Woe to the shepherds who destroy and scatter the sheep of my pasture!" declares the LORD (Jer. 23.1).

I mentioned numerous laws and policies that continue to exist to progress foundational racism. As we examine the previous one hundred years' worth of presidential administrations from 1921-2021, you will see how those laws and policies are all intertwined with the evangelical church. One of the major obstacles to justice is how American evangelicals confuse the word *justice* with a political meaning instead of a biblical responsibility. If evangelicals viewed justice as a human rights issue and not a political one, the church would take the lead of bringing justice to the oppressed. I know I keep talking about loving our neighbors as ourselves, but it is a point that we must rehash. When Jesus spoke about this concept, it was not a political statement but a biblical command. As Christ-followers, our obligation to bring equity and justice is expressed when we follow Jesus' footsteps. I mentioned that evangelicals allowed White supremacist influences to shape the American church's view of biblical justice. So, you might be wondering, how can evangelicals expel White supremacist ideas that still influence many congregations today? First, follow this command: "Thus, says the Lord: Do justice and righteousness, and deliver from the hand of the oppressor him who has been robbed. And do no wrong or violence to the resident alien, the fatherless, and the widow, nor shed innocent blood in this place" (Jer. 22.3). This verse specifically refers to the resident alien (present-day immigrants), the fatherless (orphans), and the widows who need to be protected from the oppressor (the racist).

Secondly, apprehend that God can do exceedingly, abundantly, above what can be comprehended. That is, God gives you the power to break the strongholds of White supremacy and racism through the Holy Spirit to bring healing and true biblical justice in the church and the world (Eph. 3.20). Unfortunately, too many evangelicals have chosen to neglect the gospel message in exchange for political rhetoric that makes them feel pious and super-spiritual. White evangelicals who deny that their conservative political values are problematic for minorities lack the empathy that Jesus modeled. As a result, groups of evangelicals have turned their political partisanship into idol worship as they support cult-like politicians and organizations who openly embrace racism and evil. Additionally, the continued existence of White supremacy in American evangelicalism has been suppressed for so long that many evangelicals do not see it for what it is, leaving many blinded to the effects of racism, including their churches.

The Demise of Evangelicalism through Politics and Presidents

To gain a greater understanding of evangelicalism and how it plays out in our two-party political system, you must first understand the racist history behind the Democratic and Republican parties. As mentioned previously, the Confederacy was born out of the desire for White Southerners to preserve slavery and resist the abolitionist ideals of the Northern colonies. Black Union soldiers who were captured in the South were forced back into slavery, tortured, crucified, and some were even burned alive ("Nathan Bedford Forrest"). After the Civil War, many White Christians helped newly freed Black slaves rebuild their lives. The Republican Party supported the anti-slavery laws and policies, not the Democrats. At personal risk, I must add, many White Southerners supported Reconstruction because some former Confederates grew a conscience about slavery. Those who abhorred the treatment of Black people ended up migrating to the Republican Party. Other Southerners joined the Republican Party, not because they believed in equality for Blacks, but because they thought it was better to win political power with Black Americans rather than to lose political power. During this era, the Democratic Party overtly appealed to racist Whites, which drove many Blacks into the Republican Party. Today, evangelicals who deny the existence of systemic racism represent the Democratic Party of the past and the racism represented through White supremacy in the Republican Party today. My point is that White supremacy and racism are both threaded through America's history, political system, and the church, reinforced by professing (historically, by all denominations) Christians.

The past hundred-plus years of presidential administrations, beginning with President Woodrow Wilson will reveal a connection between religious and racist presidents and the evangelical response to their policies (Loewen 21). In 1912, Woodrow Wilson was the President of Princeton University and refused to grant Black students' admission. Wilson was elected as the Democratic President from (1913-1921). He was an outspoken Presbyterian Christian who was one of the most devout Christian Presidents of his era. Wilson's father, minister Joseph Ruggles Wilson, helped found the Presbyterian Church of the Confederacy and used the Bible to defend slavery. Woodrow Wilson read his Bible daily and was an elder in his Presbyterian church. Wilson and his wife were known to be outspoken racists who believed Black people were an inferior race, and his wife was known to use ugly words to refer to their Black servants (Keating). Wilson was the first president to segregate the Navy and the federal government (Loewen 19–20). He also vetoed racial equality in the Covenant League of Nations.[22] Wilson's modus operandi was to reverse the civil rights of African Americans. He refused to allow Blacks in political positions in the Democratic Party. Wilson was sympathetic to the Ku Klux Klan, so he reinstituted Jim Crow laws, fired Black federal workers, and blocked anti-lynching laws. Most history books remain silent about the racist aspects of Wilson's legacy but only emphasize his devotion to his Christian faith. Almost one hundred years later, on July 27, 2020, Princeton University finally removed Woodrow Wilson's name from

---

[22] The League of Nations was an international diplomatic group that developed after World War I to handle disputes between countries.

their school of public policy to acknowledge the racist history of his presidency.

Next is Republican President Warren G. Harding (1921-1923). Harding was a member of the Trinity Baptist Church in Marion, Ohio. His presidency was plagued with suspicion due to an alleged induction in the Ku Klux Klan through a private ceremony in the White House Green Room. There is much controversy about whether President Harding's Klan induction is even a true story. President Harding's most vocal critic, William Eastbrook Chancellor, a professor at the College of Wooster, alleged that Harding had a Black grandmother. If President Harding had a Black ancestor and was declared legally Black, he would have been disqualified to be the presidential candidate and could not be elected President. Several states supported the one-drop rule, which meant that anyone with even one drop of African blood was considered Black, Negro or Colored and was disqualified. William Chancellor believed Harding's alleged Black status made him unfit to be the President of the United States. There is an unverified rumor that Harding allegedly joined the Ku Klux Klan to thwart William Chancellor's accusations. However, if Harding's Klan membership was factual, why was a bigger deal not made about it?

Moreover, why have a private ceremony (Straight Dope)? On October 26, 1921, Harding delivered a civil rights speech to a Klan audience in Birmingham, Alabama. In his speech, Harding talked about Black men who served in the war alongside White men and deserved equal educational opportunities and better schools, but not school integration. Harding's speech did not appeal to his White Klan audience. Although it is unknown if Harding was an outright racist like his predecessor Woodrow Wilson, or if he was inducted into the Klan, we do know that Harding proposed an anti-lynching bill later squashed in the Senate. Harding came from a family of abolitionists and was known for speaking out against the violent attacks on African Americans after the Tulsa Massacre, but he never passed any policies to eradicate segregation or to implement protections. Harding also supported restricting immigrants from coming to America. Harding's legacy is somewhat convoluted regarding the Klan and his faith.

Harding's successor, President Coolidge, was sworn in by his father in the middle of the night after President Harding unexpectedly died from congestive heart failure. Depending on the historical source of writings, Republican President Calvin Coolidge (1923-1929), is viewed as either an honorable Christian, a racist, or a hero. Coolidge and his wife regularly attended the racially integrated First Congregational Church in Washington, DC. The Congregationalist denomination was the faith of the Puritan pilgrims who came to America seeking religious freedom. Influenced by the faith of his grandparents, Coolidge embraced the teachings of the Bible. When President Harding died, Coolidge called on his pastor to counsel him before being sworn into the presidency. Two issues supporting Coolidge's reputation as a racist are his response to the Great Mississippi River Flood of 1927 and the Immigration Act of 1924. The government assisted the White families affected by the flood. However, much like the response to Hurricane Katrina under President George Bush Jr.'s administration, Black and minority families were left to fend for themselves. Even worse, their communities were flooded to take the pressure off the levees surrounding the White neighborhoods. As a result, thousands of Black people were left homeless and destitute with no governmental support. The Immigration Act of 1924 was also deemed racist because it banned the entrance of Asian and Middle Eastern immigrants into America. Other historians viewed President Coolidge as a champion for civil rights for Black and Native Americans. On June 2, 1924, President Coolidge signed into law the Indian Citizenship Act of 1924. So, you see, Coolidge's conflicting actions and policies convolute his legacy.

Unlike President Coolidge's questionable racist policies, Republican President Herbert Hoover (1929-1933) was known for being a White supremacist and racist and one of the worst presidents in our nation's history. Hoover was a Quaker and a conservative Republican. He was active in his church and served as a minister. Quakers, known as "Friends," were known for their love of humanity and the ability for everyone to access God within. However, Herbert Hoover's disdain for African Americans led him to defy Quaker's beliefs. Most African Americans supported the Republican Party, the "Grand Ole Party" (GOP), until Hoover purged Black people from GOP leadership positions and from the party itself. He fought anti-lynching laws, supported segregation, and enforced segregation in the military. Hoover did everything he could to keep the Black race poor and stripped of any means of power, and he forced the majority of African Americans to leave the Republican Party. Hoover was blamed for the Great Depression and the worsening conditions in its aftermath. Hoover was an equal opportunity offender to any race that was not White. He deported over two million American citizens with Hispanic names to Mexico and became good friends with Germany's Adolph Hitler. Hoover opposed America's involvement in

World War II. Hoover left the White House an embarrassed and embittered man after losing his reelection efforts by a landslide to Franklin D. Roosevelt. Ironically, because Hoover had driven African Americans away from the GOP, most flocked to the Democratic Party, contributing to his embarrassing loss. Despite Hoover's Quaker upbringing of love and harmony of all people, his policies and actions undoubtedly were racist.

Democratic President Franklin D. Roosevelt (1933-1945) was a life-long, devout Episcopalian and member of St. James Episcopal Church in Hyde Park, New York. Roosevelt loved the social ethics in the Bible, so he was dedicated to the Social Gospel of helping the poor, but not necessarily Black people. Even with all of FDR's accomplishments, he is still viewed by minorities as a bigot for disparaging racist remarks about African Americans, Asians, and Jews. Roosevelt was against the immigration of People of Color, often referring to them as "foreign elements." He called African Americans "semi-beasts" and had occasional use of the N-word (Medoff). Roosevelt bragged that he was not of Jewish descent and complained about too many Jews working for the government. Roosevelt refused to support anti-lynching legislation and the desegregation of the military. He also signed an executive order that forced over 100,000 Japanese Americans into inhumane prison camps during World War II. Roosevelt was praised for his work during the Great Depression, but his policies hurt minorities and ethnic communities more than they helped them. Roosevelt implemented social security, minimum wage, and unemployment benefits through his New Deal initiatives.[23] The housing discriminations built into his initiatives hurt Black communities. At the same time, it lined the pockets of the White middle-class communities. Roosevelt's policies denied African Americans the same opportunities provided to White communities to build wealth through homeownership and equity (Medoff). Clearly, this information shows that Roosevelt's legacy was clouded with racial prejudice despite his deep faith.

Roosevelt's successor, Democratic President Harry S. Truman (1945-1953), was a devout Christian who openly expressed his racist beliefs but kept his religious beliefs somewhat private. Truman was a member of the First Baptist Church of Grandview. He was one of the first presidents to support Israel as a Jewish state responding to the Holocaust. Truman believed in Christian Nationalism and that America was a Christian savior nation for the world, and he believed in the freedom of religious expression. Although Truman made civil rights a priority, he was also known for using racial slurs about African Americans and Chinese and Japanese people. Truman toned down his racial slurs before his presidency but continued to use them in private conversations even after becoming president. Truman described the African Americans in the White House as "an army of coons" and, in a letter to his wife, even referred to a "nigger picnic day" (Hampson). On July 26, 1948, Truman signed an executive order, understanding he needed the Black vote to win, that supported anti-lynching laws, anti-poll taxes,

---

[23] The New Deal was a set of programs, projects, initiatives, and financial reforms.

and desegregation of the military. He even spoke out against communism, all of which neither President Hoover nor President Roosevelt supported. Despite Truman's faith, his racial prejudice was apparent in his speech and policies.

Truman's successor was Republican President Dwight D. Eisenhower (1953-1961). Eisenhower believed Christianity was the focal point to separate America from Communist oppression. He also believed the government should be run with religious values and faith, regardless of the religion. Although he was not known for outright racism, Eisenhower was known for withholding support from the critical race and justice-related causes. Eisenhower was in office during some pivotal events of the civil rights movement. Although Rosa Parks was not the first African American to refuse to give up her seat on a bus, she was arrested, which sparked the Montgomery bus boycotts. On May 17, 1954, *Plessy v. Ferguson*, the 1896 case that allowed for segregation of public facilities, was challenged by *Brown v. Board of Education*. Eisenhower declined to endorse *Brown v. Board of Education*, which desegregated public schools, and he did little to enforce it. Some public schools closed their doors in efforts to avoid "race mixing." The lynching and subsequent death of Emmett Till also occurred under Eisenhower's watch, leaving his presidency marked by horrific events. Eisenhower did not grow up around African Americans and lived a life of privilege, which may have influenced his decisions of inaction ("Struggle for Civil Rights"). However, Eisenhower's legacy is left with a stain of racism and White supremacy even if it was not overt.

Eisenhower's successor, Democratic President John F. Kennedy's administration (1961-1963), occurred at the height of the civil rights movement. President Kennedy was known for his Catholic faith, and in fact, he was the first Catholic elected to the presidency. Kennedy was baptized in St. Aidan's Catholic Church in Brookline, Massachusetts, and attended St. Francis Xavier Church throughout his life. During his time in the Senate and presidency, Kennedy attended three different Catholic churches in Washington, DC. Kennedy ran on issues like racial discrimination, but when African Americans appealed to Kennedy's Federal government for protections, they received none. Although Kennedy was not overtly racist, the Kennedy administration was inadequate to protect Black people from the terrorism of the Klan and other racist hate groups. In many instances, the Kennedy administration sat back and did nothing, such as in the case of the Sixteenth Street Church bombing in Birmingham, Alabama, by White supremacists on Sunday, September 15, 1963. The FBI insufficiently protected Dr. Martin Luther King, Jr. even though they repeatedly received information about King's life death threats. Under the leadership of J. Edgar Hoover, the FBI refused to pass that information to Dr. King and his people to protect him. Under the Kennedy era, Black citizens faced the bombing and burning of their homes, businesses, and churches, while the FBI chose not to get involved in protecting them. Before Kennedy's death, he selected Thurgood Marshall as a federal judge and several other African American appointments ("John F. Kennedy"). Unlike many presidents before him, Kennedy was not known for being a racist, but he did not do much to fight racial violence and discrimination against African Americans either.

The assassination of President Kennedy ushered in the Lyndon B. Johnson administration (1963-1969). Johnson was a member of the National City Christian Church, also known as Disciples of Christ, in Washington, DC. Johnson grew up in a strongly religious family environment with a long line of Baptist preachers in his family. Under Johnson's administration, after passing the Civil Rights Act of 1963, the All-Star Triangle Bowling Alley in Orangeburg, South Carolina, refused to allow Black people to use their facility. Students from South Carolina State University held a demonstration in protest. State troopers fired upon two hundred unarmed, black student demonstrators, killing three and wounding twenty-eight. Johnson's administration did nothing in response to this deadly incident which came to be known as the Orangeburg Massacre (History.com). Under President Johnson's administration, the FBI opposed the civil rights movement, persecuted Black organizers, framed Black leaders, and covered up the murders of civil rights workers and police brutality. The murder of White civil rights activists forced the FBI to step in finally. On March 7, 1965, which came to be known as Bloody Sunday, six hundred protestors participated in the Selma-to-Montgomery March led by the young student organizer John Lewis. They set out to march from Selma to Montgomery, Alabama, to demand an end to racial segregation and voter suppression. State and local police officers attacked the marchers as they attempted to leave Selma on the Edmond Pettus Bridge, which, ironically, was named after a Confederate *hero*. John Lewis suffered a fractured skull in that attack but served as a U.S. Congressman from Georgia for thirty-three years. It is no secret that President Johnson often used racial slurs when referring to Black people. For example, regarding the appointment of Thurgood Marshall to the Supreme Court, Johnson referred to Justice Marshall as "a nigger" (Serwer) and the Civil Rights Act as "the nigger bill." (Serwer) President Johnson deserves credit for signing the Civil Rights Act and the Voting Rights Act into law. However, he had his racist side like previous presidents, despite being a Christian (Library Staff).

President Johnson's successor was Republican President Richard Nixon (1969-1974). President Nixon was a Quaker who often held White House worship services and was close to Evangelist Billy Graham. Nixon grew up in a highly religious community of the Quaker church in Whittier, California. Unlike evangelicals who made excuses for President Trump's unruly behavior, the Quakers National Council of Churches called for Nixon's impeachment after the Watergate scandal (Religious News). Although many considered Nixon a Christian, he was well known for his racist rhetoric and bigotry. Nixon was caught on tape spewing racial epithets as evidence of his bigotry in a conversation with Henry Kissinger, Nixon's national security adviser (Bass). Nixon did not like anyone who was not White or heterosexual, and his declaration of the "war on drugs" targeted African Americans. According to the Miller's Center Presidential Recordings Program, Nixon's had over 3,432 hours of secret recordings, many of which included racist declarations ("Reagan, Nixon and Race"). Nixon also was a proponent of states' rights revisionist history. He perpetuated the "welfare queen" stereotype that African Americans on welfare were too lazy to work and just wanted free government handouts. Nixon's term ended with his resignation over the

Watergate scandal but not before he put his racist stamp on his presidency.[24] Regardless of Nixon's religiosity, he was a racist president, and his policies confirmed it. President Ronald Reagan would pick up on Nixon's racist rhetoric in his presidency.

In his final State of the Union address, Nixon's successor, Republican President Gerald R. Ford (1974-1977), tried to influence President Nixon to talk about civil rights. Ford was a devout man of faith sworn into a presidency that he never saw coming. Ford placed his hand on the Bible at his favorite passage, "Trust in the Lord with all your heart, and don't lean on your own understanding. In all your ways acknowledge him, and he will make straight your paths" (Prov. 3:5–6). Ford was an Episcopalian and attended the Immanuel Church on the Hill in Washington, DC. While Nixon avoided Black people like the plague, President Ford was more open to inviting Black civil rights activists to the White House for regular meetings. However, Ford opposed bussing Black children to White schools and vehemently opposed *Brown v. Board of Education* to desegregate the schools. Ford quickly walked back his statements to save face. Although Ford was not an outright racist like his predecessors, he made significant blunders on critical civil rights issues that caused some critics to view him as a racist despite his faith.

On the other hand, Ford's successor, Democratic President Jimmy Carter (1977-1981), was specifically known for his faith in Jesus Christ. Carter attended Maranatha Baptist Church in Plains, Georgia. Carter, a consistent devout

---

[24] Watergate was a political scandal where the federal government covered up its involvement in the break-in of the Democratic National Committee.

Baptist, taught Sunday School when evangelical Christianity was not automatically associated with the Republican Party. Carter was known as the Jesus-loving Democrat who often talked about his relationship with Jesus and his temptation to lust (Shirley). Historically, Carter also had a history of racist behavior during his time in Georgia state politics. Before Carter's ascent to the presidency, he praised life-long segregationist Democratic Governor Lester Maddox, who endorsed Carter for Governor. Carter openly criticized his Democratic challenger Governor Carl Sanders for locking arms with Black NBA players. Sanders was part-owner of the Atlanta Hawks and supported Dr. Martin Luther King, Jr. Carter even told a reporter he could win an election without a single Black vote. In truth, Carter won the Georgia Governorship without hardly any of the Black vote. He also said he would not force integration of neighborhoods and saw nothing wrong with maintaining "ethnic purity." Carter did not allow for racist campaign tactics in his bid for the White House, but his past actions contradicted his Christian beliefs. Carter's presidency ended with a loss to Republican presidential candidate, Ronald Reagan.

Republican President Ronald Reagan (1981-1989) did not try to hide his racist White supremacist views. Reagan was known as a devout Christian raised in the Disciples of Christ Church. He also embraced the Catholicism of his father's faith. At age fifteen, Reagan began teaching Sunday School at Dixon's First Christian Church. Reagan's faith encouraged him to speak out against abortion, support school prayer and shaped his foreign policy views. Although Reagan was rarely seen inside a church, he constantly appealed to the evangelical community throughout his presidency. Reagan was also known for holding private prayer before his Cabinet meetings. Regardless of his religious affiliations, Reagan upheld his racist beliefs. For example, in a call with President Nixon, then-Governor Reagan referred to people from African countries as "monkeys" (Naureckas). Reagan sided with Bob Jones University in their attempt to maintain the tax-exempt status they lost for refusing to desegregate their school. Reagan continued President Nixon's "welfare queen" rhetoric and hired segregationist-loving, race-baiting Lee Atwater as the political director of his presidential campaign. Lee Atwater later became the presidential campaign manager for George Bush, Sr., in 1988 and went on to chair the Republican National Committee (RNC). Reagan was hostile toward affirmative action, welfare, social programs for the poor, and supported a state ballot initiative that discriminated against Black people in the housing sector. Reagan was also opposed to the Civil Rights Act and the Voting Rights Act (Rossinow). Reagan opposed any policy that allowed for equity between the White and Black races. Reagan's politics ridiculed the homeless and oppressed and valued the rich over the poor, which is contradictory to the teachings of Jesus. Reagan used racially charged words like "states' rights," "strapping young buck," "Chicago welfare queen," and "the South shall rise again" to feed into the White supremacy of his base, much like President Trump did forty years later (Haney-Lopez). Even with all of the overt racism toward African Americans, most evangelicals embraced Reagan's views, and they celebrated Reagan as a fellow evangelical.

 Under Reagan's presidency, the middle class shrunk, and much of the middle class found themselves in the lower class. His "war on drugs," disproportionately increased mass incarceration of Black and Brown people through his 1986 Anti-Drug Abuse Act. The Act imposed longer sentences to Black and Brown people than their White counterparts received for the same crimes. Reagan used racially coded rhetoric to attract voters who felt threatened by the advancements of People of Color, much like the racist rhetoric used by future President Donald Trump. There is a direct correlation between how Reagan's policies affected African Americans and the increased number of poor African Americans, which grew by 2.2 million under his presidency (Kendi "11 Most"). Reagan portrayed a message to White evangelicals that their privilege, jobs, colleges, and way of life would be in jeopardy if minorities reached equal status. In 1980, Reagan made an appearance at the Neshoba County Fair held in a small town where the Ku Klux Klan murdered three civil rights activists in 1964, and the fair was known for attracting racists (Young, N). Despite Reagan's White supremacist views, his racist policies, rhetoric, and illegal foreign activities like the Iran-Contra scandal,[25] Reagan is still revered as a champion of the evangelical Religious Right.

Reagan's successor, Republican President George H.W. Bush (1989-1993) in many ways piggy-backed many of Reagan's racist policies in his one-term presidency. Bush (Sr.) was known as a devout Episcopalian, and his policies were more in line with the evangelicals who supported him. Bush, Sr. often quoted the Scriptures in his prayers and speeches from the White House. He encouraged

---

[25] The Iran-Contra Affair was a political scandal of the secret sale of arms to the Khomeini government of the Islamic Republic of Iran.

Americans to volunteer their time and to embody a life like Jesus. Bush, Sr. was a member of St. Martin's Episcopal Church in Houston and revered as a godly man of faith. He commissioned a volunteer organization called Points of Light to give resources to those less fortunate. Bush, Sr. even publicly denounced former Grand Wizard of the Ku Klux Klan David Duke and appointed General Colin Powell as the first Black Chairman of the Joint Chiefs of Staff. Bush, Sr. also appointed Dr. Louis Sullivan, Founding President of Morehouse School of Medicine, to be the Secretary of Health and Human Services. He also replaced retiring Thurgood Marshall with another Black Justice appointment Clarence Thomas. However, Thomas's views were not welcomed by most of Black America.

Under Bush Sr.'s administration, the rich became richer through his tax cuts aimed explicitly at decreasing taxes for the wealthy. Lee Atwater led his presidential race against Michael Dukakis. Bush Sr.'s campaign ran a racist newspaper ad Atwater later apologized for on his death bed, but Bush never did. The campaign ad attempted to capitalize on White fear of Black men by prominently featuring a photo of a Black convicted murderer named Willie Horton. Bush, Sr. also continued Reagan's "war on drugs," which, as I mentioned, under Reagan's administration disproportionately incarcerated Black and Brown men by the thousands. Another stain on Bush's legacy was his reference to his biracial grandchildren (by his son Jeb Bush and Jeb's Mexican-born wife) as "the little brown ones" (Associated Press). In Bush's last year in office, the race riots from the Rodney King beating were the ultimate test to his presidency. Bush, Sr. called for "law and order" while at the same time saying the beating was revolting to him. George Bush, Sr., had a complicated legacy that seemed to play both sides of the coin, either racist or a sympathetic antiracist.

Bush, Sr.'s successor Democratic President Bill Clinton (1993-2001), was a self-proclaimed Methodist. Clinton accepted Jesus at nine years of age. During his presidency, Clinton attended a Methodist church; but in the 1980s, he joined Immanuel Baptist Church, sang in the choir, and regularly attended Bible study. Truthfully, many evangelicals denounced Clinton's faith as a political stunt because of his views on abortion, sexuality, and sexual misconduct. Many evangelicals did not believe Clinton was a Christian. Other evangelicals led a rallying cry for the impeachment of Clinton because of his "character" in what they perceived as a moral decline. When sexual allegations against Clinton's White House aide Monica Lewinsky surfaced, evangelicals publicly crucified Clinton as morally unfit for the office of the President of the United States of America. For example, Televangelist Pat Robertson said Clinton made the Oval Office into his sexual playpen (Merritt).

Interestingly, those same evangelicals who supported the morally unfit candidacy of Donald Trump owe Bill Clinton an apology. While many African Americans viewed Clinton as the "first Black President" for the policies and promises they thought would help People of Color, Clinton's 1994 Violent Crime Control Act unjustly profiled People of Color. The Act led to over 250,000 mass incarcerations and put thousands of non-violent offenders in jail. Clinton's crime bill included:

- the three-strikes provision that mandated life in prison,

- grants for the construction of prisons, and
- a federal ban on assault weapons.

Today, the 1994 crime bill is seen as a racist bill that unfairly targeted Black and Brown communities. Another stain to Clinton's legacy was his racist comment about President Barack Obama in 2008. Clinton's faith, morality, and racist policies make you question if he really supported the advancement of People of Color or if he were just merely a politician doing what he thought would win him another election.

Clinton's successor was Republican President George W. Bush (2001-2009), the son of Former President George H.W. Bush. Bush Jr. is an openly devout Christian who believed his religion shaped his worldview and political career. Bush Jr. and his wife Laura faithfully attended a United Methodist Church in Texas before he became President. Bush read the Bible every morning and was fundamentally conservative in his views of Christianity. Although his Methodist church was part of mainline Protestantism, his religious views were more conservative and traditional, so evangelicals claimed President Bush as one of their own. Bush was probably one of the most vocal Christian presidents besides Jimmy Carter in our lifetime. Many African Americans viewed Bush as a racist after thousands of New Orleans Black residents were left stranded, and over a thousand died, waiting for federal aid after Hurricane Katrina. A rumor that stained Bush's presidency stated the government intentionally flooded the poor parts of New Orleans to save the wealthier White districts, similar to what had occurred under President Hoover's administration after the Mississippi flood.

The Bush administration's lack of oversight and regulation of the banking and financial industries are typical of conservative Republican economic policies, and led to the Great Recession of 2008. While large corporations deemed "too big to fail" received government bailouts, millions of Americans, especially the poor and People of Color, were left unemployed, and many lost their homes. Once again, the working poor and People of Color were disproportionately impacted. In addition, Bush's No Child Left Behind Act (NCLB) was also racially biased and prejudicial because it broadened the stranglehold of standardized testing on children. Many activists argue that standardized testing is too biased because it is from a White-biased perspective. Schools that did not do well on the standardized tests were denied funding, thus broadening the already large chasm in schools with children of Color (Kendi "11 Most"). However, after the death of George Floyd in 2020 former President Bush Jr. spoke out against the police brutality against African Americans and praised the protestors (Fredericks). Like many of his presidential predecessors, Bush has a complex history concerning his faith and racist policies.

When the first biracial Presidential nominee of both Black and White parents became the President of the United States, many began to believe that racism in America was a thing of the past. Those hopes died by the backlash that was soon to come out. After the Democratic President Barack Obama's election (2009-2017), the Ku Klux Klan increased throughout the South. White nationalists and White supremacist hate groups were emboldened to come out in the open and recruit new members, and racist hate speech flooded social media. Instead of embracing the intelligent, talented, and faith-filled career of Barack Obama, evangelical journalists, talk show hosts, and pastors maligned, ridiculed, and repeated racist stereotypes. Instead of defying racist stereotypes, "no drama Obama" as he was often referred to, brought out White rage, especially the White evangelical Religious Right. Obama often referenced Scripture in his speeches. He expanded the White House faith-based initiatives to include the evangelical's perspective. Still, Obama was met with racist taunts and cartoons of him and his wife Michelle, and he was accused of being a Muslim terrorist by evangelical leaders. Obama was baptized as an adult in the Trinity United Church of Christ Chicago, Illinois, despite all the Muslim rumors. Obama is a man of compassion and faith. He had a presidential legacy that reflected his family values. Obama defended the rights of all people regardless of race, gender, or sexual orientation, advocated for gun control, the working poor, and for equality in the workplace. Obama supported affordable healthcare for all Americans, stood up against prominent corporate lobbyists, and spoke against the death penalty.

While President Obama was giving a speech to a joint session of Congress in September 2009, Senator Joe Wilson, Jr. shouted out "You lie!" in the middle of his speech. No American President in modern history was ever treated with such utter disrespect. Senate Majority Leader Mitch McConnell boasted on FOX News how he blocked Obama's attempt to fill federal judicial vacancies for two years, leaving them open for President Trump to fill instead (Mazza). The same level of disrespect that made McConnell pledge to do everything in his power to make Obama's presidency fail echoed from the pulpits of many evangelical churches.

Evangelicals blamed Obama for the legalization of same-sex marriage and for passing the Affordable Care Act or Obamacare. Although Obama's presidency was a significant milestone in American History and a proud moment for African Americans, Obama's policies were often seen as racist for the Hispanic communities. Obama was known as the "Deporter in Chief" because of the millions of immigrants his administration deported to Mexico and other countries. Under the Obama Administration, over 2.5 million immigrants were deported, which was more than any president before or after him. I will admit I was proud to see the first African American man elected to the Presidency two times, just as I am proud to see the first Black-Asian American elected to the Vice Presidency in 2020. However, in all honesty, I cannot say I am proud of all the policies of Obama's administration, especially if they are deemed racist to my brothers and sisters of Hispanic heritage.

After Obama's two terms in office, evangelicals vowed never to let the Democratic candidate, former Secretary of State Hillary Clinton, step foot in the Oval Office. Evangelicals opened the door for Obama's successor, one of the most racist and vindictive Presidents in America, Donald John Trump. There is so much to say about President Trump's policies and racist rhetoric that I have dedicated the next chapter to him. I will, however, mention a few examples about the Trump Administration to end this chapter's illustrations of racist policies and White supremacy in the past hundred years of presidential administrations. Under Republican President Donald Trump's administration (2016-2020), he gave significant tax cuts to corporations and the wealthy. Just like under his predecessors Reagan and Bush, there was also a significant increase in poverty. President Trump's actions were not typical of a conservative evangelical, but he did play to the hearts of conservative evangelicals' political beliefs and values. For a long time, Trump identified with the Presbyterian denomination but changed to non-denominational Christianity. Regardless of Trump's religious affiliation, he did not try to hide his racist comments. For example, Trump posted a racist Twitter rant against several Democratic congresswomen of Color, telling them to go back to fix their crime-infested places. Trump complained on FOX News, conspiracy theory outlets, and Twitter that predominately Black Democratic counties are cheaters or illegal voters. Trump called the city of Baltimore a rat- and roach-infested place where no human would want to live (Crockett, Jr.). Trump encouraged excessive use of deadly force on peaceful Black Lives Matter protesters and called COVID-19 "the China virus," treating it as a political issue instead of a humanitarian crisis.

Interestingly, evangelicals who voted against Bill Clinton's second presidential term because of his moral failures and character voted for Trump in large numbers despite his moral failures and character. White evangelicals were loyal to President Trump and were pleased with his policies. Trump promised to promote evangelical values like opposing abortion, appointing conservative Supreme Court Justices, restricting immigration, bringing law and order, presenting a solid military presence in the Middle East, and putting more money in their pockets. For the most part, Trump kept most of his promises, which made White American evangelicals extremely happy. Many evangelicals believed Trump was the most pro-Christian president the United States has had in the past hundred years. The reason is Trump appointed three conservative pro-life Republican Judges to the Supreme Court. Trump took credit for increasing the national GDP (gross domestic product), the stock market's rise, and low unemployment numbers. Trump recognized Jerusalem as the capital of Israel and ordered the relocation of the U.S. Embassy from Tel Aviv to Jerusalem. Trump also signed the First Step Act of 2018, a bipartisan sentencing and prison reform bill spearheaded by his son-in-law Jared Kushner. Trump's prison reform bill went further than any prison reform from his predecessors. However, none of Trump's accomplishments excuse the consistent racist rhetoric or his character issues.

I began authoring this book in 2019 before the presidential candidates for the 2020 election were confirmed. No one had insight into the events that would unfold between election day and Congress certifying the election results. Vice President Biden and Senator Kamala Harris won the election and were sworn in on January 20, 2021. President Biden and the first female in the history of the United States, a Woman of Color of African and Asian descent, Vice President Kamala Harris, ran on decency, unity, and better leadership for the COVID-19 pandemic. President Biden has not been in office long. However, he has received his fair share of criticism for his policies besides his approach to managing the pandemic, the economic downturn, the Capital insurrection, and the mishandling of the military withdrawal from Afghanistan. Instead, we will look at Biden's record as a Senator and Vice President. President Biden is a practicing Catholic and the first Catholic elected to the presidency since President Kennedy. Biden attended St. Joseph on the Brandywine in

Wilmington, Delaware, and rarely missed Sunday Mass. Biden still carries his deceased son Beau's rosary in his wallet, prays regularly, and often uses the Catholic Scriptures in his speeches. However, I would be remiss if I did not mention the legacy of racism from Biden's past that must be addressed as President.

For example, Biden praised a former Ku Klux Klan leader as a mentor, and he praised segregationist George Wallace as someone who speaks his mind (Margolis). Biden collaborated with several segregationist Democrats in 1977 to fight the federally mandated school busing and desegregation. Biden said he did not want his children growing up in a "jungle" (Caldera, *1977 Biden Said*). While campaigning in 2008 with Senator Barack Obama, Biden had to walk back his statements as if no intelligent, clean-cut Black man had ever run for president. He called Barack Obama "articulate and bright and clean" (Ryan). Biden also used the anti-Semitic slur "shylock" at the fortieth-year celebration of the Legal Services Corporation, in which he publicly apologized after the Anti-Defamation League rebuked him. Moreover, during an appearance on *The Breakfast Club* radio show, Biden famously said, "you ain't Black," referring to Black Americans who chose to vote for Trump instead of voting for him (Bradner et al.).

Despite Biden's racist comments, the Biden Administration on paper is a highly diverse administration. By far, historically, Biden has the most female leaders as cabinet picks. Only time will tell if President Biden's past statements will dictate his future policies or if Biden genuinely wants diversity to break the barriers of systemic racism. However, if Biden holds to his campaign promises, then there should be a notable change. Below is the initial list of President Biden's diverse cabinet picks, not all of which were confirmed by the Senate.

- The first female Treasury Secretary Janet Yellen
- African American retired four-star Army General Lloyd Austin
- Climate Czar Gina McCarthy
- The first Native American Secretary of Interior Deb Haaland
- The first Latino immigrant for Secretary of Homeland Security Alejandro Mayorkas
- The first openly LGBTQ Secretary of Transportation Pete Buttigieg
- The Secretary of Energy former Michigan Governor Jennifer Granholm
- US Ambassador to the United Nations Linda Thomas-Greenfield
- The first female Director of National Intelligence, Avril Haines
- Office of Management and Budget Neera Tanden
- White House Press Secretary Jennifer Psaki (The first all-female White House Communications team)
- US Trade Representative Katherine Tai
- Twice-appointed U.S. Surgeon General Vivek Murthy
- White House Domestic Policy Council Director Susan Rice
- Secretary of Housing and Urban Development Representative Marcia Fudge

- First Puerto Rican Secretary of Education Miguel Cardona
- Center for Disease Control and Prevention Director Rochelle Walensky

When we look at the past hundred years of presidential administrations, I will caution anyone who would declare someone is not a Christ-follower. Only God can judge the heart, and since none of us are the Holy Spirit, Jr., we cannot know if a person has had a spiritual conversion and accepted Jesus as their Lord and Savior. However, I do believe that as Christ-followers, we can judge a person's fruit. Jesus said, "For no good tree bears bad fruit, nor again does a bad tree bear good fruit, for a tree is known by its own fruit. For figs are not gathered by thornbushes, nor are grapes picked from a bramble bush. The good person out of the good treasure of his heart produces good, and the evil person out of his evil treasure produces evil, for out of the abundance of the heart his mouth speaks" (Luke 6.43–45). As for judging the lives and policies of our past "Christian" Presidents, we must hold them to the standards of the Bible and judge them by their fruit. Unfortunately, many politicians feel they have to pretend to be Christian to appease evangelicals, which leads to hypocrisy.[26] Pretending to be a Christian for the sake of getting evangelical votes is deceitful and downright offensive. Only a life that genuinely represents the fruit of the Spirit: love, joy, peace, patience, kindness, goodness, faithfulness, gentleness, and self-control is the life that Christians should emulate (Gal. 5.23). The fruit of the Spirit produces a

---

[26] Conversation with Gail Clayworth, June 2021

genuine love for our neighbor, which is the proper standard for Christianity. Only God knows which presidents had a personal relationship with Jesus.

For many of them, Christianity conflicts with their policies and character. The significant patterns of racism and White supremacy represented in the past one hundred years of presidential administrations show this dichotomy. Most conservative evangelicals claim their political choices are based on their religion but willingly or unwittingly advocate policies that continue to hurt the poor and People of Color. The body of Christ is meant to be different. We are supposed to love when it is hard, give grace when it is not deserved, and always live to bring righteousness and justice to the poor and the oppressed. To those of you who say you are allied to People of Color, let me remind you of God's words, "For I the Lord love justice; I hate robbery and wrong" (Isa. 61.8).

CHAPTER 7
PRESIDENT TRUMP & THE MODERN-DAY EVANGELICAL

"Who among you fears the LORD and obeys the voice of his servant? Let him who walks in darkness and has no light trust in the name of the LORD and rely on his God" (Isa. 50.10).

Before you read this chapter, I ask that you take a moment to stop and pray this prayer. "Lord, we are living in a culture that is hateful and divided. Father, help me to hear and see Your truth. Help me to discern what is evil and when my intellect tells me to disregard what I see, I pray that you show me the way. Convict my heart and show me the areas in my life I need to change. Show me where I lack empathy and compassion or harbor anger and bitterness. Help me to challenge what I have learned over the course of my life that is in opposition to Your love. Show me those leaders who plot to do evil. Help me to see how the modern-day evangelical's behavior has moved away from your message of love and justice. Lord, I lament over the condition of our country, our political system, the mistreatment of the poor and People of

Color, and the state of the church. I desire to bring change, but I do not always know how to do it. If there be any sin in me, or pride in my heart, forgive me of my sins. I pray all these things in Jesus' name, Amen."

I asked you to pray before reading this section because I will disclose a lot of facts about Donald John Trump that may anger you if you are one of his followers. However, my prayer is that your heart and eyes will be open to the truth. In the early 1990s, Trump was the cool, rich, pro-choice Democrat White guy who appeared in rap videos, flaunted beautiful women, and claimed to have a ton of money, hotels, and casinos. Trump became famous for his reality T.V. shows, *The Apprentice* and *Celebrity Apprentice.* He continuously flaunted himself as a self-made businessman. Still according to the *New York Times,* Trump borrowed money for his casinos at extremely high interest rates resulting in no margin to make a profit (Berke). The "self-made businessman" had a notorious history of not paying his vendors. As far back as the 1970s, Donald Trump and his father, Fred Trump, were fighting charges of violating the Fair Housing Act of 1968 (Zirin). Trump purchased a fourteen-story building near Central Park in New York City to convert into luxury condominiums. Trump was often accused of being a slumlord by his tenants. To get rid of them, Trump cut off the apartment building's water and heat in the middle of the winter. He even proposed to put homeless people in the building and allowed a rodent and roach infestation to drive out the tenants. In October of 1973, the *New York Times* ran a front-page story with the headline "Major Landlord Accused of Anti-Black Bias" about Trump's business practices (Dunlap). In a class-action lawsuit, Trump was sued by his tenants, who said Donald Trump scammed them illegally and unfairly imposed steep increases in their rent (Jacobs).

In a later lawsuit, the Ninth Circuit Court of Appeals awarded a 25-million-dollar settlement to students defrauded by Trump University, which collected large tuition payments but failed to provide the promised real estate investment training. Donald Trump had a long racist history before Democrats and Liberals began calling him a racist during his first presidential campaign. People of Color, especially those in New York City, were well aware of Trump's racism long before that. For example, on April 19, 1989, a Hispanic boy and four Black boys were wrongly convicted of raping and beating a White female jogger, Trisha Meili. These boys, called *The Central Park Five*, were slandered by Trump. He spent $85,000 on full-page newspaper ads calling for the death penalty for those underaged boys. Trump said the teenagers should "be forced to suffer." He even said they should be "executed for their crimes" (Devega).

Another example was during President Barack Obama's term in office, where Trump's racism was on full display. Trump went on a crusade on social media, talk shows, and FOX News claiming Obama was not born in the United States but Kenya, which would have disqualified him from the presidency. Trump demanded Obama show his birth certificate and made baseless claims that Obama was a Muslim. Referring to Obama as a Muslim translated to White Americans, especially White evangelicals, that Obama was a terrorist. Trump's lies led to a movement against Obama that later became known as birtherism. Birtherism was a way for White Americans to denounce Barack Obama's presidency.

During Obama's second term in office, Donald Trump decided to denounce his Democrat status to run as a Republican for President of the United States. While on the campaign trail, he mocked a disabled reporter, made a derogatory comment about commentator Megyn Kelly being on her menstrual cycle, and incited violence against protesters at his rallies. Trump even bragged about standing in the middle of Fifth Avenue and shooting people (Flores). His supporters, including evangelicals, were seen laughing, cheering, and encouraging candidate Trump's injurious behavior even at the expense of Christianity's reputation. On October 7, 2016, the *Washington Post* released the *Access Hollywood* tape with Donald Trump and Billy Bush crudely talking about women sexually. Trump was bragging on the video about sexually assaulting women saying he would just kiss them at will and just "grab them by the pussy" (Smidt). But this was not the only damaging piece of evidence against Trump, as several women came forward to say that he had sexually assaulted them. Much of the evangelical community ridiculed those women, questioned their credibility, and overlooked multiple allegations.

Despite all the allegations, foul-mouthed, and racist comments, the evangelicals supported Donald Trump as their 2016 presidential candidate for the Republican Party. Eight out of ten White evangelicals voted for Trump, and they were one of Trump's most substantial bases of support (Lemon). As a candidate, Trump coined the phrase, "Make America Great Again" (MAGA). What was Trump referring to by this phrase? For most People of Color, MAGA is a cruel joke and a constant reminder that White supremacy is still alive and well, especially in the church. How can anyone say with a straight face that America has been great? Even the "good ole days," for People of Color, specifically African Americans, Native Americans, Asians, and Hispanics, have never been great. What do White evangelicals mean by "great" when they repeat the phrase? America was not great when White Christian settlers murdered over 56 million Native Americans who refused to assimilate and give up their lands (Kent). America was not great when Texas Rangers murdered and lynched hundreds of Mexicans and Mexican Americans in Porvenir, Texas, from 1910 to 1920 (Reyes).

America was not great when over 12.5 million Africans were brought to the New World as slaves, separated from their families, language, culture, and religion. America was not great when immigrant communities were used for low-waged jobs and experienced prejudice and unjust, illegal deportations. America was not great after the bombing of Pearl Harbor when thousands of Japanese Americans were held in concentration camps while evangelicals turned a blind eye. America was not great when thousands of Black men were infected with syphilis in the Tuskegee experiment. As a result, many Black men became sterile, and some died without the proper medical treatment. In 2019, America was not great when a gunman walked into a crowded Walmart in El Paso and murdered twenty-three Hispanics citing President Trump as his motivation for his heinous act. Nor was America great when the evangelical Christian crowdfunding site, GiveSendGo, raised $500,000 after GoFundMe refused to do so for a seventeen-year-old vigilante named Kyle Rittenhouse (Cowen). After killing two White Black Lives Matter protesters in Kenosha, Wisconsin, Rittenhouse claimed self-defense and was acquitted of all the charges. Shortly after Rittenhouse's acquittal, he was seen posing with extremist groups like the Proud Boys.

Donald Trump's America is not great when his administration removed protections for People of Color in home ownership.[27] America is not great as long as our judiciary system remains extremely unbalanced due to Trump's overwhelmingly White male conservative judges appointed to the courts. America is not great as long as excessive over-policing remains and minorities are unjustly killed by police or treated like animals. America is not great as long as the Ku Klux Klan, White nationalists, and White supremacist organizations infiltrate law enforcement and the military (Levin). America is not great as long as evangelicals and Republican's support President Trump's unfounded lies of a stolen 2020 election. America is not great as long as President Trump incites hate speech against Asian Americans because of COVID-19. America was not great when Trump supporters issued death threats against poll workers and Republican elected leaders. America was not great when White supremacist groups incited an insurrection at the U.S. Capitol. The list goes on and on about how America has not been great, especially for People of Color. What is even more problematic is that evangelicals have not been great either. Evangelicals who supported Trump as he displayed debase behavior are worse than Trump because they know

---

[27] On July 30, 2020, the Trump Administration overturned the Affirmatively Furthering Fair Housing rule from 2015 that upheld the Fair Housing Act of 1968 identifying racial segregation patterns.

better and have no excuse. The phrase "Make America Great Again" comes from a White perspective and indicates the White person's unwillingness and inability to consider the experiences of People of Color. From my perspective as a Person of Color, "Make America Great Again" means "Make America White Again."

The Apostle Paul gives a prescription of how to live a life that represents Christ. I mentioned in the previous chapter that Galatians 5.23-24 explains what a Christ-follower's life should look like through the power of the Holy Spirit. More importantly, Paul gives us an example of what a leader's life should look like, especially one who claims to be a follower of Christ. Paul said, "The fruit of the Spirit is joy, peace, patience, kindness, goodness, faithfulness, g entleness, s elf-control; against such things there is no law." There are nine different fruit of the Spirit that Paul mentions in this verse. The first three examples of fruit are love, joy, and peace. These are internal qualities but are seen when they are outwardly expressed. Love, joy, and peace are attributes from God because God is love (1 John 4.8,16). God provides joy despite the circumstances we are facing (Jas. 1.2). God gives us peace that surpasses all human comprehension even during dark times in our lives (Phi. 4.7). Paul mentions the following six fruit are outward expressions of our faith, which are easily recognizable in a true Christ-follower. We will compare this fruit with President Trump's character during his four years in office. The six fruit in Paul's list are patience, kindness, goodness, faithfulness, gentleness, and self-control. I am not saying that Trump did not do anything good during his presidency, but his bad character outweighed the good. Trump's lousy behavior includes rude, racist, unethical, and immoral actions, support for outlandish conspiracy theories, affirming racist cult-like groups like QAnon (Associated Press, *Trump*) and The Proud Boys (Lee), inciting chaos and violence, and turning COVID-19 into a political issue.

Since Trump claims he is a Christian, we can judge his actions by his fruit. Patience means to suppress restlessness or annoyance, to be without complaint or the loss of one's temper. King Solomon said, "A patient spirit is better than a proud spirit" (CSB, Ecc. 7.8). Trump was impatient with the Federal Drug Administration's delayed approval of the Pfizer COVID-19 vaccine. Allegedly, Chief of Staff Mark Meadows, under the direct orders of President Trump, threatened to fire the head of the FDA if he did not clear approval by that Friday (Lovelace, Jr.). Trump was extremely impatient with the public health officials leading the COVID-19 task force (Salon). But most specifically, Trump did not hide his annoyance with Dr. Anthony Fauci for his direct contradictions to Trump's false claims about COVID-19 (Miller). Trump was impatient with the Russia investigation (Dupree) and fired FBI Director James Comey in hopes that the investigation would go away (Pace). Special Counsel Robert Muller was appointed to head the Russia investigation due to Trump's interference ("Robert Muller"). Trump repeatedly threatened to fire Robert Muller on Twitter amid the investigation (Robinson, W.). Trump was impatient with several Republican leaders (Morgan) and fired what he considered "disloyal" career civil servants and whistleblowers (Stracqualursi). I will admit it is not always easy to be patient, but as the leader of the free world, Trump's impatience was deadly. Trump's impatience with the vaccine's approval undermined the public's confidence in the medical experts. It also set a precedence for other leaders in our country to be just as impatient and impulsive. Impatience in any influential leader is a dangerous character flaw, and it has a ripple effect on the people under their leadership. Patience is not a fruit of the Spirit Donald Trump displayed while in office.

I could spend an entire chapter on the fruit of the Spirit, kindness. Kindness is displaying good behavior, being considerate, helpful, gentle, loving, and affectionate. Kindness is not rude, arrogant, impulsive, nor vile. One way Christians can display kindness is by showing generosity and compassion towards others. Paul said, "Put on then, as God's chosen ones, holy and beloved, compassionate hearts, kindness, humility, meekness, and patience" (Col. 3.12). Even now, as a private citizen, Trump is still spewing hate speech and lies. On July 18, 2015, Trump publicly humiliated and demeaned the military service of Senator John McCain. McCain was a decorated Vietnam Prisoner of War and Trump ridiculed that McCain was captured by the enemy (Cillizza). Trump's mean comments were not only aimed at U.S. citizens. Trump publicly ridiculed and maligned world leaders like the President of Syria Bashar al-Assad, calling him "Animal Assad." Trump also called the Supreme Leader of North Korea, Kim Jong-un "Little Rocket Man." Trump's mouth was constantly filled with mocking, lies, misinformation, and outright deceit. He told over 18,000 lies in the first three and a half years of his presidency (Markowitz). Trump's lies are a great reminder as to why the Apostle James said, "No human being can tame the tongue. It is a restless evil, full of deadly poison.

With it we bless our Lord and Father, and with it we curse people who are made in the likeness of God" (Jas. 3.8–9).

Proverbs 12.18 says, "There is one whose rash words are like sword thrusts, but the tongue of the wise brings healing." Trump's words were like sword thrusts as he used his words to hurt people. For example, he famously called Mexicans "rapists" and NFL players who chose to kneel during the National Anthem "sons of bitches" (Edelman). Trump used his bully pulpit at press briefings to speak nasty words towards Women of Color and talked down to journalists from media outlets he felt were unfavorable to him. Before Trump became President, he assigned derogatory nicknames to each of his presidential opponents. He publicly ridiculed, humiliated, and bullied the other candidates on camera and social media. For example, Trump repeated the phrases, "Lyin' Ted" referring to Senator Ted Cruz, "Pocahontas" referring to Senator Elizabeth Warren, "Low energy Jeb" referring to former Governor Jeb Bush, and "Little Marco" referring to Senator Marco Rubio. Trump called former Secretary of State Hillary Clinton "Crooked Hillary" (Itkowitz) and incited his followers to chant "lock her up" over and over at his rallies (Samuels). Trump called the former Director of the United States Secret Service Randolph Alles "Dumbo." Joe Biden had several names like "Sleepy Joe," "Basement Biden," "Corrupt Joe," and Michael Bloomberg was called "Mini Mike." President Trump called Senator Maxine Waters "Low-IQ Maxine Waters" and Michigan Governor Gretchen Whitmer "Gretchen Half-Whitmer." Trump's most hated Senator Adam Schiff had names like "Shifty Schiff," "Pencil Neck," and "Watermelon Head" ("List Nicknames").

Kindness is not a fruit of the Spirit that Donald Trump displayed throughout his presidency. Thankfully, at least pastor and author Max Lucado publicly spoke out against Donald Trump's bullying and crude statements (McFarland Miller).

The fruit of the Spirit, goodness, is moral excellence, kindness, and generosity. Speaking to the church at Rome, the Apostle Paul said, "I myself am satisfied about you, my brothers, that you yourselves are full of goodness, filled with all knowledge and able to instruct one another" (Rom. 15.14). It is difficult to say that Trump's actions, threats, tweets, and speech were good. Ironically, his wife Melania Trump ran an anti-bullying campaign when her husband, President Donald Trump, was the most prominent public bully our country has ever seen. Donald Trump would say or do anything to embarrass, offend, belittle, and disgrace those he did not like. Trump impulsively fired anyone who would not agree with him or publicly contradicted anything that he had said. There is nothing good about how Trump allowed his administration to put migrant children in cages like dogs ("Trump Migrant Separation"). Trump even suggested shooting migrants in the legs to keep them from crossing the border (Kelly). He is a habitual liar who spews falsehoods and misleading claims daily to the media and through conspiracy theory outlets. No wonder why Proverbs 12.22 reminds us that "Lying lips are an abomination to the Lord." Trump's consistent lies only hurt the people whom he said he would lead and protect. One of the biggest and most baseless lies perpetrated by President Trump was the 2020 election fraud. Proverbs 12.20 says, "Deceit is in the heart of those who devise evil." So, why would anyone be surprised about these lies when Trump started claiming election fraud almost two years before the 2020 election? He declared that any paper ballot cast for his opponent was fraudulent except for his absentee ballot. I keep highlighting Trump's bad behavior because the Bible says, "If anyone thinks he is religious and does not bridle his tongue but deceives his heart, this person's religion is worthless" (Jas. 1.26).

Additionally, Trump's nasty behavior encouraged his followers to mistreat anyone seen as the opposition, including those in their party. For example, Trump's followers made death threats to election officials and threatened Republican governors and delegates who certified the 2020 election on the premise of Trump's baseless lie. What makes Trump's lies worse is that he knew they would incite violence, yet he continued to perpetuate the lies anyway. Trump fired the Department of Homeland Security's Head of Cybersecurity, Christopher Krebs, to refute his false election fraud and hacking claims. Krebs is just one person in a long list of officials Trump fired and dehumanized by tweet. Trump humiliated Defense Secretary Mark Esper, White House Counsel Don McGahn, Secretary of State Rex Tillerson, and Acting U.S. Attorney General Sally Yates.

Another debacle of Trump's presidency was his downplaying of the deadly COVID-19 virus. Trump lied to the American people saying that COVID-19 was more like the flu and there was no need to wear a mask. In a recorded interview with Bob Woodward, Trump admitted that he knew COVID-19 was a considerable threat even before he downplayed it on national television (Gernoble). Trump consistently mocked journalists wearing masks at press briefings and turned COVID-19 into a political issue instead of a humanitarian crisis. Do not worry, Trump will be held accountable in this life or the next for Jesus said, "I tell you, on the day of judgment people will give account for every careless word they speak, for by your words you will be justified, and by your words you will be condemned" (Matt. 12.36–37). In Donald Trump's final act of obstruction of justice, he pardoned known criminals associated with the Mueller investigation who refused to testify against him like George Papadopoulos, Alex van der Zwaan, Paul Manafort, Roger Stone, and Michael Flynn. Trump also pardoned Charles Kushner, his son-in-law Jared Kushner's father, and disgraced former Republican Representatives Duncan Hunter, Steve Stockman, and Chris Collins. In the most scandalous and outrageous defiance of justice, Trump unashamedly pardoned the four Blackwater guards who murdered twelve civilians in Baghdad (Shackford). During a raging pandemic, Trump also had attorneys from his administration sue to repeal the Affordable Care Act, also known as Obamacare. If overturned, this would leave millions of Americans without healthcare and remove protections for pre-existing conditions. Anyone who has been infected with COVID-19 now has a pre-existing condition and would lose protection. The fruit of the Spirit, goodness, has been hard to find throughout President Trump's four years in the White House.

The fruit of the Spirit, faithfulness, means being faithful to one's words, promises, or vows, and constant and consistent. Faithfulness also means to be loyal, dependable, trusted, and believed. Trump was not just unfaithful to his wives; he publicly humiliated them by parading his extramarital affairs in the media. His first marriage to Ivana

Trump fell apart because of his public affair with model Marla Maples in the 1990s. Trump's attorney Michael Cohen revealed some of Trump's sexual activities resulting in several women coming forward to confirm their sexual relationships with Donald Trump while he was married to his wife Melania Trump (Tegna). Shortly after that, news broke of Donald Trump's adultery with porn star Stormy Daniels and *Playboy* magazine model Karen McDougal who he paid to cover up their affairs. Nineteen women came forward and accused Trump of sexual harassment, most of which occurred while he was married (Delkic).

Trump was unfaithful to the American people and the office of the President of the United States. He attempted to bribe Ukraine to find dirt on Joe Biden, leading to Trump's impeachment in the House of Representatives ("President Impeached"). President Trump consistently denied Russian influence and interference in the 2016 election and the 2020 Russian hacking of multiple government agencies and private contractors. Trump blamed the government hacking on China instead of affirming Secretary of State Mike Pompeo and Attorney General Bill Barr's statements that Russia was to blame (Sink). Trump tried to weaponize the United States Postal Service and the U.S. Census Bureau (Brownstein). He tried to bribe State representatives to change the election results (Colarossi), encouraged his supporters to commit violence, and entertained talks of martial law to overturn the election (Johnson). Trump sided with Russia and President Putin rather than believing the findings from U.S. Intelligence Agencies (Satlin). Trump was willing to work back channels, bribe to hurt an opponent, and steal the 2020 election. Trump's actions revealed his unfaithfulness to our country and his oath of office. Despite Trump's unfaithfulness to the American people, thankfully, God is faithful, for the Bible says, "If we are faithless, he remains faithful—for he cannot deny himself" (2 Tim. 2.13). It is safe to say that faithfulness was not a fruit of the Spirit in President Trump's arsenal.

The fruit of the Spirit, gentleness, is remarkably similar to kindness. Gentleness means being kind, amiable, mild-mannered, and courteous; not severe, forceful, and rough. Gentleness is also showing a humble and sweet attitude towards others. As Christ-followers, we should continuously "Pursue righteousness, godliness, faith, love, steadfastness, gentleness" (1 Tim. 6.11). After Trump's loss of the 2020 election, sources within his administration said he was like a ticking time bomb, yelling and screaming profanity at his White House Aides and close advisors. This behavior is contrary to the word of God, for it says, "Let every person be quick to hear, slow to speak, slow to anger, for the anger of man does not produce the righteousness of God" (Jas. 1.19–20). Ever since Trump's loss of the 2020 election, Trump waged war on his party, with continued name-calling. Trump abused his power in the past by sexually harassing women who participated in the Miss USA pageants. Many complained that Trump entered the dressing rooms while they were half-dressed ("Pageant Contestants"). Other women complained about Trump's inappropriate sexual behavior like kissing them without their consent, inappropriate touching, and sexual harassment. Trump violated the emoluments clause of the United States Constitution with foreign diplomats ("Federal Court Rules"). He also signed a travel ban on Muslim majority countries, except countries where he held business interests, and he indefinitely prohibited Syrian refugees from entering the United States (Schallhorn). Lastly, Trump threatened and berated Vice President Pence for not rejecting the 2020 election results (Hadfield). Gentleness is a fruit of the Spirit that was not displayed by President Trump at all.

The final fruit of the Spirit is self-control. Self-control is restraint of oneself or one's actions. Self-control is not reacting or overreacting but being able to act in a disciplined manner under the guidance of the Holy Spirit. The Holy Spirit is there to quicken our hearts when we are not operating consistently with his righteousness. The Holy Spirit dwells within us and directs us on the right path if we yield to his will. The Apostle Peter said, "Make every effort to supplement your faith with virtue, and virtue with knowledge, and knowledge with self-control, and self-control with steadfastness, and steadfastness with godliness" (2 Pet. 1.5-6). Trump consistently lacked self-control, especially on his Twitter account. Trump's actions eventually got him banned from Twitter. On Trump's Twitter feed, he constantly made racist comments, bullied his so-called enemies, dehumanized, and ridiculed females, routinely spewed lies and misinformation about losing the 2020 election, and refused to denounce racist White supremacists and White nationalist groups. Trump's vendetta against his predecessor, President Barack Obama, is another area where Trump lacked self-control. He called Obama names and made it a point to repeal all of Obama's policies to destroy Obama's legacy out of spite. Trump rescinded Obama's Stream Protection Rule, which kept companies from dumping toxic chemicals into lakes and streams ("Trump Administration Revokes").

He repealed Obama's ban on transgender military service ("Repeal Don't Ask") and Obama's Deferred Action for Parents of Americans (DAPA) program protecting illegal immigrants (Funes). Trump pulled the U.S. out of the Paris Accord (Jung) for Climate Change and the Iran Nuclear Deal that the Obama Administration negotiated (Rogers). Under the direction of National Security Advisor John Bolton, the Trump Administration disbanded Obama's pandemic response task force implemented after the Ebola epidemic, which created the playbook for dealing with diseases like COVID-19 (Caldera, *White House Didn't Fire*). Trump lacked self-control when he notoriously posted videos that promoted extremist conspiracy theories of Anti-Muslim and Anti-Semitic propaganda (Swasey). What is mind-blowing is how hard Trump fought to keep his presidency and denounce Biden's win, but he stopped fulfilling his presidential duties long before he lost the election. For example, without explanation, Trump delayed signing a COVID-19 relief bill and a military spending bill (O'Neil). Self-control is not one of Trump's virtues and was not displayed as one of his fruit of the Spirit either.

Luke 14.28-33 paints an even greater picture of why Christians should produce fruit as evidence of our salvation. "For which of you, intending to build a tower, does not sit down first and count the cost, whether he has enough to finish it—lest after he has laid the foundation, and is not able to finish, all who see it begin to mock him saying, 'This man began to build and was not able to finish?' Or what king, going to make war against another king, does not sit down first and consider whether he is able with ten thousand to meet him who comes up against him with twenty thousand?

Or else, while the other is still a great way off, he sends a delegation and asks conditions of peace. So likewise, whoever of you does not forsake all that he has cannot be My disciple" (Luke 14.28–33). Have you ever driven past a lot where you can see the foundation, but the building was never completed? The builder miscalculated, had poor planning, and ran out of money to finish the job in the planning stages. Jesus said, if you are not going to see it through to the end, then why even start the process? In other words, if you are not willing to grow and produce fruit, then do not even call yourself a follower of Jesus.

In addition to not operating in the fruit of the Spirit, Trump made too many racist and offensive comments to deny that he is not a racist. If you have to say, "I'm the least racist person in the room," then there is something wrong. Some people argue Trump is not a racist but an equal opportunity offender, but as the old saying goes, "If it walks like a duck, and it quacks like a duck, it's a duck." This applies to Trump as a racist. What is disheartening about those who claim Trump is not a racist is that they are either White, employed by Trump, or benefited from him somehow. The other saying, "sticks and stones may break my bones, but words will never hurt me," is one of the biggest lies ever told to children along with the Tooth Fairy, the Easter Bunny, and Santa Claus. Trump's words hurt; they are debasing and offensive. After Hurricane Maria, Trump treated Puerto Ricans as second-class citizens instead of American citizens by delaying his response for aid and mocked them by throwing rolls of paper towels into the crowd (Ocasio). While campaigning in Charlottesville, Trump refused to disavow former Ku Klux Klan Grand Wizard David Duke (Chan). He picked a fight on social media with gold-star immigrant military families (Walker, J.). Trump's hard-line on immigration dehumanized immigrants who are image-bearers of God too. Trump's treatment of immigrants is opposite to how the Bible tells us to treat immigrants. God said, "I will come to you in judgement, and I will be ready to witness against sorcerers and adulterers; against those who swear falsely; against those who oppress the hired worker, the widow, and the fatherless; and against those who deny justice to the resident alien" (Mal. 3.5 CSB).

Billions of people all over the world have cleaned dirty laundry since the beginning of time. In every culture, ethnicity, and country, dirty laundry is hang-drying outside, moving through washing machines, inside laundry mats, or homes. Dirty laundry is stinky and filthy, and it comes with sweat stains, dirt stains, and other unpleasant stains. Every time your laundry is dirty, you wash it to remove the filth and make it clean. Most people would not deliberately walk around wearing dirty, stinky laundry. But evangelicals, you are walking around in the dirty laundry of guilt by association. That is, evangelicals are guilty of their association with Donald Trump. The worst part of the evangelical's guilt is that most of Trump's followers do not know how bad they stink. Evangelicals, your laundry is reeking of the sins of slander, arrogance, greed, and White supremacy. Your injustice and lack of empathy are tone-deaf to the outside world. Evangelicals, you are referred to as hypocrites who set double standards, who are disingenuous, in cahoots with fraudulent and criminal activity, and are complicit in racism and White supremacy. The world believes these things to be true because of evangelicals who willingly support immoral and racist candidates.

For the four years that Trump was in office, the evangelical's stench increased in their unwavering support for him. I mentioned in previous chapters overt support for Trump from pastors like Franklin Graham and Robert Jeffress. Still, I am sickened by so many prominent evangelical leaders who publicly supported Trump despite his character. For example, some of those leaders include former Senators Michele Bachmann and Kelly Loeffler, Pastors Paula White-Cain, Greg Laurie, Jerry Falwell Jr., Samuel Rodriguez, and Robert Morris. Also included in this list are televangelist Kenneth Copeland, Dr. James and Shirley Dobson, Dr. Jay Strack, Ralph Reed, Mike Lindell, Tony Perkins, and Christian musical artists Michael W. Smith, Michael Tait, Kari Jobe, Sean Feucht, and Cody Carnes. These prominent evangelicals supported Trump despite his immoral, illegal, and racist behaviors. For example, Trump refused to call out White supremacist and White nationalist hate groups in Charlottesville by saying, "there are good people on both sides." Trump operated in unethical business dealings, including violating the Hatch Act (Solender) and soliciting foreign dignitaries to his hotels. Many of these evangelicals that I mentioned supported Trump and perpetuated his election fraud lies. Unashamedly, the majority of these same evangelicals hypocritically ostracized the LGBTQ community. However, they accepted Trump with absolute allegiance and showed loyalty to a president whose character is questionable at best and treasonous at worse.

Continued evangelical support for Trump has pushed away Millennials, Gen Z's, non-Christians, and non-Trump supporters from the message of Christ. For example, evangelicals like Kayleigh McEnany and Sarah Huckabee Sanders, Trump's White House Press Secretaries, and self-proclaimed evangelicals are very outspoken about their faith. Kayleigh routinely repeated the President's lies to the press and the American people. She consistently made excuses, reiterated Trump's racist rhetoric, all while her gold cross dangled from her neck for all viewers to see. Sarah Huckabee Sanders is just as guilty of repeating President Trump's lies but with a nasty attitude toward the press day after day. "Do not be deceived: 'Bad company ruins good morals'" (1 Cor. 15.33). People like Kayleigh and Sarah allowed Donald Trump's nasty behavior to corrupt their reputation, not to mention put a stain on Christianity. Proverbs says, "He who justifies the wicked and he who condemns the righteous are both alike an abomination to the LORD" (17.15). American evangelicals, if you continue to defend wicked leaders like Trump, the Bible says you are an abomination to the LORD and a stench to His nostrils. Unfortunately, non-Christians and atheists are laughing in our faces because of evangelicals like Kayleigh and Sarah, who have selective degrees of ethics and morality.

Despite Trump's immoral behavior, racist comments and tweets, downright criminal behavior, and unethical acts of sedition, White evangelicals continue to remain at his side with unwavering allegiance. President Trump will go down in American History as twice Impeached and the most immoral President surpassing President Herbert Hoover for inciting an insurrection to steal the 2020 presidential election. The U.S. Capitol had not been invaded since August 24, 1814, until January 6, 2021, under the direction of Donald J. Trump. The world watched in shock while thousands of Trump terrorists, White supremacists, and White nationalist supporters stormed, raided, and destroyed the Capitol building. These individuals were incited by President Trump, his children, personal attorney Rudy Giuliani, and several Republican lawmakers. News outlets like FOX News tried to paint a different picture of the events of that day. FOX wanted to make you believe that you did not see what you saw by claiming the rioters wearing MAGA paraphernalia were not "real" Trump supporters. Before the Capitol invasions, Trump told his supporters, "If you don't fight like hell, you're not going to have a country anymore." He urged the crowd to head down to the Capitol to protest the certification process and that is what they did and even more. The most despicable protestors urinated on the floors, shattered windows, and doors, while some smeared poop down the hallway walls (Sommerfeldt). Those insurrectionists and thugs desecrated the U.S. Capitol with their Confederate flags and Trump flags. Some Trump supporters wore racist Holocaust paraphernalia while others carried Bibles and "Jesus loves" signs (Smith). Trump supporters looted several offices and ransacked Speaker Nancy Pelosi's offices, tearing her nameplate off the wall. One rioter propped his feet up on Speaker Pelosi's desk and posed for the camera. Rioters hung from the rafters, scaled the walls, terrorized Senators, Congress, and staffers, leaving some to hide behind their seats or lock themselves in their offices. When the enraged Trump supporters breached the Senate floor, shots were fired, and a rioter lost her life off the lie of a "stolen election." Trump supporters have always claimed that they "Back the Blue," but on this day, they beat the Capitol police officers with flag poles and fire extinguishers and sprayed them with pepper spray. Unfortunately, one officer died, and in the aftermath, several officers committed suicide.

The Congress and Senate fled through hidden tunnels in the Capitol, while the mob yelled profanities attempting to break down the wall (Dozier). One rioter carried plastic handcuff restraints, while others wore tactical gear, shouting "kill Nancy Pelosi," and "hang Mike Pence." A noose was erected just for Mike Pence and any other "traitor outside the Capitol building." One protester held a mannequin with a noose around its neck with "traitor" written on the shirt, referring to Mike Pence (Mahbubani). Instead of stepping in to tell his supporters to stop the raid, Trump used his Twitter feed to incite and encourage them in a video by saying that he loved them (Kroll). To bring insult to injury, Trump even delayed calling the National Guard to help the Capitol police, who the mob had overrun. After all the chaos, Senator Lindsey Graham, one of Trump's "election fraud" supporters and advocate to stop the certification of the election, said, "All I can say is count me out, enough is enough" (Weber).

After the dust settled, the Capitol looked like America had gone to war with a foreign country. It took six days for President Trump to call Vice President Pence after his life was threatened by Trump's supporters (Colvin). Major social media companies like Twitter, Facebook, and Instagram took the unprecedented step of banning President Trump's account. Not long after, Google removed Parler, a conservative social media platform, due to the riots and continuous White supremacists and terrorist chatter (Shead). Official merchandise was also removed from Shopify (Thorbecke).

The evangelicals, especially evangelicals who were present at the Capitol that day, you have blood on your hands. You are responsible for the monster that you created and whom you allowed to put a "bullet into our country" (Chapman). You are responsible for the injuries suffered and the deaths of Capitol police officers as a result of the insurrection. But the world should have seen this coming as Trump was staging a coup to overturn the election and force Congress to change the election results in his favor. For example, Trump illegally called Republican election officials to bribe them to change the election results and give him the 11,000+ votes he needed to overturn Georgia's results (Fausset). Claiming election fraud for years before the election even happened is another sign that should have warned us that Trump would not take the loss like a normal adult. In my opinion, the terrorist mob at the Capitol and President Trump's incitement borders on the crime of sedition. Sedition is a conspiracy committed by two or more people to conspire war against the U.S. government and advocate organizing or overthrowing the government by force ("Sedition"). The penalty for the crime of sedition is up to twenty years of imprisonment. Quite frankly, Trump should serve time in prison for his role in the January 6th insurrection or be banned from ever holding public office for the rest of his life.

    In contrast, during the 2020 BLM protests, Trump ordered police to violently remove peaceful protesters who were protesting the death of George Floyd so he could have a photo op. Trump walked across the street to the St. John's Episcopal church and posed for the cameras while holding a Bible upside down in the exact resemblance of an Adolph Hitler photo (Gjelten). Trump also said, "When the looting starts, the shooting starts" (Sprunt) to the BLM protesters protesting in the streets. But when it came to the White nationalists, the Proud Boys and White supremacist mob terrorists, the disparities in how they were treated versus how BLM protesters were treated was appalling. What was especially nauseating was how many evangelicals spoke out against BLM protestors over the years but were silent about the insurrection.

Unfortunately, many evangelicals refuse to acknowledge that minorities live in two different Americas—White America versus the America that People of Color experience daily. White people are almost always given the benefit of the doubt because of their skin color. The Capitol police did not consider the Trump protesters a threat because they were not prepared for the crowds (Malone). There is a clear distinction between the treatment of white protestors at the Capitol insurrection versus Black Lives Matter protesters in the summer of 2020. White protestors and rioters were given grace, like those allowed to "walk" out of the Capitol after raiding it. At the same time, BLM protestors were seen as a threat and were tear-gassed and shot with rubber bullets. Had those rioters been majority Black, Hispanic, or Muslims raiding the Capitol, they would have been shot and killed on the scene. There is a double standard of how peaceful People of Color are treated as aggressive animals that need to be put down, but armed and aggressive White men are treated as friendlies. For White people shocked by Trump's supporters, understand that People of Color saw this coming even if the Capitol police and FBI did not.

The examples I mentioned are many reasons why non-Christians question how American evangelicals can put morality on the shelf in the name of voting for a second Trump presidential term. I initially believed the Republican leaders were solely responsible for allowing Trump to get away with all his illegal activities, misuse and abuse power, and obstruct justice. Actually, American evangelicals are to blame. Evangelicals enabled Trump's bad behavior and cult-like activities. How can we dare expect non-Christians, who rightfully see Christianity as a group of hypocrites, to fall in love with Jesus when we align with a persona like Trump? Even worse, evangelicals who are following Trump have offended those of us who are genuinely trying to pursue the righteousness of Christ. The elevation of politics, patriotism, and American exceptionalism has emboldened the average evangelical to not listen to anyone who disagrees with them. This is a problem because it portrays Christians as self-centered people who are more concerned with winning than being a witness for Christ. By not calling out Trump's character publicly, evangelicals are just as complicit as he is.

The evangelical's unwavering support and loyalty to Trump, despite his dishonoring of our democracy, is a form of idol worship. This cult-like behavior turned Trump into the god of evangelicalism instead of Jesus. Even if Trump (mis)quoted Scripture, pun intended, and said he believes in God, this does not make him a leader that evangelicals should pledge their loyalty to and get behind. More importantly, this is a sign of the American evangelical's demise when partisanship is equated to a relationship with our risen Savior. No wonder why non-Christians and non-Trump following Christians are fed up with evangelicals. Speaking of which, I read an article about the evangelical's hypocrisy by author and pastor John Pavlovitz. Many evangelicals consider his views on abortion too liberal, and some even perceive John as a heretic. However, when John wrote explicitly about the world's view of White American evangelicals, Pavlovitz's words were so profound that they left an impression on me.

To sum up his synopsis, Pavlovitz said that evangelicals demonized President Obama for eight years, denied that Obama was a Christian, refused to believe he was born in America, called him a Muslim, and used racial stereotypes to malign his character (Pavlovitz). Pavlovitz is correct in his analysis. Never once did White evangelicals openly gather to pray for President Obama. Instead, they ridiculed, berated, maligned, and character-assassinated Obama. Evangelicals turned their backs on him when there was not one scandal in eight years of Obama's presidency. Instead of embracing the man of character (Obama), evangelicals embraced a man of maleficence (Trump). And let us just be truthful, most White evangelicals do not believe Trump is a Christian. However, they would rather support a man with incendiary intentions than a Democrat with godly character and principles.

Just as evangelicals twisted the Scriptures to support slavery in the past, today, evangelicals twist Scripture to support Trump. Many evangelicals choose to believe the lie that God used Trump as America's vessel to accomplish His kingdom ministry on earth. For example, evangelicals make comparisons to Trump and the pagan leader King Cyrus. King Cyrus was the King of Persia between 539-530 B.C., and he famously ended the Babylonian captivity for the Jews. Cyrus was an evil pagan King, but God prompted him to bring the Jews back from their seventy-year captivity to rebuild the temple in Jerusalem. God said, "Thus says the

LORD to his anointed, to Cyrus, whose right hand I have grasped, to subdue nations before him and to loose the belts of kings, to open doors before him that gates may not be closed: I will go before you and level the exalted places" (Isa. 45.1–3). King Cyrus' decree was a fulfillment of prophecy recorded multiple times in the Bible (2 Chr. 36.22–23; Ezra 1.4–11, 6.4–5 and Dan. 6.28, 10.1). Some evangelicals continue to believe that God used King Cyrus in the same way he used Donald Trump to bring about a conservative agenda that protects religious freedoms and pro-life values. How can evangelicals justify Trump's misconduct as an excuse of him being "a baby Christian," flawed, or simply not perfect? (Gabbatt). Famous evangelical leader and Bible teacher Beth Moore spoke out against Trump to evangelicals saying that our King is Jesus, not Cyrus (@BethMooreLPM). Unlike King Cyrus, King Josiah, the sixteenth King of Judah, was called "The Great Reformer" because he cleansed the temple of pagan worship. King Josiah centralized worship in Jerusalem and brought the Word of God back to the people. That is the kind of King that evangelicals should want our "Christian" presidents to emulate, King Josiah, not King Cyrus, and not Trump.

Some evangelicals also compare President Trump to a modern-day King David because God used David despite of his sins. For those reading this chapter unfamiliar with the story of King David, Psalm 51 explains how many evangelicals make the parallel between David and Trump. Unaddressed sins take us down a dark and dangerous path, just like they did for King David. But there is a stark difference between King David and President Trump. David was a worshipper, and he was quick to repent because he had a genuine relationship with God. The Bible says that David was known as a man after God's own heart (1 Sam. 13.14; Acts 13.22). But when David fell into a series of sins, it led him to write Psalm 51. King Saul, the first king of Israel, was anointed King before David became his successor. God rejected King Saul because he willfully disobeyed God's commands, so instead, God gave the throne of Israel to David. The prophet Samuel appointed David to replace King Saul. David was a highly successful King of Israel. David killed Goliath (before he became king) and fought the Amalekites, the Philistines, the Ammonites, and the Syrians. But when the time of the year that it was customary for kings to go out to war came, for some reason, David decided to stay home. Instead of being on the battlefield fighting with his men, David's decision to stay home was the first sin that led to many other sins.

While King David was standing on his balcony at home, he looked over and spotted a beautiful woman bathing. David sent his messengers to find out who she was. Bathsheba was that beautiful woman's name, and she was married to one of David's soldiers named Uriah. Bathsheba was also the granddaughter of a man named Ahithophel, one of David's faithful advisors. None of that mattered to David when he sent his messengers to bring Bathsheba to his palace to have sex with her. Now let me interject this note that Bathsheba was not the one who sinned. If the King summoned you in those days, you would risk death if you did not comply. Bathsheba did not have the choice, and she was forced to have sex with David. Today, David's actions would be considered rape. Not long after their sexual encounter, Bathsheba found out she was pregnant. To save himself the embarrassment and the shame, David conjured up a scheme to bring Uriah,

Bathsheba's husband, home from war. David's goal was to get Uriah to sleep with Bathsheba to pass the baby off as his. But David's plan did not work. Uriah came home, but he never had sex with Bathsheba. When David realized his plan was not working, he ordered his Commander Joab to let Uriah be intentionally killed on the battlefield. Uriah was killed on the battlefield. David married Bathsheba, and she had his baby. The prophet Nathan confronted David to explain that the baby would die because of David's sins. David was remorseful after Nathan's confrontation, and he understood that he had to confess his sins.

The prophet Nathan let David know that God was displeased with his actions. This confrontation led to David's brokenness and repentance. There is a stark difference between King David and President Trump, for David was remorseful and confessed his sins. On the other hand, President Trump said he "doesn't need to ask for forgiveness" (Jefferson). David wrote Psalm 51 out of remorse for his sins and prayed to God, saying, "Blot out my transgressions and Wash me whiter than snow." David wanted God to erase his past and cleanse him entirely from his sins. His sins not only cost Uriah's life, but they also cost the life of his baby. President Trump's sins have cost over 750,000 American lives to the COVID-19 pandemic. The Apostle John said, "If you confess your sins, God is faithful and just to forgive you of your sins, and to cleanse you of all your unrighteousness" (1 John 1.9). And that is what David did; he confessed his sins because his fellowship with God was disrupted. David understood that God requires truth, total confession, and repentance. My mom used to say to us, "your sins will find you out." In other words, what you do in secret always finds a way to the light. David recognized that he needed to come clean. God is concerned that our hearts are broken over sin. David's sins were forgiven, but the consequences of those sins would follow him for the rest of his life. Forgiveness removes the guilt from our sins, but it does not mean that God will withdraw the consequences. David's sin was not just against himself; it also affected the lives of the entire nation of Israel because he was the King. Similarly, President Trump's sins are like equating masks with politics and downplaying how COVID-19 hurt our country. King "David reigned over all Israel. And David administered justice and equity to all his people" (2 Sam. 8.15). This verse reminds us that President Trump had an obligation to administer justice to ALL people, not just one race, political party, agenda, base, or White supremacist groups. Trump is a race-baiting, hate-promoting, violent-mob-inciting, habitual liar, conman, and crook who does not deserve the support of God-fearing Christians.

Many evangelicals also compare Trump to Mordecai and Haman from the biblical story of Esther. Esther was a beautiful Hebrew virgin, raised by her cousin Mordecai because her parents had died. She was selected to be one of the virgins for King Ahasuerus's harem to replace Queen Vashti. "The king loved Esther more than all the other women, and she obtained grace and favor in his sight more than all the virgins; so, he set the royal crown upon her head and made her queen instead of Vashti" (Esth. 2.17). King Ahasuerus had a ruler named Haman who was jealous of Mordecai. But the King showed favor to Mordecai, which enraged Haman that he planned Mordecai's murder by issuing a decree to kill all the Jews. Meaning, Mordecai, Esther, and all her people were supposed to be eradicated (3.9–15). Mordecai pleaded with Esther to go to the King to save the Jews from annihilation. Esther knew that approaching the King without being summoned first could result in her death. Although King Ahasuerus loved Esther, it was against protocol for anyone, including the queen, to approach him without being summoned or risk being put to death. Esther was desperate to plead for her life and the lives of her people. After several days of fasting and prayer, Esther approached the king and found favor with him. Esther invited the King and Haman to dinner so that she could reveal Haman's plan to kill the Jews, which meant killing her as well.

Haman was so excited about Esther's dinner invitation that he went home and bragged to his wife. And Haman thought that he would finally be able to be rid of Mordecai once and for all. Haman ordered his servants to create gallows on which to hang Mordecai after Esther's banquet. The next day, the King could not sleep and asked for the book of deeds to be read aloud. The attendee read about a coup attempt on the king's life that Mordecai thwarted. So, the king inquired if Mordecai had been rewarded for saving his life. At that moment, Haman entered the court, and King Ahasuerus asked Haman how he should reward someone for doing a good deed. Haman was so self-absorbed that he thought the king was referring to him. "So Haman said to himself, 'Whom would the king delight to honor more than me?' And Haman said to the king, "For the man whom the king delights to honor, let royal robes be brought, which the king has worn, and the horse that the king has ridden, and on whose head a royal crown is set. And let the robes and the horse be handed over to one of the king's most noble officials." Funny enough, everything that Haman said to the king, the king ordered for Mordecai (Esth. 6.6–10). Of course, this enraged Haman because he thought the king was referring to him, not Mordecai. Haman attended Esther's banquet, and the king asked Esther what her request was? Esther revealed to King Ahasuerus Haman's plot to kill all the Jews, including herself. The King was so upset that he had to walk out of the room, but he found Haman literally on top of Queen Esther, begging for his life. When King Ahasuerus returned and saw Haman grabbing Queen Esther, he was so mad that he ordered Haman's execution on the gallows that Haman had prepared for Mordecai (7.7–10).

After reading the story of Esther, you may be wondering how this story relates to President Trump? Here are several analogies created by evangelicals. First, some evangelicals think that Donald Trump resembles Haman (Cusey). Trump, like Haman, is a power-hungry man, likes to brag about his accomplishments, and wants all the glory bestowed on him. Trump, like Haman, used his position of power to enforce his will with no regard for anyone else. Haman was enraged with Mordecai because Mordecai refused to bow down to him. Trump, like Haman, became enraged with anyone he did not deem "loyal," even those in his party, especially the media. Trump bullied, dehumanized, demeaned, and did whatever he could to destroy those who would not bow down to his will. The second analogy sees President Trump as King Ahasuerus in Esther's story. King Ahasuerus and Trump put their wealth on display. Both hosted a beauty pageant, loved, and divorced beautiful women, blamed immigrants for the problems in their countries, and used others as scapegoats for their sins. Finally, both demonstrated compassion toward those they loved. For King Ahasuerus, it was compassion to Queen Esther's request, and for President Trump, it was compassion for his children Ivanka, Eric, and Don Jr.'s requests (Burns). The third analogy in Esther's story is President Trump represents Mordecai and Haman represents the Democrats. When I researched this analogy, several articles about this theory all said the same statement, "Democrats will hang on the gallows they prepared for Trump." Each evangelical blog and article I read claims that the Democrats represent the Deep State of Washington DC who desire nothing else but to wage war against Donald Trump. Trump is like Mordecai because they both were outsiders who rose to power and were also deemed a threat. For example, on the Arizona GOP News, editor Frank Aquila wrote about debunked claims stating that the Deep State is like Haman. Mr. Aquila claimed that the Democrats planted fake evidence of Russian collusion through a fake whistleblower. He also claimed that the 2020 election was filled with the fraud perpetrated by Democrats (Aquila). Evangelicals can try to use biblical characters to compare and esteem Trump. But every one of those analogies is just a disturbing excuse to advance their political agenda and pervert Scripture.

    Unfortunately, evangelicals who make these ridiculous analogies are being deceived by the devil, or they are willingly submerging in the deception. Congressmen and Senators in the Republican Party who claim they are "evangelical Christians" and affirmed Trump's baseless claims of election fraud are just as guilty. Senators Ted Cruz, Josh Hawley, and disgraced Rudy Giuliani betrayed the GOP by their undemocratic antics and posturing, which were an affront to the democratic process and a disgrace to

Christianity. The Apostle Paul explained how easy it is for people, even Christians, to be deceived. Paul laid out some simple principles about deception in the first chapter of Romans. First, Paul said, "For the wrath of God is revealed from heaven against all ungodliness and unrighteousness of men, who by their unrighteousness suppress the truth" (18). Those who are only concerned about their political agenda will do everything to suppress the truth. Secondly, "For although they knew God, they did not honor him as God or give thanks to him, but they became futile in their thinking, and their foolish hearts were darkened" (22). Many of our political leaders use Christianity as leverage to play on the heartstrings of evangelical agendas. Next, "They exchanged the truth about God for a lie and worshiped and served the creature rather than the Creator" (25). Republicans and Trump evangelicals exchanged the truth about the 2020 election for lies of election fraud and worshiped at the altar of Trump. Finally, "They were filled with all manner of unrighteousness, evil, covetousness, malice. They are full of envy, murder, strife, deceit, maliciousness. They are gossips, slanderers, haters of God, insolent, haughty, boastful, inventors of evil, disobedient to parents, foolish, faithless, heartless, ruthless. Though they know God's righteous decree that those who practice such things deserve to die, they not only do them but give approval to those who practice them" (29–32). Unfortunately, many evangelicals selfishly supported not certifying the 2020 election. Both Senators Cruz and Hawley lied to the American people about "election fraud," saying it nullified Biden's presidential election.

To the evangelicals who approved Trump's madness, here is a warning to you. God knows all and sees all. You will be held accountable for your actions in this life or the next. God said, "I have this against you, that you have abandoned the love you first had. Remember therefore from where you have fallen; repent and do the works you did at first. If not, I will come to you and remove your lampstand from its place unless you repent" (Rev. 2.4–5). Before you saw the entire picture that I laid out about Trump, you possibly thought he was a decent man for upholding your favorite policies. But now, after seeing the whole picture, if you continue to deny that allegiance to Trump is dangerous to the body of Christ, you are part of the problem. My plea is that evangelicals will listen to the voice of the Holy Spirit and not harden their hearts to His plea of relinquishing support for Trump for the sake of the gospel. The Holy Spirit is trying to protect you from the lies of the enemy, but the devil wants Christianity to remain a laughingstock in the eyes of non-Christians.

Ephesians 5.11 states, "Have no fellowship with the unfruitful works of darkness, but rather expose them." I have no issues with evangelicals who support the Republican Party or consider themselves Republicans because of its traditional roots as the party of "Christian morality" and capitalism. I have no problems with evangelicals who choose to vote for Republican candidates because of their support of the pro-life movement, even if misguided. But supporting the Republican Party as it stands does not mean that you ignore the policies that continue to hurt the poor, the oppressed, People of Color, or damage Christianity's reputation. Evangelical support for the Republican Party does not mean supporting people like President Trump or other Republicans who orchestrated a legislative coup d'état to overthrow the 2020 election results and disenfranchise millions of voters. Politicians like Senators

Ted Cruz (TX), John Kennedy (LA), Josh Hawley (MO), Marsha Blackburn (TN), Mike Braun (IN), James Lankford (OK), Bill Hagerty (TN), Cynthia Lummis (WY), Roger Marshall (KA), Tommy Tuberville (AL), Steve Daines (MT), Ron Johnson (WI), and Representatives Louie Gohmert (TX), Marjorie Taylor Greene (GA), and Lauren Boebert (CO) are all responsible for their lies, deceit, and unwavering loyalty to Trump's lies about a "stolen election." These politicians are only concerned with their commitment to Trump for their political gain, and they could not care less what they were doing to diminish our democracy or hurt their constituents. For example, politicians like Marjorie Taylor Greene, who calls herself a "Christian" but consistently repeats evil conspiracy theories and racist rhetoric, are why non-Christians think we are all hypocrites. These politicians are not worried about the welfare of the people, or at least not the poor and People of Color. Nor do they seem concerned if their rhetoric defames the name of Christ. If you are a Christ-follower, then you cannot continue to blindly support President Trump or other evil politicians and think that your actions do not damage Christianity's reputation. Sin always has consequences. The Holy Spirit speaks, guides, and gives wise counsel even when you do not want to listen. The Holy Spirit's small voice that you can almost audibly hear is probably saying, "Don't follow the lies," "Don't believe the conspiracy theories," "Don't do anything to destroy America's democracy," "Don't trust cults like QAnon," "Turn away from the liars on FOX and other social media outlets," and "Turn away from your allegiance to Trump."

There was a time in Israel's history where over ninety percent of the Jewish people in the northern kingdom stopped worshipping God and worshipped a god made with human hands named Baal. The children of Israel completely turned their backs on God, but the LORD told the prophet, Elijah, that seven thousand people had not bowed down to Baal (1 Kings 19.18). Unfortunately, the children of Israel look much like present-day Trump evangelicals. Fortunately, like the seven thousand Israelites who did not bow down to Baal, there are life-long Republican evangelicals who have chosen to break away from the craziness going on in their party. Despite of death threats and political fallout, Representatives Liz Cheney and Adam Kinzinger have bravely spoken out against the shenanigans of Trumpism, the insurrection, and the lies insisted upon by the Republican Party. *HuffPost* surveyed life-long evangelical Republican voters who voted for candidate Trump in 2016 but found his behavior and character unacceptable afterward. These individuals considered voting Democrat for the first time in their lives because they could not justify President Trump's behaviors. A seventy-seven-year-old, life-long Republican woman considered voting against the Republican candidate for the first time in her life because of all the lies and divisiveness (Kuruvilla, *These Evangelicals*).

This woman represents many life-long Republican evangelicals who chose to stop supporting their party due to the election fraud "big lie" or because of the attacks on the U.S. Capitol. I am pleased to know that there are other evangelical leaders in the Republican Party who value character and country over party, and they refused to support President Trump's reelection. Thankfully, these Republican leaders courageously stood out against their party's outrageous actions and denounced their alliance with Trump. For example, Nebraska Senator Ben Sasse said that Trump mocked evangelicals and flirted with White supremacists (Ward). According to a Christian website dedicated to preventing Donald Trump's reelection called *Vote Common Good*, they inspired evangelical voters to oppose the Trump administration because of his behavior. *Pro-life Evangelicals for Biden* is a group of evangelicals who would generally vote Republican but chose to break away, primarily due to Donald Trump's character issues. The *Evangelicals for Biden* website states that "poverty, lack of accessible healthcare services, smoking, racism, and climate change are all pro-life issues" ("Join Movement"). Therefore, they advised evangelicals not to vote for Trump on a one-party issue like abortion.

In addition to *The Common Good* and *Pro-life Evangelicals*, prominent leaders endorsed Democrat candidate Joe Biden, not for his policies but his decency. Evangelical leaders like President Emeritus of Fuller Seminary John Richard Mouw, Board Chair Emeritus of Christianity Today John Huffman, Billy Graham's granddaughter Jerushah Duford, Baylor University Professor George Yancy, former Republican Congressman Reid Ribble, Scholars of Messiah College Peter Wehner and John Fea, Republican Senator Ben Sasse, Republican Senate Candidate John Kingston, Republican political strategist Joel Searby, former South Carolina Republican Representative Bob Inglis, former Governor and Congressman John Kasich, Wheaton College Professor of Theology Vincent Bacote, Ron Snider, Amy Sullivan, Tim Keller, John Piper, Max Lucado, and Assistant Secretary for Counterterrorism at the Department of Homeland Security Elizabeth Neumann should all be applauded for their bravery and standing for character and decency. They are brave, not for endorsing Biden, but for standing up against the evils of Trumpism. These evangelical leaders have put their lives, livelihood, families, ministries, and reputations on the line to stand up for the truth. If Trump, who claims he is a Christian, continues to wreak chaos and havoc on our democracy through his election fraud lies, greed, and criminal behavior, then he is not being led by the Holy Spirit. Trump continues to be led by his flesh, that is, his debased sin nature.

The evangelical's blind allegiance to Trump, the "election fraud" lies, overt racism, White supremacy, and bias against People of Color, and the insurrection are the reasons why I cannot align myself with evangelicalism. Evangelicalism continues to stand in the way of racial reconciliation between the church and People of Color. Conservativism is not linked to ethics and morality but bigotry. Either evangelicalism is aligned with Christ, the One and living God who came to save us all from sin, or evangelicalism supports a form of an anti-Christ, a demigod, the one who came to wreck America's Democracy, Donald Trump. But one thing is for sure; evangelicalism cannot be both. My friend, author, and blogger Bob Dickinson said, "To those I say, you get what you wish/vote for! You, in your support, are just as responsible. You can say how awful the attack on the Capitol was. You can say how democracy must prevail. You can say those actions aren't American. You can say those don't reflect the feelings of most citizens. But you put him in that position. And after watching that for four years, you still voted for him" (Dickinson).

The Republican Party has been permanently fractured. White supremacist groups, militia, and vigilantes feel emboldened. There is no affirming of his actions, excusing erratic behavior, or attributing Trump to King Cyrus, King David, King Ahasuerus, or Mordecai. No one can blame the Capitol insurrection on BLM, Antifa, Democrats, socialism, leftwing media, or fake news. Only President Trump, Republican politicians, and those who continued to support him while knowing the truth are to blame. Evangelicals, you supported an evil, deranged, narcissistic, delusional liar. You endorsed a con artist, a White supremacist racist bigot who is a criminal. If you say you did not vote for him based on his character, my dear evangelical brothers, and sisters, you are deceiving yourself. Character is everything for a Christ-follower. Character was important to you during the Clinton Administration, so why isn't it essential now? So, my question to those reading this that still refuse to denounce Trump despite all you know about his behavior; how will you justify this before the Lord? How will you explain how your support turned non-Christians away from the message of Christ? (Psa. 94.15). We all have the responsibility to call out people, organizations, and leaders whose actions support racism, White supremacy, lies, and criminal activity (Williams, R.). But more importantly, as Christ-followers, we must defend the name of Christ, and that means calling out sin and evil for what it is. My dear evangelicals, all I can say is, you must do better because the name of Christ deserves better.

CHAPTER 8
WHERE DO EVANGELICALS GO FROM HERE?

_____

"Let justice roll down like waters, and righteousness like an ever-flowing stream" (Amos 5.24).

In 1989, a rap group called Public Enemy put out a profanity-laced song called *Fight the Power*. The song spoke out about racism and inequalities against People of Color. The song also brought Public Enemy tons of backlash from mainstream media and evangelicals. Realistically, whenever you speak out publicly against racism and injustice, it almost always comes with criticism and backlash. Many of the pastors and politicians I mentioned in the previous chapter who spoke out against Trump and racism were attacked with hostile responses on their social media posts. They experienced a type of backlash called "cancel culture." Cancel culture is the withdrawal of support or canceling of the opposition if someone says or does something that you do not like. Cancel culture via social media is unfriending or blocking someone's posts. It is so easy to participate in cancel culture today. However, I want to warn you how detrimental cancel culture is for Christianity. Cancel culture sews division in churches, in families, amongst friends and party lines. Cancel culture has caused Millennials, Gen Z, and non-Christians to see Christianity as an unviable option due to evangelical hypocrisy. Cancel culture is not a twenty-first-century phenomenon because it was happening in Jesus' day. The Pharisees and Sadducees thrived in cancel culture, but they took it a step further. They declared certain groups like the tax collectors, prostitutes, and lepers "sinners." But Jesus never looked at "sinners" as his enemies but as people to reach, love, and to whom to build a bridge. My dear Christians, the people we disagree with are not our enemies but are our mission's field. We cannot afford to participate in cancel culture because it tarnishes the name of Christ and makes Christians look intolerant and unapproachable. We must strive for unity, not division, and seek to love, not be dismissive.

Change must first begin with the church. I briefly mentioned the church of Antioch in a previous chapter where the Apostle Paul confronted the Apostle Peter for his discrimination (Gal. 2.11–12). Antioch was also the first multicultural and multiethnic Gentile church. Antioch was a pivotal city east of the Mediterranean inside the Roman empire that consisted of different ethnicities, diversities, and backgrounds. Believers were first called Christians at the church of Antioch in Acts 11.6 and 13.1. There were diverse, multicultural leaders of different ethnicities, prophets, and preachers in Antioch. These leaders were Paul, Barnabas, Simon called Niger (which means Black or dark), Lucius of Cyrene, and Manaen. For evangelicals, understanding true multiculturalism is essential to growing as an ally for People of Color. The Apostle John described what heaven would look like. He said, "After this I looked, and behold, a great multitude that no one could number, from every nation, from tribes and peoples and languages, standing before the throne and before the Lamb, clothed in white robes, with palm branches in their hands" (Rev. 7.9). This verse describes an international, multiethnic, multicultural, multiracial group of Christ-followers worshipping God in heaven.

Today many evangelical churches are striving for multiculturalism in their congregations. Nevertheless, true multiculturalism is an intentional engagement of diverse cultures and not just a church of different races. Multiculturalism does not stop at diverse cultures but focuses on social policies and programs that bring equity to all people. Numerous churches today consider themselves multicultural, but most churches deemed multicultural are primarily dominated by one race. These churches may have a small segment of members representing different ethnicities, but often most churches are absent of varying cultural expressions. I would argue that most evangelical churches who pride themselves as multicultural are, in fact, multiracial or multiethnic churches because they have not embraced the different cultures in their worship music, teaching styles, or volunteer events. There are many problems with today's evangelical multicultural church because so many churches are not meeting the needs of the minority races in their congregations. Although these churches may consider themselves multicultural churches, not many consider themselves antiracist churches. As a result, minorities are forced to conform to the traditions, worship music, and preaching styles of the majority race instead of experiencing a church that emphasizes a multicultural experience. Suppose everyone in the congregation is listening to the same kind of music and one preaching style. In that case, this is not a multicultural church but a monocultural (assimilation to one culture) church.

The standard for the evangelical multicultural church experience in America is typically a predominately White church with a small minority, usually less than 30% of the congregation, of different ethnicities. The worship music and worship style feature songs and music genres predominately from White Christian music artists. The preaching style is culturally White. Even if there are preachers of other ethnicities, they are coached to assimilate to the preaching style of the majority White preachers on staff. The volunteering, activities, and entertainment is typically culturally White and feature things that a predominately White culture would enjoy. One of the problems with the evangelical's perspective of multiculturalism is that most of these things are usually not appealing to the minorities in the congregation. While some evangelical churches may have their own Chinese, Korean, or Spanish services, other ethnicities like Native Americans, African Americans, and some other Asian cultures are expected to assimilate to the majority culture, which can be perceived as insensitive.

Paul explained in the letters to the Galatian Christians that walking in the Spirit of God is one way to apprehend a multiethnic, multicultural, antiracist perspective. The goal of accomplishing multiculturalism is often tricky and frustrating, so this is an important concept. People may say or do things that may cause you to want to respond in your flesh. However, we must "Walk by the Spirit, and you will not gratify the desires of the flesh. For the desires of the flesh are against the Spirit, and the desires of the Spirit are against the flesh, for these are opposed to each other, to keep you from doing the things you want to do" (Gal. 5.16–21). I am not saying that Christians do not sin because we all sin. "If we say we have not sinned, we make Him a liar, and His word is not in us" (1 John 1.10). Sinning is not the issue, but "Christians" who ignore racially ethnic disparities in the church and racial inequality in society are willfully or inadvertently sinning. As Christ-followers, we will always struggle against sin, even the sins of inherent biases and racism, but that is no excuse not to work on these issues collectively. The desire to achieve heaven on earth should help drive your church's longing to establish a truly multicultural, multiracial, multiethnic, antiracist church.

As Christ-followers, walking in the Spirit means not allowing your flesh to control you, but instead, the Holy Spirit dictates how you live as a representation of His love. When we yield to the Holy Spirit, He will help us examine what is lacking to bring true multiculturalism and antiracism to our churches. In other words, when we submit ourselves to God's will and not our own, then we can allow the Holy Spirit to show us our blind spots. In order to achieve multiculturalism in our churches, Christian businesses, and ministries, I have decided to list action steps to help us achieve our goals. You can use this list for personal accountability and help your organization track continuous progress. By no means is this list exhaustive, nor am I suggesting you should try to accomplish everything at once. These simple suggestions will help you establish a timeline toward antiracism and multiculturalism in your church. If you are anxious and ready to get started, jump in with both feet.

Nevertheless, I do want to warn you not to rush to complete the list for the sake of completing it. Some reading this have already begun working on many of the items in this list, which is excellent. For others, this list (items are bolded in the remaining text) may seem foreign to you and maybe a little scary at first. I want you to pray over each step. God will show you which areas you need to focus on first. Based on these items, I suggest putting together a one-day, one-month, six-month, and one-, three-, and five-year plan. Finally, make sure you have someone in your organization or a friend who is a Person of Color to help hold you accountable for accomplishing and working through these steps.

Before you do anything, you must first identify sins that lie within your heart and then **Repent.** Repentance is the acknowledgment of wrong. In this case, repentance is the acknowledgment of biases and participating in overt or unintended racism and lack of diversity in your organization. Although many scholars believe that only White people can be racist, I do not believe this is true. We all have a propensity towards sin, including racism. Therefore, we all can show racist or at least biased tendencies. So, we must repent for the times when we did not step up to call out racism or call out our friends, family, or fellow evangelicals. Now is the time to dig in deep, soul search, and come before the altar of Jesus and repent. The work of restoring the name of Christ, being a consistent antiracist, and being a genuinely multiracial, multiethnic church cannot begin unless repentance is completed first. Repent if you have allowed politics to take over your social media threads. Repent if you supported politicians like

President Trump despite his character. Repent for turning a blind eye toward the needs of the poor, the homeless man on the street corner, the oppressed, and People of Color. Repent if you have ever been insensitive towards another race. Repent if you have canceled, unfriended, or blocked someone who does not share your political views. Repentance is a continuous process because we are not perfect, and we will always miss it. Thankfully, the Bible says, "If we confess our sins, He is faithful and just to forgive us of our sins, and to cleanse us of all unrighteousness" (1 John 1.9).

Along with repentance is a need to acknowledge personal **Spiritual Growth** in the area of antiracism. Collectively the body of Christ needs to grow more spiritually in this area. For example, a vine is essential for growth, and it acts as a conduit for the nutrients that a plant needs as its source of life. The roots of the vine are anchored in the soil. As with all plants, some produce crops while others do not, and this analogy is similar to the church today. You may grow from this book, but it will not be because you gained knowledge; instead, you will acknowledge areas that you need to change. Each spring, I am always excited to see the bulbs that I planted in the fall grow into beautiful flowers. Amazingly, not every bulb I plant produces a flower, and it puzzles me how some produce multiple bulbs while others produce nothing. On the flip side, some plants have so many flowers and leaves there is insufficient room for growth. The plant must be pruned so that it continues to grow. Pruning involves the selective removal of plant leaves by removing overgrowth. Pruning prepares the plant for harvest to produce a large crop which allows the plant to flourish. After several weeks of pruning, the leaves turn into flowers; but if the flower is not getting enough nutrients from the vine or the soil, eventually it dies off.

Jesus said, "I am the vine; you are the branches. Whoever abides in me and I in him, he it is that bears much fruit, for apart from me you can do nothing" (John 15.5). Jesus is the True Vine, the source of all life, including plants, animals, and most importantly, human beings. When we are not connected to the True Vine, we become like the plants that die and fall off the vine because they were never really connected to it in the first place. Those plants wither and die because they were never getting the proper nutrients. In other instances, the growth of those plants only grows to a certain level, and they never produce fruit. However, when we stay connected to Jesus, we will produce a harvest for the kingdom. Jesus said, "If anyone does not abide in me, he is thrown away like a branch and withers; and the branches are gathered, thrown into the fire, and burned" (6). This verse does not refer to losing your salvation, but to those who continue to act like Christians while never making a true confession of faith. We cannot bear fruit independent of being connected to Vine, and that vine is Jesus. We cannot be antiracists and accomplish true multiculturalism without being connected to Jesus. Those who are not connected to the Vine are vulnerable and are more inclined to fall away from the faith rather than bear fruit.

You must personally **Confront Racism**. I must elaborate on this point because this step is crucial and cannot be skipped. Starting with my fellow People of Color, I implore you to openly support our allies who bravely speak out against racism in their congregations, their social media groups, and with their families and friends.

We need our pastors and leaders of Color to speak out and lead from the front lines and hold our fellow evangelical pastors accountable. The time is now to show our evangelical brothers and sisters support because their allegiance to antiracism comes with a cost. For evangelicals who have embraced antiracism through uncomfortable conversations for the first time, I understand that it may be scary or even frustrating. As long as People of Color continue to be gunned down by police and White supremacy exists in the church, this is not the time to take your foot off the gas but plow forward. As the Psalmist says, "The mouth of the righteous utters wisdom, and his tongue speaks justice" (Psa. 37.30). We should not expect over four hundred years of racism, inequalities, and discrimination in this country to go away overnight. However, this is not an excuse to put antiracism on the backburner either. My brothers and sisters are in a race for change; it is not a sprint but a marathon.

In businesses and church settings, when you witness racism, you are obligated to confront the person. Too often, we fall into the trap of slapping leaders on the wrist for racist infractions and microaggressions, which only cause issues down the road for potential lawsuits against your organization. Also, not confronting racism can lead to grieving and quenching the Holy Spirit. The Apostle Paul said, "Do not grieve the Holy Spirit of God, by whom you were sealed for the day of redemption" (Eph. 4.30). Grieving the Holy Spirit pushes aside His warnings, willfully choosing to ignore His counsel, and rejecting guidance. An example of grieving the Holy Spirit is those who consciously supported shameful conspiracy theories of "election fraud" or participated in the insurrection at the Capitol. Paul also said, "Do not quench the Spirit" (1 Thes. 5.19). The best way I can describe quenching the Holy Spirit is like pouring water onto a fire to distinguish the power of the flames. Quenching the Holy Spirit occurs when we have gone past the point of ignoring the truth and the warnings not to continue to engage in sin, and we consciously do it. Quenching the Spirit means that we have made up our mind that "we are going to do what we want to do," and the Spirit's influence is no longer significant, nor is it a driving force, in our life. At this point, when we quench the Spirit, we have entirely put out His power over our lives and have deliberately turned our backs to engage in sin. An example of quenching the Spirit is when evangelicals supported the one hundred and forty House Representatives and thirteen Senators who objected to the certification of President Biden. Alternatively, the evangelicals who protested and promoted a coup to take over the election certification with the Proud Boys, QAnon, and White supremacist groups in Washington also quenched the Spirit.

Jesus said, "Salt is good; but if the salt has lost its taste, how shall its saltiness be restored? It is of no use either for the soil or for the manure pile. It is thrown away. He who has ears to hear, let him hear!" (Luke 14.34-35). Jesus addressed his disciples with what it takes to be a committed follower. Although Jesus had a large crowd following him, He was not interested in drawing the large crowds. Jesus was concerned with developing true disciples who would spread the gospel message to the ends of the earth. Jesus turned to the crowd and said, "If anyone comes to Me and does not hate his father and mother, wife and children, brothers and sisters, yes, and his own life also, he cannot be My disciple" (Luke 14.26).

The Greek word that Jesus used for hate is *miseo*, which means "hate, detest, abhor." Jesus used this word to make his statement shocking, jolting, and thought-provoking. To hate something or to detest something is not a neutral feeling. Those feelings go against our natural tendencies. This kind of hate does not mean that you are ignoring someone, nor does it imply disinterest. *Miseo* means to despise someone or something actively. Christians should hate and detest racism and White supremacy. Jesus used hyperbole as an overstatement in order to make a point with the maximum impact. Jesus is not saying he wants us to hate our family members. As Americans, we view hate as something repulsive or loathsome. Whereas hate in the Eastern world means to place something or someone in a lower position. In other words, a genuinely committed disciple of Christ will place his family, friends, job, hobbies, possessions, policies, and politics in a lower position than God. Again, this is not a license to mistreat people because we love our neighbors as ourselves. Nothing and no one should take your allegiance over God, for He must be first in your life and not secondary to your political party allegiances or your loyalty to a persona.

In the ancient East, family lineage was the most important thing to survival. It was more important than anything because the family was the backbone of their financial structure, support system, and community. So, the idea of forsaking your family to follow Jesus was not only a foreign language to them, but it was also a radical statement. This kind of talk completely went against the grain of society. If you wanted to be one of Jesus' disciples, then you had to be willing to make God the center. You might have to separate from family and friends who refuse to be antiracists. Jesus, says, "So likewise, whoever of you does not forsake all that he has cannot be My disciple" (Luke 14.33). Forsake means to give up, renounce, and abandon our right to have ownership. It also implies that we must become good stewards of our resources. Jesus also says, "Salt is good; but if the salt has lost its flavor, how shall it be seasoned? It is neither fit for the land nor the dunghill, but men throw it out. He who has an ear to hear, let him hear!" (14.34). In the ancient world, salt was an essential element used to preserve and season food. Unlike today's pure sodium chloride, salt in the Bible days came with impurities that could render it useless. How can we say we are disciples of Christ when many of our actions are not producing salt? Salt preserves what is wholesome and good, but Jesus is saying that un-salty salt is useless.

I have lived in Texas for twenty-three years, but I grew up in cold and snowy Cleveland, Ohio. If you are familiar with the northern states, then you know the winter months are brutal. People say you get used to it, but I never got used to the cold and snow in Cleveland for twenty-four years of my life. One year Cleveland received over four feet of snow. In order to drive on the roads and highways, the city trucks distributed rock salt onto the streets, so your tires had traction to drive on the snow and ice. Rock salt can penetrate snow and ice, and it preserves the streets by making a clear path. In the same manner, evangelicals should be like rock salt. Our lives should represent Christ so that it penetrates the hearts and minds of non-Christians around us to clear the path for the Holy Spirit to do His work of salvation in their lives. When I moved to Dallas, I laughed when the city workers put dirt and sand on the icy streets instead of using rock salt. Sand and dirt only made the street dirty, and cars continued to slide on the roads. You see, sand and dirt are cheap substitutes for rock salt. Unfortunately, I believe many evangelicals live like cheap substitutes for rock salt because they are just pretending to be antiracists when they are not. Jesus is saying, consider whether or not you are willing to be his follower, and if so, the will of God must be your priority. If you do not have the ability or willingness to follow Jesus and sacrifice everything for him, including being an antiracist, then just stop while you are ahead, and stop embarrassing the name of Christ.

After you confront the racism or racial bias in your heart, you must **Speak Out**. When an injustice occurs, you should defend the oppressed person immediately. Either way, a strong rebuke or a soft reprove may be necessary; but you must make sure the wounded person is addressed. "Better is open rebuke than hidden love" (Pro. 27.5). In other words, this means that you cannot worry about the fallout. Doing the right thing means, as a Christ-follower, not remaining silent. When applicable, you must defend the Person of Color in their presence when witnessing a racist or oppressive incident. Next, you must **Protect the Wounded.** After implementing policies and procedures, decide who will advocate for the person the racist incident has wounded. In other words, is it the responsibility of the wounded person to confront the person who caused the incident, or will your organization bring in an outside, unbiased individual to handle the incident? What individual will be appointed to ensure that the racist action is handled above board? How will you make sure that the offender does not just get a slap on the wrist? Ensure your organization determines what kind of counseling and training programs will be provided for the wounded person and the person who engaged in the offense. In writing a handbook, list infraction policies, training, and repercussions for the person accused of the racism. Make sure you document *every* incident. Suppose the person who was wounded is emotionally traumatized from the event. In that case, you have a responsibility to determine the appropriate paid counseling sessions that will be provided through your organization, for God says, "I hate robbery and wrong; I will faithfully give them their recompense" (Isa. 61.8).

    Continue to **Look for Personal Biases**. Consistently check your heart against your evangelical worldview and look for racial, cultural, and ethnic biases. Do as King David did when he said, "Search me, O God, and know my heart! Try me and know my thoughts!" (Psa. 139.23). Check to see if your political and racial views line up with Scripture. Ask questions and have thought-provoking conversations with People of Color that may not share the same views. Do not be easily offended or defensive by the responses to your questions, nor feel the need to explain yourself and make it about your feelings. Move past your emotions so you can hear the hearts of People of Color and be true champions for change both racially and politically. **Challenge Yourself**. Pray for God to show the areas where you need to be challenged for People of Color. In other words, "Pray without Ceasing" (1 Thess. 5.1). Pray, fast, and allow the Holy Spirit to lead you in these areas of change. Remember, racism is purely a sin issue that can only be changed through heart change. The power of the Holy Spirit will help you lean into His guidance, and you will be an ally and an anti-racist.

Have **Intentional Conversations.** Deliberate conversations help build relationships with People of Color. For, "Evil men do not understand justice, but those who seek the Lord understand it completely" (Pro. 28.5). Therefore, surround yourself with new people who are not like you. Serve, work together on ministry teams, and pray with them. Support them as they speak out against injustices by showing solidarity. Encourage them both privately and publicly. Practice **Intentional Interactions.** Similar to intentional conversations, intentional interactions are essential for your growth. "For you were called to freedom, brothers. Only do not use your freedom as an opportunity for the flesh, but through love serve one another" (Gal. 5.13). Ensure that your circles of friends and associates are diverse by going out of your way at work and at church to connect with people of different ethnicities. Invite People of Color to lunch or dinner with you so that you can get to know them personally. Again, to expose yourself to different nationalities, get out of your comfort zone and meet new people. Have **Deliberate Uncomfortable Conversations** so that you can talk about the complex issues at work, in your small groups at church, and with your family members. You must, "Destroy arguments and every lofty opinion raised against the knowledge of God, and take every thought captive to obey Christ" (2 Cor. 10.5). Be intentional about these conversations at least once monthly. Participate in a unity table where you invite groups of different ethnicities to engage around complex and polarizing topics. Challenge them to talk about what they have learned and what changes they perceive should take place. Do not forget to invite younger people in these conversations and value their input.

Continue to practice **Empathy and Compassion.** It is essential to work on your empathy meter, so that you can see disparities from the eyes of the poor, the oppressed, or People of Color. Complete a spiritual evaluation of your heart. Stop letting the news, social media, and political preferences be your final standard instead of the Bible. This means many evangelicals need to pull away from social media, politics, and patriotism to search the Scriptures apart from these manufactured systems. "For the Lord will vindicate his people and have compassion on his servants" (Psa. 135.14). Empathy also requires you to listen from a position of grace and not from knowing what you think people need. Seek **Godly Counsel** and collaborate on how you should address the issues of racism and politics. "For justice will return to the righteous, and all the upright in heart will follow it" (Psa. 94.15). Therefore, do not make assumptions about what you might think People of Color want or need. Instead, ask them and put in the necessary work that is required to make the environment inclusive and racially sensitive, which requires flexibility on your behalf.

Hold your **Leaders Accountable** for "Not many of you should become teachers, my brothers, for you know that we who teach will be judged with strictness" (Jam. 3.1). This verse mandates our church leaders and Christian business owners be accountable for extending the olive branch and being a more diverse church or business. Schedule time to meet with your leaders, email them, call them to talk about these issues, and ask their plans to implement the changes needed at your church or business. Find ways to measure progress, and do not let your leaders off the hook. Set quarterly meetings to review the new changes, and do not be afraid to tweak these changes and discuss ways to do more.

Implement **New Policies & Procedures.** Church leaders and business owners cannot afford to miss this critical step. You will potentially place your church or business in jeopardy of a lawsuit if you do not have specific written policies and procedures that address and document racial incidents that occur with your staff, members, volunteers, or guests. "When justice is done, it is a joy to the righteous but terror to evildoers" (Pro. 21.15). In other words, if you need to address racial incidents, it is better to have written policies and procedures explained and trained with your executive leadership teams before you fall into a situation that your organization is not prepared to deal with properly. In addition to written policies and procedures, you should interview the People of Color on your staff to find out how they feel about your organization's diversity and give them space to be open with their responses. Now is not the time to be concerned about feelings but about your staff's emotional state. Secondly, your organization should invest in hiring an outside independent counsel who has no ties to the executive leadership at your organization so that an unbiased diversity and inclusion audit is performed to find areas where your organization needs to improve. Another suggestion is to allow your staff to complete a 360 survey specifically about each executive business leader, senior manager, pastor, and elder at your church or business by a person of color so they can be transparent about their thoughts without fear of retribution. Pastors and teachers, create **Sermons and Lessons.** Pastors and teachers must begin months of sermons and lessons on these complex subjects through the

Scriptures and unbiased history books. "For justice return to the righteous, and all the upright in heart will follow it" (Psa. 94.15). Your sermons cannot be a single lesson but must be a series of messages and lessons to change the hearts of your members and students. Find new textbooks with more accurate history and provide Bible studies and discipleship training that deals with these issues.

Actively Participate by making sure you are doing things to keep the issue of anti-racism in the forefront and not in the background. "Learn to do good; seek justice; correct oppression; bring justice to the fatherless, plead the widow's cause" (Isa. 1.17). For example, get involved in writing, reading, studying, talking, protesting, and advocating. These actions will help build trust with your friends of Color. Schedule a date on your calendars to do something weekly in this area as a challenge. Talk with your spouse as to how your family will be antiracist, pro-justice, and actively help the poor and the oppressed. Active participation must be intentional as this is probably not a natural process, but change will not happen on its own. Have **Community Impact.** Just like Paul said, "We urge you brothers, admonish the idle, encourage the fainthearted, help the weak, be patient with them all" (1 Thes. 5.14). Actively seek ways to impact unity in your community. Find out what kind of community unity events are in your areas, like peaceful protests, prayer vigils, council meetings, community groups, neighborhood watch, and small group gatherings (use wisdom for your risk of COVID-19, of course). Volunteer to be in conversations and community panel discussions to talk about these issues. Do not forget you can write your congressman about areas in your community that need to change.

Try new **Cultural Experiences.** This step will take you out of your comfortability. Deliberately connect with People of Color of different ethnicities by listening to different genres of music other than White Christian music such as Traditional Gospel, Contemporary Gospel, Christian Latin, Christian Caribbean, Christian Asian, Christian Indigenous music. Ask your friends of Color for suggestions of songs and artists of Color to listen to on streaming apps. Choose a church of different ethnicity and intentionally visit or view a worship service online different from your own culture. Even if the service is in another language, you can still enjoy worship music and unique styles and sounds even if you do not understand the preaching in a foreign language. Participating like this will expose your mind to a vision of heaven when you see people worshiping and praising God from every nation and every tongue. For, "All the earth worships you and sings praises to you; they sing praises to your name" (Psa. 66.4).

Get Involved for "The Lord loves justice; he will not forsake his saints. They are preserved forever, but the children of the wicked shall be cut off" (Psa. 37.28). Volunteer to serve on church committees or Christian activist groups to help implement change. If there are no groups available in your community, start your own group by getting your leadership on board while you lead the charge. Do not stop at the first no or not yet. Ask for help and ask questions with People of Color. If you are finding that cliques exist, expose them and work towards inclusivity instead of exclusivity.

Help minorities and **Use Your Privilege.** Understand the areas where you have the privilege and use those privileges to glorify God and help the poor and People of Color.

Privilege does not suggest all White people are wealthy, have never struggled in life, or have always had it easy. Privilege does not assume that everything you accomplished was unearned, nor mean that you cheated to obtain what you possess. Privilege means that the world is seen from a White vantage point, and everyone else is expected to assimilate. "For there will never cease to be poor in the land. Therefore, I command you, 'You shall open wide your hand to your brother, to the needy and to the poor, in your land'" (Deu. 15.11). In other words, use your privilege, your sphere of influence, your financial ability, and your connections to make lasting change in your church, your job, and your community. **Patronize Minority-Owned Businesses.** Try shopping or patronizing Black and Brown minority-owned businesses, restaurants, stores, and non-profits you would not usually patronize. Seek out these businesses through social media outlets or by asking your friends of Color for recommendations of their favorite stores and restaurants. Be intentional about supporting at least one of these organizations regularly. For "We ought to support people like these, that we may be fellow workers for the truth" (3 John 1.8).

Educate Your Family. Make sure you educate your children to be anti-racists and empathize with the poor and the oppressed. Education starts at home, in the schools, as well as in the church. King Solomon said, "Train up a child in the way he should go; even when he is old he will not depart from it" (Pro. 22.6). Make sure your children's youth ministry addresses these issues and teaches from a biblical perspective. Talk about the positive things People of Color are doing, and do not just talk about famous athletes or celebrities. Education is essential for a journey towards antiracism, establishing a multicultural church, and making political decisions. Arm yourself with knowledge by reading books written by People of Color to help you learn and identify blind spots. This step will take years of unlearning false truths to replace them with absolute truths, so do not stop reading and learning new things. Maybe think about starting a book club or reading a book with a friend or spouse to collaborate on what you are reading and learning.

Just remember, your political choices have consequences that can hurt People of Color. Make sure you are doing things to help see the needs of others. Plenty of organizations are working in the areas of racial reconciliation, antiracism, and multiculturalism. Some organizations are already working with the poor and needy to help churches meet their communities' needs. For example, I started my ministry called Royalty Ministries in 2012 to serve homeless women and single mothers. After a divorce, I lost my home. My credit was ruined, and I was denied approval to rent an apartment. I slept on the couches of friends until I was able to rebuild my credit score. Going through that unbearable time in my life gave me a more profound passion for the poor and the oppressed. I am not saying that you have to lose everything to develop a passion for those hurting. However, serving in those environments will change your outlook on life. Go on a short-term mission trip to a war-torn or underdeveloped country. Serve in inner-city programs, volunteer at homeless shelters, single moms' organizations, or start your cause. Remember, many organizations in your community need your support so find ways to volunteer your time and contribute your resources.

As you work through the points listed in this chapter, educate yourself as an antiracist, and bring justice for the poor and the oppressed by remembering, "The Lord sits enthroned forever; he has established his throne for justice" (Psa. 9.7). As Christ-followers, we are all heirs to God's throne of justice and coheirs with Jesus. We are all brothers and sisters in Christ's family, so when one of your fellow family members in Christ is wounded by racism, treated unjustly, or oppressed, you have a responsibility to uphold justice for your family. We each have a responsibility to work on our own racial biases and do whatever we can to work on racial reconciliation in our churches and communities. Remember, "Commit your way to the Lord; trust in him, and he will act. He will bring forth your righteousness as the light, and your justice as the noonday" (Psa. 37.5–6).

CONCLUSION

"A light has dawned on those living in the land of darkness" (Isa. 9.2).

"I charge you in the presence of God and of Christ Jesus, who is to judge the living and the dead, and by his appearing and his kingdom: preach the word; be ready in season and out of season; reprove, rebuke, and exhort, with complete patience and teaching. For the time is coming when people will not endure sound teaching but having itching ears they will accumulate for themselves teachers to suit their own passions and will turn away from listening to the truth and wander off into myths. As for you, always be sober-minded, endure suffering, do the work of an evangelist, fulfill your ministry" (2 Tim. 4.1-5). I end this book with a broken heart for the state of the American evangelical. Too many of my evangelical friends have lost their way. They have turned their backs on the righteousness of God and have accepted the lies of the devil instead. As a fellow minister of the gospel, I must rebuke American evangelical Christians for their allegiance to President Trump, Marjorie Taylor Greene, QAnon, or any other conspiracy theories, over their allegiance to Christ. It is like the sign inside the store that says, "you break, you buy." Well, evangelicals, you broke it, and now you buy it. You broke the trust of non-Christians when you decided to sell out to a con artist, an insurrectionist, a White supremacist, and a racist. You broke it when you turned your backs on the poor and the needy in favor of policies that put more money in the pockets of the wealthy. You broke it when you sided with the oppressor instead of protecting the oppressed by pushing away immigrants fleeing for their lives. You called terrorists "patriots." You continue to push "the big lie" about an election that was not stolen by People of Color in Georgia. Woe to you hypocrites! Babies were caged like animals on your watch, and now your words are like whitewashed walls and empty tombs, "which outwardly appear beautiful, but within are full of dead people's bones and all uncleanness. So you also outwardly appear righteous to others, but within you are full of hypocrisy and lawlessness" (Matt. 23.27-28). You called evil good. You "exchanged the truth about God for a lie and worshiped and served what has been created instead of the Creator, who is praised forever" (CSB Rom. 1.25). Now you must buy, you must reap what you sow—that which has left our nation and the church in peril. For that reason and all the other reasons I explained throughout this book, I denounce today's evangelicalism for it is not of God.

Remember Judas, Jesus' disciple who was so focused on power and greed that he was willing to sell out Jesus? In the same manner, evangelicals you have been so focused on political power and policies that keep you comfortable, that you have sold out the church in the process. You hide behind support for your political preferences under the guise of Christian nationalism and morality. How can this be? Christian nationalism is NOT godly but a faulty attempt to bring Christianity back to America. You must have forgotten that "Our citizenship is in heaven, and from it we await a

Savior, the Lord Jesus Christ" (Phi. 3.20). Although I should be happy when prominent evangelicals speak out against White nationalism, Christian nationalism, Trumpism, and police brutality against People of Color, I am tired, honestly. Realistically, it is too little too late for words of shock and awe. Evangelicals, you must deal with the genuine issues of White supremacy and racism in the church and in your hearts. To the Southern Baptist Convention leaders and the six Southern Baptist seminary presidents who condemned critical race theory,[28] this solidifies what People of Color already knew existed. You still have racism in your hearts because you continue to ignore that race motivates many political views and policies.

Black and Brown people are dehumanized and criminalized before you can begin to tell their story. I pray that you desire to understand better the disparities between people who look like you versus the treatment of People of Color. I pray that what you learned about evangelical involvement with White supremacy in this book has made you uncomfortable. I pray that the events at the U.S. Capitol and the disparities in the police presence at the BLM protests have grieved your heart. I pray that the Holy Spirit convicts your heart to see the truth, to see the evil and violence that has emerged from the Trump administration as well as previous administrations based on racism and White supremacy.

---

[28] Critical Race Theory is a view that the law is inherently racist, and race is a social construct to maintain elitism by the dominant race. It is a secular viewpoint but has validity in the areas of structural and systemic racism. The church has an obligation to bring justice to the poor and the oppressed, and address racism. How the Southern Baptist Convention could come to this conclusion to denounce CRT baffles me.

Remember, no one is above the law, and no one is above God's law, not the President, and not the church.

With that said, I decided to end this book by listing several names of People of Color who died at the hands of the police or a White supremacist in rage. Each of these individuals has a story. Some of these individuals came from a troubled past, came from single-mother homes, or lived in poverty. Others on this list came from modest means, were middle class, taxpayers, and regular U.S. citizens contributing to society. The majority of the names on this list were not bad people but, unfortunately, were put in life-altering situations. Regardless of what circumstances led to their deaths, these individuals were all created in God's image, just like you and me. They are all God's children, but regrettably, their lives were cut short because of the actions of a rogue police officer or a racist mass shooter who killed them. I end this book with a dedication to the families of People of Color killed by police officers, "concerned citizens," and racist hate groups. As you read these names, I want you to imagine that these people look like you, live next door to you, attend your church, or are your friends. I hope that you read these names, and you will read their stories. Please do not skip over this section, but I challenge you to read each name aloud. I pray that you "see" their faces as another person created in the image of God like you.

Adam Toledo
Adolfo Cerros Hernandez
Ahmaud Arbery
Aiyana Stanley-Jones

Akai Gurley
Akeelah Jackson
Akiel Denkins
Alberta Spruill

Alex Nieto
Alexander Gerhard Hoffman
Alfred Olango
Alton Sterling
Amilcar Perez-Lopez
Andre Anchondo
Andres Guardado
Andy Lopez
Angelina Silva Englisbee
Antonio Zambrano-Montes
Anthony Hill
Anthony Lemar Smith
Antwon Rose
Ariane McCree
Arturo Benavidez
Atatiana Jefferson
Aura Rosser
Bettie Jones
Billy Ray Davis
Botham Jean
Brandon Keith Gray
Brandon Webber
Brendon Glenn
Breonna Taylor
Channara Tom Pheap
Charly Keunang
Chief Greg Allen
Christian Taylor
Christopher Whitfield
Rev. Clementa Pinckney
Corey Jones
Cynthia Hurd
D'ettrick Griffin
Daniel Prude
Rev. Daniel Simmons
Danny Ray Thomas
Dante Parker
Daoyou Feng
Darius Tarver
Darnisha Harris
Daunte Wright
David Alvah Johnson
David McAtee
DeAndre Ballard
DeJuan Gillory
Delaina Ashley Yaun Gonzalez
Rev. DePayne Middleton-Doctor
De'Von Bailey
Dominique White
Dontre Hamilton
Eleanor Bumpers
Elena Mondragon
Elijah McClain
Elsa Mendoza de la Mora
Emantic Fitzgerald Bradford, Jr.
Emmett Till
Ethel Lance
Eric Garner

Eric Harris
Eric Logan
Erik Salgado
Ezell Ford
Fermin Vincent Valenzuela
Finan Berhe
Frank Smart
Freddie Gray, Jr.
Gabriella Nevarez
George Floyd
Gloria Irma Marquez
Gregory Gunn
Gregory Hill
Guillermo 'Memo' Garcia
Hyun Jung Grant
Ivan Filiberto Manzano
Jamar Clark
Jamarion Robinson
Jamee Johnson
Jamel Floyd
JaQuavion Slaton
Javier Amir Rodriguez
Jemel Roberson
Jerame Reid
Jeremy McDole
Jimmy Atchison
John Burris
John Crawford III
Jonathan Ferrell
Jonathan Hart
Jordan Anchondo

Jordan Baker
Jordan Davis
Jordan Edwards
Jorge Calvillo Garcia
Juan de Dios Velazquez Chairez
Julius Johnson
Justin Howell
Kajieme Powell
Kathryn Johnston
Keith Lamont Scott
Kendra James
Kendrec McDade
Korryn Gaines
Kwame Jones
Lamontez Jones
Laquan McDonald
Larry Jackson, Jr.
Lavante Biggs
Leonardo Campos, Jr.
Luis Alfonzo Juarez
Magdiel Sanchez
Manuel Loggins, Jr.
Margie Reckard
Maria Eugenia Legarreta Rothe
Maria Flores
Marco Cardoza
Maribel Campos
Mario Woods
Marvin D. Scott III

Maurice Granton
Melissa Ventura
Melissa Williams
Melvin Watkins
Michael Brown
Michael Dean
Michael Donald
Michelle Cusseaux
Miles Hall
Miriam Carey
Myra Thompson
Natosha McDade
Oscar Grant
Pamela Turner
Patrick Harmon
Paul Andre Michels
Pedro Villanueva
Philando Castile
Phillip White
Quintonio LeGrier
Ramarley Graham
Raul Flores
Raul Saavedra-Vargas
Rayshard Brooks
Rekia Boyd
Rev. Sharonda
   Coleman-Singleton
Robert Lawrence White
Rumain Brisbon
Ryan Twyman
Samuel David Mallard

Samuel DuBose
Sandra Bland
Sara Esther Regalado Moriel
Sean Monterrosa
Sean Reed
Sergio Reyes
Shantel Davis
Shelly Frey
Soon Chung Park
Stephon Clark
Steven Demarco Taylor
Suncha Kim
Susie Jackson
Tamir Rice
Tanisha Anderson
Janisha Fonville
Tarika Wilson
Terence Crutcher
Teresa Sanchez
Terrance Franklin
Tommy Smith
Tony Robinson
Trayvon Martin
Tshyrad Oates
Tyisha Miller
Tywanza Sanders
Victor White III
Vinson Ramos
Walter Scott
Wendell Allen
William Chapman

William Green
Willie McCoy
Xiaojie Tan
Yassin Mohamed

Yong Ae Yue
Yvette Smith

There is no question that White supremacy continues to exist in evangelicalism today. Suppose the church grieves, laments, and repents for the state of evangelical Christianity, although we may not be able to eradicate racism everywhere. In that case, we can at least make progress to restore the evangelical's reputation in the world and work towards reconciliation with People of Color. As Christ-followers, we are called to live a life that represents Christ. We are called to be set apart for God's kingdom for service to *all* humankind and to love our neighbors as ourselves. For God "loves righteousness and justice" (Psa. 33.5). Evangelicals (more specifically, our White Christian brothers and sisters) must love righteousness and justice just as much as God does. That love will enable you to lead the charge for antiracism and justice, and it will give the church the courage to make wrongs right.

Evangelicals, you are being held responsible for calling out evil, upholding justice, protecting the poor and oppressed, and standing up for People of Color. You have a personal obligation to expose racism in the church and the injustices in our society. I close with this; how can the church be influential if Christians do not stand against evil? How can we defend the faith if Christians do not clearly understand God's Word about justice? How can we share the gospel with others if Christianity is a laughingstock?

Conclusion

How can we call ourselves followers of Christ if we are not following Him by our actions and loving our neighbors as ourselves? Christianity is not a set of dos and don'ts. Christianity is a personal acceptance of our sinful nature, our need for an intimate relationship with God, and a life striving for holiness and righteousness. You should "Be diligent to present yourself approved to God, a worker who does not need to be ashamed, rightly dividing the word of truth" (2 Tim. 2.15). In other words, study your Bible so that you can defend your faith against the schemes of the devil that align Christianity to a persona, a political party, and politics. Be diligent in understanding your Bible so that you can live like Christ, take care of the poor and needy, and bring justice to the oppressed. Following Christ means to stand for justice and the truth. As the prophet Micah said, "He has told you, O man, what is good; and what does the Lord require of you but to do justice, and to love kindness, and to walk humbly with your God" (Micah 6.8)?

As this country becomes more politically divisive, fellow leaders and pastors, this is an opportunity to use your platform for change. Pastors, this is a great occasion to address racism and White supremacy in your sermons. Business owners, you can change your policies and speak to the lack of diversity and inclusion in your companies and upper-level leadership. School leaders, you can advocate for more minority teacher representation in your schools. The minority voice cannot lead this charge because change can only happen when the evangelical recognizes the poor, the oppressed, and People of Color as their equals. The phrase "history repeats itself" is an understatement of what is being witnessed in our world today. Will you allow history to repeat itself, or will you be a change agent? Evangelicals, please do not miss this opportunity and unique time in our history to make things right because the non-believing world is watching your response.

APPENDIX

If you are wondering about a list of resources that you can reference to help you through the process of multiculturalism in your church and being an antiracist, below are some suggestions. This by no means is an exhaustive list. Note: Not all of these suggestions are written or created by Christians but most of them are faith-based.

BOOKS:
A People's History of the United States by Howard Zinn
Be the Bridge by Latasha Morrison
Between the World and Me by Ta-Nehisi Coates
Black Religion Black Theology by Deotis Roberts
Blindspot: Hidden Biases of Good People by Mahzarin R. Banaji and Anthony G. Greenwald
Bound for the Promised Land by Kate Clifford Larson
Divided by Faith: Evangelical Religion and the Problem of Race in America by Michael Emerson & Christian Smith
Disunity in Christ: Uncovering the Hidden Forces that Keep us Apart by Christena Cleveland
How to be an Antiracist by Ibram X. Kendi
How to Fight Racism by Jemar Tisby
I'm Still Here: Black Dignity in a World Made for Whiteness by Austin Channing Brown

Insider Outsider: My Journey as a Stranger in White Evangelicalism and My Hope for Us All by Bryan Loritts

Jesus and the Disinherited by Howard Thurman

Jesus and John Wayne, How White Evangelicals Corrupted a Faith and Fractured a Nation by Kristin Kobes Du Mez

Just Mercy: A Story of Justice and Redemption by Bryan Stevenson

Letters to a Birmingham Jail: A Response to the Words and Dreams of Dr. Martin Luther King, Jr. by John Piper, John Perkins, Matt Chandler and Bryan Loritts, and others

Lies my Teacher Told Me by James W. Loewen

Let Justice Roll Down by John Perkins

Me and White Supremacy: Combat Racism, Change the World, and Become a Good Ancestor by Layla F. Saad

One: Healing the Racial Divide by Dennis Rouse

Right Color, Wrong Culture: The Type of Leader Your Organization Needs to Become Multiethnic by Bryan Loritts

Slavery by Another Name by Douglas Blackmon

Stamped from the Beginning by Ibram X. Kendi

Stamped: Racism, Antiracism, and You by Jason Reynolds and Ibram X. Kendi

Still Evangelical?: Insiders Reconsider Political, Social & Theological Meaning by Shane Claiborne, Lisa Sharon Harper, Soong-Chan Rah, Jim Daly, Karen Swallow Prior and others

So You Want to Talk About Race by Ijeoma Oluo

The Color of Compromise by Jemar Tisby

The Color of Law by Richard Rothstein
The Cross and the Lynching Tree by James Cone
The Founding Myth: Why Christian Nationalism is Un-American by Andrew Seidel
The Mis-Education of the Negro by Carter G. Woodson
The New Jim Crow by Michelle Alexander
Weep with Me: How Lament Opens a Door for Racial Reconciliation by Mark Vroegop
White Awake by Pastor Daniel Hill
White Fragility by Dr. Robin DiAngelo
White Lies by Pastor Daniel Hill
White Rage by Carol Anderson
Why are All the Black Kids Sitting Together in the Cafeteria? by Beverly Daniel Tatum
Woke Church: An Urgent Call for Christians in America to Confront Racism and Injustice by Eric Mason

MOVIES & DOCUMENTARIES:
Clemency
Dear White People
Detroit
Do the Right Thing
Emperor
Fruitvale Station
Hidden Figures
If Beale Street Could Talk
Just Mercy
Kettle
King Richard

Maya Angelou: And Still I Rise
Race in America
Reconstruction: America after the Civil War (on PBS)
Say Her Name: The Life and Death of Sandra Bland
Selma
13th
The Black Power Mix Tape 1967-1975
The Central Park Five
The Good Lord Bird
The Hate U Give
The House I Live In
The Kalief Browder Story
The Skin We're In
Watchmen (HBO series)
Who Killed Malcolm X?
When They See Us
Who We Are: A Chronicle of Racism in America
Whose Streets?

YouTube Videos:
https://www.youtube.com/watch?v=1mcCLm_LwpE&t=1000s A Class Divided (full film) | FRONTLINE
https://www.youtube.com/watch?v=Sojf8D5WH00 A Conversation on Race and Privilege Jane Elliott & Angela Davis
https://www.youtube.com/watch?v=ebPoSMULI5U Blue Eyes/Brown Eyes Anti-Racism Exercise by Jane Elliott
https://www.youtube.com/watch?v=zuvxhPIm4dA How Can You Talk to Your Child About Racism by Jane Elliott

Appendix

https://www.youtube.com/watch?v=AGUwcs9qJXY Race in America by Phil Vischer

https://www.youtube.com/watch?v=j84RWjr8lM8 The Church's Complicity in Racism with Jemar Tisby & Holy Post

https://www.youtube.com/watch?v=K0e4ROSH-Hg Southern Shame Culture & How to Fight Racism w/Jemar Tisby

https://www.youtube.com/watch?v=Gln1JwDUI64 The New Jim Crow by Michelle Alexander

https://youtu.be/h8jUA7JBkF4 Uncomfortable Conversations with a Black Man by Emmanuel Acho

https://www.youtube.com/watch?v=NiiRnO7UTTk What is an Evangelical? By Phil Vischer

https://www.youtube.com/watch?v=RvWD7ykNjCc What about Abortion? Should this One Issue Determine How Christians Vote? By Phil Vischer

https://youtu.be/45ey4jgoxeU White Fragility by Dr Robin DiAngelo

https://www.youtube.com/watch?v=W4eS2E-P0G0 Why do White Christians Vote Republican and Black Christians Vote Democrat? By Phil Vischer

Below is a list of local organizations that I support financially or volunteer with that need your support.

Gift for Moms is a non-profit organization that supports single moms and children through a peer-to-peer support group, resource referrals, educational seminars, and counseling groups. You can learn more or donate at www.gfmsinglemoms.org

Krush Careers helps students make transitions from college to the business world. You can learn more about Krush Careers at www.krushcareers.com

Local Good Center partners with the community of Plano, TX, to provide opportunities for transformation. You can learn more about the Local Good Center at localgoodcenter.org/job-readiness

The North Texas Food Bank is an organization that helps meet the needs of those who are food insecure. During the COVID-19 pandemic, the need is especially great. You can learn more about the North Texas Food Bank or donate at www.ntfb.org

The Salvation Army is a Christian organization that helps meet the needs of the poor and the oppressed without discrimination. They provide food, clothing, shelter, educational programs, life skills and counseling to assist those in need. You can learn more or donate at www.salvationarmyusa.org

The Samaritan Inn is a comprehensive homeless program that provides shelter and teaches self-sufficiency and life skills to meet the needs of homeless individuals and families in Collin County. You can learn more or donate at www.saminn.org

WORKS CITED LIST

"40 Top Jefferson Davis Quotes That Reflect His Mind.: *The Famous People,* 2021, https://quotes.thefamouspeople.com/jefferson-davis-1795.php Accessed 7 Sept. 2021.

Aaro, David. "What is Stop and Frisk? Controversial Policing Technique Explained." *FOX News,* 11 Feb. 2020, https://www.foxnews.com/us/what-is-stop-and-frisk Accessed 20 Dec. 2020.

"Abraham Lincoln: The Prairie Years." *Encyclopedia.com,* 2019, https://www.encyclopedia.com/arts/encyclopedias-almanacs-transcripts-and-maps/abraham-lincoln-prairie-years. Accessed 15 July 2020.

"Abraham Lincoln Speech in the Lincoln-Douglas Debate." *The Slave Heritage Resource Center,* Son of the South, 2018, http://sonofthesouth.net/slavery/abraham-lincoln/abraham-lincoln-speech-debate.htm. Accessed 15 July 2020.

Acevedo, Z. "Abortion in Early America." *Pubmed.gov,* https://pubmed.ncbi.nlm.nih.gov/10297561/. Accessed 7 Sept. 2020.

"African Americans and Heart Disease, Stroke." *Heart.org*, 31 July 2015, https://www.heart.org/en/health-topics/consumer-healthcare/what-is-cardiovascular-disease/african-americans-and-heart-disease-stroke. Accessed 12 Oct. 2021.

"African Americans: Overview." *Encyclopedia.com*, 2019, www.encyclopedia.com/history/encyclopedias-almanacs-transcripts-and-maps/african-americans-overview. Accessed 1 Oct. 2020.

Alexander Stephens. "Cornerstone Speech," *Battlefields.org*, 2021, https://www.battlefields.org/learn/primary-sources/cornerstone-speech. Accessed 1 Aug. 2021.

Anderson, Richard. "Jonathan Edwards, Sr." *Princeton & Slavery*, Trustees of Princeton University, 2021, https://slavery.princeton.edu/stories/jonathan-edwards. Accessed 9 Sept. 2021.

Associated Press. "Bush Defends 'Little Brown Ones' Term for Grandchildren, Tells 'Pride and Love.'" *Los Angeles Times*, 17 Aug. 1988, https://www.latimes.com/archives/la-xpm-1988-08-17-mn-655-story.html. Accessed 21 June 2021.

Associated Press. "Trump Praises QAnon Conspiracists, Appreciates Support," *US News & World Report*, 19 Aug. 2020, https://www.usnews.com/news/politics/articles/2020-08-19/trump-praises-qanon-conspiracists-appreciates-support. Accessed 13 Sept. 2021.

Works Cited List

Baldwin, James. "Letter from a Region of My Mind." *Thenewyorker.com,* 17 Nov. 1962, https://www.newyorker.com/magazine/1962/11/17/letter-from-a-region-in-my-mind. Accessed 15 June 2021.

Bass, Gary J.. "The Terrible Cost of Presidential Racism." *The New York Times,* 3 Sept. 2020, https://www.nytimes.com/2020/09/03/opinion/nixon-racism-india.html. Accessed 5 Dec. 2020.

@BethMooreLPM (Beth Moore). *Twitter,* 13 Dec. 2020, 8:50 am https://twitter.com/bethmoorelpm/status/1338134290647953410 https://religionnews.com/2020/12/13/evangelical-leader-beth-moore-trends-on-twitter-after-calling-trumpism-seductive-and-dangerous/ Accessed 1 Jan. 2021.

Berke, Jeremy. "Donald Trump's Casino Business in Atlantic City Was a 'Protracted Failure.'" Business Insider, 11 June 2016. https://www.businessinsider.com/trumps-casinos-were-failures-2016-6 Accessed 1 Aug. 2021.

BGEA. "Billy Graham's Answers on Race, Inequality," *Billy Graham Evangelistic Association,* 14 Jan. 2021, https://billygraham.org/story/billy-grahams-answers-on-race-inequality. Accessed 31 Jan. 2021.

History.com Editors. "Birth of a Nation Opens, Glorifying the KKK" *History.com,* A&E Television Networks, LLC, 9 Feb. 2010, https://www.history.com/this-day-in-history/birth-of-a-nation-opens Accessed 8 Nov. 2021.

"Black Panthers." *History.com,* A&E Television Networks, LLC, 3 Nov. 2017, https://www.history.com/topics/civil-rights-movement/black-panthers. Accessed 8 Nov. 2021.

Bloesch, Donald. *Essentials of Evangelical Theology.* vol. 1, HarperCollins Publishers, 1998, pp. 7. Print.

Bradner, Eric, et al. "Biden: 'If You Have a Problem Figuring Out Whether You're for Me or Trump, Then You Ain't Black.'" *CNN Politics,* 22 May 2020, https://www.cnn.com/2020/05/22/politics/biden-charlamagne-tha-god-you-aint-black/index.html. Accessed 25 Sept. 2020.

Brownstein, Ronald. "Just How Far Will Trump Go?" *The Atlantic*, 14 Aug. 2020, https://www.theatlantic.com/politics/archive/2020/08/trumps-weaponization-usps-and-census/615235/. Accessed 24 Sept. 2020.

Burns, Rev. John. "Mordecai, Esther, and the President." *The Christian Citizen*, 22 May 2018, https://medium.com/christian-citizen/mordecai-esther-and-president-trump-54da01b35589. Accessed 25 Sept. 2020.

Caldera, Camille. "Fact Check: In 1977, Biden Said Without Orderly Integration, His Kids Would Grow up in a 'Racial Jungle.'" *USA TODAY,* Gannett Satellite Information Network, LLC., 27 Oct. 2020, https://www.usatoday.com/story/news/factcheck/2020/10/27/fact-check-post-partly-false-biden-1977-racial-jungle-remark/6045749002/. Accessed 5 Dec. 2020.

Works Cited List

Camille Caldera, "Fact Check: White House Didn't Fire Pandemic Response Unit When It Was Disbanded in 2018." *USA TODAY*, Gannett Satellite Information Network, LLC., 10 Sept. 2020, https://www.usatoday.com/story/news/factcheck/2020/09/10/fact-check-white-house-didnt-fire-pandemic-response-2018/3437356001/. Accessed 8 Oct. 2020.

Carlton, Genevieve. "Meet J. Marion Sims, the 'Father of Modern Gynecology' Who Experimented on Slaves." *ATI.com*, 6 June 2020, https://allthatsinteresting.com/j-marion-sims. Accessed 9 July 2021.

Carson, E. A., and Sabol, W. J. "Prisoners in 2011." *U.S. Department of Justice*, Dec. 2012, pp. 11. https://bjs.ojp.gov/content/pub/pdf/p11.pdf. Accessed 2 Aug. 2021.

Casper, Jayson, "Why Many Christians Want to Leave Palestine and Why Most Won't." *Christianity Today*, 4 Aug. 2020. https://www.christianitytoday.com/news/2020/august/palestinian-christians-survey-israel-emigration-one-state.html. Accessed 13 Jan. 2020.

Chan, Melissa. "Donald Trump Refuses to Condemn KKK, Disavow David Duke Endorsement." *Time*, 26 Feb. 2018, https://time.com/4240268/donald-trump-kkk-david-duke/. Accessed 12 Aug. 2021.

Chapman, Matthew. "Trump Will 'Put a Bullet Into the Country' Before He Lets a Court Say He Lost The Election: NYT Columnist." *Raw Story*, 30 Sept. 2020, https://www.rawstory.com/2020/09/

trump-will-put-a-bullet-into-the-country-before-he-lets-a-court-say-he-lost-the-election-nyt-columnist/. Accessed 4 Dec. 2020.

"Christian Democracy." *Encyclopedia Britannica*, www.britannica.com/topic/Christian-democracy. Accessed 30 Oct. 2020.

"Christianity." *Fanack.com.* 28 Apr. 2016, https://fanack.com/society-in-the-middle-east-and-north-africa/religions-in-the-middle-east-and-north-africa/christianity/. Accessed 13 Jan. 2020.

Cillizza, Chris. "The Awful Reality That Donald Trump's Repeated Attacks on John McCain Prove." *CNN Politics*, 19 March 2019, https://www.cnn.com/2019/03/19/politics/donald-trump-john-mccain-dead/index.html. Accessed 7 June 2020.

Clark, Simon. "How White Supremacy Returned to Mainstream Politics." *Americanprogress.org.* 1 Jul. 2020. https://www.americanprogress.org/article/white-supremacy-returned-mainstream-politics/. Accessed 14 Nov. 2021.

Clarke, Adam. "Commentary on Ephesians 6." *"The Adam Clarke Commentary." StudyLight.org*, 1832, https://www.studylight.org/commentaries/acc/ephesians-6.html. Accessed 4 May 2020.

Clarke, Adam. "Commentary on 1 Timothy 1." *"The Adam Clarke Commentary." StudyLight.org*, 1832, https://www.studylight.org/commentaries/acc/1-timothy-1.html. Accessed 4 May 2020.

Colarossi, Sean. "Rachel Maddow: Trump Is Committing a Crime by Pressuring Officials to Falsify Election Results." *Politicus USA*, 7 Dec. 2020, https://www.politicususa.com/2020/12/07/rachel-maddow-trump-is-committing-a-crime-by-pressuring-officials-to-falsify-election-results.html. Accessed 15 Dec. 2020.

Cole, Nicki Lisa, Ph.D., "Definition of Systemic Racism in Sociology." *Thought Co.* 21 July 2020, https://www.thoughtco.com/systemic-racism-3026565. Accessed 5 Sept. 2020.

Collman, Ashley. "Michelle Obama Was Told She Wasn't 'Princeton Material', But She Applied Anyway and Got In." *Businessinsider.com* 17 Jan. 2019, https://www.businessinsider.com/michelle-obama-wasnt-princeton-material-college-counselor-told-her-2018-11. Accessed 21 Sept. 2021.

Cone, James H. *Martin & Malcolm & America: A Dream or a Nightmare*, HarperCollins, 1993, pp. 169. ebook.

"Conservative." *Dictionary.com*, 2021, https://www.dictionary.com/browse/conservative?s=t. Accessed 30 Oct. 2020.

"Conservatism." *Encyclopedia Britannica*, 2021, www.britannica.com/topic/conservatism. Accessed 31 Jan. 2020.

Colvin, Jill and Miller, Zeke. "After a Frosty Few Days, Pence, Trump Appear to Reach Détente." *Yahoo!News*, 11 Jan. 2021, https://news.yahoo.com/frosty-few-days-pence-trump-012747266.html. Accessed 2 Feb. 2021.

Cowen, Trace William. "Christian Group Raises More Than $500,000 for Kyle Rittenhouse's Legal Defense." *COMPLEX*, 29 Sept. 2020, https://www.complex.com/life/2020/09/christian-group-raises-more-than-500-hundred-thousand-dollars-kyle-rittenhouse. Accessed 5 Nov. 2021.

Crockett, Jr., Stephen A. "Surprise! Beloved President Ronald Reagan Was a Racist: Unearthed Call to Then-President Nixon." *The Root*, G/O Media Inc., 31 July 2019, https://www.theroot.com/surprise-beloved-president-ronald-reagan-was-a-racist-1836848286. Accessed 12 Aug. 2021.

Curry, Thomas. "Critical Race Theory." *Britannica.com*, 2021, https://www.britannica.com/topic/critical-race-theory. Accessed 4 Sept. 2021.

Cusey, Rebecca. "Trump as God's Instrument: A Fairy Tale of Biblical Proportions." *The Hill*, 11 Oct. 2016, https://thehill.com/blogs/pundits-blog/presidential-campaign/300266-trump-as-gods-instrument-a-fairy-tale-of-biblical. Accessed 7 Jan. 2021.

Delkic, Melina. "How Many Times Has Trump Cheated on His Wives? Here's What We Know." *Newsweek*, 12 Jan. 2018, https://www.newsweek.com/how-many-times-trump-cheated-wives-780550. Accessed 9 July 2020.

Devega, Chauncey. "Racist Then, Racist Now: The Real Story of Bill Clinton's Crime Bill." *Salon*, 16 Apr. 2016, https://www.salon.com/2016/04/16/

racist_then_racist_now_the_real_story_of_bill_clintons_crime_bill/. Accessed 15 July 2020.

Dickinson, Bob. "Not Shocked by Insurrection." *Like the Dew*, 7 Jan. 2021, https://likethedew.com/2021/01/07/not-shocked-by-insurrection/#.X_pcd9hKg2w. Accessed 10 Jan. 2021.

"δουλος (doulos)." *Servitude and Lymphedema,* Abarim Publications. 24 Aug. 2021, https://www.abarim-publications.com/DictionaryG/d/d-o-u-l-o-sfin.html#.XzdEqOhKg2w. Accessed 4 Oct. 2021.

"Dr. Robert Jeffress: We Thank God Our President Doesn't Hesitate in the Confronting & Eliminating of Evil." *Harbingers Daily,* 4 Jan. 2020, https://harbingersdaily.com/r-robert-jeffress-thanks-god-for-presidents-strength-in-protecting-the-nation. Accessed 10 Jan 2021.

Dozier, Kimberly and Vera Bergengruen. "Incited by the President, Pro-Trump Rioters Violently Storm the Capitol." *Time Magazine,* 7 Jan. 2021, https://time.com/5926883/trump-supporters-storm-capitol/. Accessed 10 Jan. 2021.

"Dred Scott Decision." *Dictionary.com,* 2021, https://www.dictionary.com/browse/dred-scott-decision#. Accessed 15 Oct. 2020.

Duford, Jerushah. "I'm Billy Graham's Granddaughter. Evangelical Support for Donald Trump Insults His Legacy." *Usatoday.com,* 27 Aug. 2020, https://www.usatoday.com/story/opinion/voices/2020/08/25/

billy-graham-evangelicals-support-donald-trump-hypocrisy-column/5625617002/. Accessed 4 Sept 2020.

Duignan, Brian. "Gerrymandering." *Britannica.com* 2021, https://www.britannica.com/topic/gerrymandering. Accessed 30 Oct. 2021.

Dunlap, David W. "1973, Meet Donald Trump." *Times Insider*, The New York Times Company, 30 July 2015, https://www.nytimes.com/times-insider/2015/07/30/1973-meet-donald-trump/. Accessed 21 Aug. 2021.

Dupree, Jamie. "Trump Expresses More Frustration Over Russia Investigation." *The Atlanta Journal-Constitution*, 15 June 2017, https://www.ajc.com/blog/jamie-dupree/trump-expresses-more-frustration-over-russia-investigation/07UjteAA2NhBjrDfB2VMZP/. Accessed 9 Jan. 2021.

Editors. "White Nationalism." *Facinghistory.org*, 2021, https://www.facinghistory.org/educator-resources/current-events/explainer/white-nationalism. Accessed 6 Nov. 2021.

Edelman, Adam. "Trump Rips NFL Players after Anthem Protests During Preseason Games." *NBC NEWS*, NBC UNIVERSAL, 18 Aug. 2010, https://www.nbcnews.com/politics/donald-trump/trump-rips-nfl-players-after-protests-during-preseason-games-n899551. Accessed 7 Aug. 2021.

Ellis, Philip. "New Study Links Trump's 'Chinese Virus' Tweet to Rise in Anti-Asian Hate Speech."

Works Cited List

Yahoo Life, Yahoo!, 18 Mar. 2021, https://www.yahoo.com/lifestyle/study-links-trump-chinese-virus-200000276.html. Accessed 5 May 2021.

"Evangelical." *Dictionary.com,* 2021, https://www.dictionary.com/browse/evangelical. Accessed 9 Sept. 2020.

"Fair Housing Act." *History.com,* A&E Television Networks, LLC, 27 Jan. 2010, https://www.history.com/topics/black-history/fair-housing-act. Accessed 1 Aug. 2021.

"Fair Maps, Fair Representation, and a Fair Say." *Common Cause,* https://www.commoncause.org/our-work/gerrymandering-and-representation/gerrymandering-redistricting/. Accessed 1 Aug. 2021.

Falwell, Jerry. *An Autobiography: The Inside Story.* Liberty House Publisher, 1997.

Fausset, Richard and Katie Benner. "Georgia Officials Reveal Third Trump Call Seeking to Influence Election Results." *New York Times,* 9 Jan. 2021, updated March 15, 2021, https://www.nytimes.com/2021/01/09/us/georgia-presidential-election-results.html. Accessed 5 Sept. 2021.

"Federal Court Rules Trump Violated the Constitution's Emoluments Clauses." *Politicus USA,* 14 May 2020, https://www.politicususa.com/2020/05/14/federal-court-rules-trump-violated-the-constitutions-emoluments-clauses.html. Accessed 7 Aug. 2021.

"FFRF Asks IRS to Probe Megapastor Jeffress' Endorsement of Pence/Trump." *Freedom From Religion Foundation*, 28 July 2020, https://ffrf.org/news/news-releases/item/37741-ffrf-asks-irs-to-probe-megapastor-jeffress-endorsement-of-pence-trump. Accessed 7 Aug. 2021.

Flores, Reena. "Donald Trump: I Could 'Shoot Somebody and I Wouldn't Lose Any Voters.'" *CBS NEWS*, CBS Interactive Inc., 23 Jan. 2016, https://www.cbsnews.com/news/donald-trump-i-could-shoot-somebody-and-i-wouldnt-lose-any-voters/. Accessed 8 Aug. 2021.

Foley, Ryan. "Abortion Shouldn't Determine How Christians Vote in a Presidential Election." *Thechristianpost.com*, 29 Oct. 2020, https://www.christianpost.com/news/podcaster-pro-lifers-focus-on-national-politics-is-misplaced.html. Accessed 3 Jan. 2021.

Frank, Aquila. "Democrats Will Hang on the Gallows they Prepared for Trump." AZgop.news, 2021, https://az-gop.news/blog/2020/12/07/democrats-will-hang-on-the-gallows-they-prepared-for-trump/. Accessed 12 Feb. 2021.

Franklin Graham. Praise of President Trump Actions Recommending Trump for Nobel Peace Prize, *Facebook*, 26 Oct. 2020, 10:27 am, www.facebook.com/FranklinGraham/posts/3804824096240410. Accessed 29 Oct. 2020. This post has since been deleted from Franklin Graham's page.

Works Cited List

Fredericks, Bob. "George W. Bush on George Floyd's Death, Racism: It's the Time to Listen." *New York Post*, 2 June 2020, https://nypost.com/2020/06/02/george-w-bush-on-george-floyds-death-its-the-time-to-listen/. Accessed 15 June 2020.

French, David. "Do Pro-Lifers Who Reject Trump Have 'Blood on Their Hands?'" *The Dispatch*, 23 Aug. 2020. https://frenchpress.thedispatch.com/p/do-pro-lifers-who-reject-trump-have. Accessed 1 Sept. 2020.

Funes, Yessenia. "Trump Administration Keeps DACA in Place but Revokes DAPA." *Colorlines*, 16 June 2017, https://www.colorlines.com/articles/trump-administration-keeps-daca-place-revokes-dapa. Accessed 23 Aug. 2020.

Gabbatt, Adam. "'Unparalleled Privilege:' Why White Evangelicals See Trump as Their Savior." *The Guardian*, 11 Jan. 2020, https://www.theguardian.com/us-news/2020/jan/11/donald-trump-evangelical-christians-cyrus-king. Accessed 1 Sept. 2020.

Gernoble, Ryan. "Trump Admits That He Lied About COVID-19 Threat in New Woodward Book." *HuffPost*, BuzzFeed, Inc., 9 Sept. 2020, https://www.huffpost.com/entry/trump-coronavirus-bob-woodward_n_5f58fd32c5b6b48507fabc99. Accessed 15 Sept. 2020.

Gjelten, Tom. "Peaceful Protestors Tear-Gassed to Clear Way for Trump Church Photo-op." *NPR*, 1 June 2020, https://www.npr.org/2020/06/01/867532070/

trumps-unannounced-church-visit-angers-church-officials. Accessed 4 June 2020.

Grimsley, Edwin. "African American Wrongful Convictions Today." *Innocence Project*, 29 Mar. 2013, https://innocenceproject.org/african-american-wrongful-convictions-today/. Accessed 2 Aug. 2021.

Hackett, Erna Kim. "Why I Stopped Talking About Racial Reconciliation and Started Talking About White Supremacy." *Inheritancemag.com*, 25 Mar. 2020, https://www.inheritancemag.com/stories/why-i-stopped-talking-about-racial-reconciliation-and-started-talking-about-white-supremacy. Accessed 15 Apr. 2020.

Hadfield, Jack. "Trump Infuriated by Pence 'Not Fighting Hard Enough' for Election Integrity." *National File*, 23 Dec. 2020, https://nationalfile.com/report-trump-infuriated-by-pence-not-fighting-hard-enough-for-election-integrity/. Accessed 3 Jan 2021.

Holloway, Kali. "Time to Expose the Women Still Celebrating the Confederacy." *The Daily Beast,* 2 Nov. 2018, https://www.thedailybeast.com/time-to-expose-the-women-still-celebrating-the-confederacy. Accessed 9 Nov. 2021.

Hamm, Ryan. "Patriotism and Christianity." *Christianity Today,* 26 June 2012, https://www.christianitytoday.com/biblestudies/articles/churchhomeleadership/patriotism.html. Accessed 5 Nov. 2020.

Hammer, Josh. "Overrule Stare Decisis." *Nationalaffairs.com,* Fall 2020, https://www.nationalaffairs.com/publications/detail/overrule-stare-decisis. Accessed 2 Jan. 2021.

Hampson, Rick. "Truman Revisited: Historian Says Harry Gave 'Em Racism." *AP NEWS,* The Associated Press, 24 Oct. 1991, https://apnews.com/article/ab0d537a112c3554373a97dff54c0e60. Accessed 15 July 2021.

Haney-Lopez, Ian. "The Racism at the Heart of the Reagan Presidency: How Ronald Reagan Used Coded Racial Appeals to Galvanize White Voters and Gut the Middle Class." *Salon.com,* 11 Jan. 2014, https://www.salon.com/test/2014/01/11/the_racism_at_the_heart_of_the_reagan_presidency/. 16 July 2021.

Harper, Douglas. "Slavery in New Jersey." *Slavery in the North,* Slavenorth.com., 2003, http://slavenorth.com/newjersey.htm. Accessed 20 Mar. 2021.

Helin, Kurt. "Doc Rivers: 'We Keep Loving This Country, and This Country Does Not Love Us Back.'" *NBCsports.com,* 26 Aug. 2020, https://nba.nbcsports.com/2020/08/26/doc-rivers-we-keep-loving-this-country-and-this-country-does-not-love-us-back/. Accessed 27 Aug. 2020.

History.com Editors. "The Orangeburg Massacre." *History.com,* A&E Television Networks, LLC, 6 Apr. 2018, www.history.com/topics/1960s/orangeburg-massacre. Accessed 5 Dec. 2020.

Hopfensperger, Jean. "Black Pastor Takes Stand Against Southern Baptist Race Statement." *Star Tribune*, 2 Jan. 2021, https://www.startribune.com/black-pastor-takes-stand-against-southern-baptist-race-statement/600006144/. Accessed 4 Jan. 2021.

Itkowitz, Colby. "Little Marco, Lyin' Ted, Crooked Hillary, How Donald Trump Makes Name Calling Stick." *Washington Post*, 20 Apr. 2016, https://www.washingtonpost.com/news/inspired-life/wp/2016/04/20/little-marco-lying-ted-crooked-hillary-donald-trumps-winning-strategy-nouns/. Accessed 31 Oct. 2021.

@JackGraham (Jack Graham). Twitter, 24 July 2020, https://twitter.com/jackngraham/status/1286627797109284864 Accessed 8 Nov. 2021.

Jacobs, Shayna. "Trump Sued by NY Apartment Tenants Alleging Years-old Rent Scheme." *The Washington Post*, 5 Dec. 2020, https://www.washingtonpost.com/national-security/trump-tenants-lawsuit/2020/12/04/db4a82e6-367a-11eb-8d38-6aea1adb3839_story.html. Accessed 1 Nov. 2021.

James, Ryan. "A History of Racial Remarks: Is Joe Biden a Racist?" *Freedom Wire*, 24 July 2020, https://freedomwire.com/is-biden-a-racist/. Accessed 25 Sept. 2021.

Jefferson, Andrea. "Trump Says He's a Christian, But That 'He Doesn't Need To Ask For Forgiveness' For His Sins." *Political Flare*, 24 Dec. 2019, https://www.politicalflare.com/2019/12/

Works Cited List

trump-says-hes-a-christian-but-that-he-doesnt-need-to-ask-for-forgiveness/. Accessed 3 Jan. 2021.

"Jim Crow Laws." *History.com,* A&E Television Networks, LLC, 28 Feb. 2018, https://www.history.com/topics/early-20th-century-us/jim-crow-laws. Accessed 7 Dec. 2020.

"Jim Crow Museum of Racist Memorabilia." *Ferris State University,* https://www.ferris.edu/HTMLS/news/jimcrow. Accessed 8 Nov. 2021.

"John F. Kennedy- Civil Rights." *World Biography U.S. Presidents,* 2021, https://www.presidentprofiles.com/Kennedy-Bush/John-F-Kennedy-Civil-rights.html#ixzz6fzy7Ca2W. Accessed 30 Dec. 2021.

Johnson, Jake. "Trump Reportedly Entertained Michael Flynn's 'Martial Law' Proposal in Meeting." *Truthout,* 20 Dec. 2020, https://truthout.org/articles/trump-reportedly-entertained-michael-flynns-martial-law-proposal-in-meeting/. Accessed 3 Jan. 2021.

"Join the Movement." *EvangelicalsforBiden.com,* 2020, https://www. evangelicalsforbiden.com/. Accessed 31 Oct. 2020.

Jones, Robert. P. "Racism Among White Christians is Higher than Among Nonreligious." *NBC NEWS,* NBC UNIVERSAL, 27 July 2020. www.nbcnews.com/think/opinion/racism-among-white-christians-higher-among-nonreligious-s-no-coincidence-ncna1235045. Accessed 4 Feb. 2021.

Jung, Helin. "Why did Trump Leave the Paris Agreement? What You Need to Know About the Climate Pact." *Cosmopolitan.com*, 4 Nov. 2020, https://www.cosmopolitan.com/politics/a9659229/paris-climate-agreement-trump/. Accessed 9 Sept. 2021.

Keating, Joshua. "The Accidental Anti-Imperialist." *Slate*, The Slate Group, a Graham Holdings Company, 30 June 2020, https://slate.com/news-and-politics/2020/06/woodrow-wilson-racism-self-determination.html. Accessed 4 Feb. 2021.

Kelly, Caroline. "New York Times: Trump Suggested Shooting Migrants in the Legs." *CNN Politics*, 1 Oct. 2019, https://www.cnn.com/2019/10/01/politics/new-york-times-trump-shoot-migrants-legs/index.html. Accessed 9 Sept. 2021.

Kendi, Ibram X. "The 11 Most Racist U.S. Presidents." *HuffPost*, BuzzFeed, Inc., 28 May 2017, https://www.huffpost.com/entry/would-a-president-trump-m_b_10135836. Accessed 4 June 2021.

Kendi, Ibram X. *Stamped from the Beginning: The Definitive History of Racist Ideas in America*. New York. Hachette Book Group. 2016.

Kent, Lauren. "European Colonizers Killed So Many Native Americans That It Changed the Global Climate." *CNN World*, Cable News Network. A Warner Media Company, 2 Feb. 2019, https://www.cnn.com/2019/02/01/world/european-colonization-climate-change-trnd/index.html. Accessed 9 Sept. 2021.

Works Cited List

Kobes Du Mez, Kristin. *Jesus and John Wayne: How White Evangelicals Corrupted a Faith and Fractured a Nation.* Liveright Publishing Corporation, Independent Publishers, 2020, pp. 2.

Kristian, Bonnie. "How to have Patriotism without Nationalism." *Christianitytoday.com,* 21 June 2021, https://www.christianitytoday.com/ct/2021/july-august/how-to-have-patriotism-without-nationalism.html. Accessed 14 Nov. 2021.

Kroll, Andy. "Trump Responds to Attack on Capitol by Telling the Mob He 'Loves' Them." *Yahoo.com,* 6 Jan. 2021, https://www.yahoo.com/entertainment/trump-responds-attack-capitol-telling-225639675.html. Accessed 7 Jan. 2021.

Kuruvilla, Carol. "Billy Graham's Granddaughter: Evangelicals' Excuses for Trump Hurt their Reputation." *HuffPost,* 10 Oct. 2020, https://www.huffingtonpost.ca/entry/jerushah-duford-trump-evangelicals_n_5f89f16cc5b67da85d1deaa8. Accessed 31 Oct. 2021.

Kuruvilla, Carol. "These Evangelicals Voted for Trump in 2016. They Refuse to Do It Again." *HuffPost,* BuzzFeed, Inc., 2 Nov. 2020, https://www.huffpost.com/entry/white-evangelical-trump-election-2020_n_5f625059c5b6ba9eb6e89d7d. Accessed 3 Nov. 2021.

Lamothe, Dan. "I Can't Even Look at the Atrocities: Us Troops Say Trump's Syria Withdrawal Betrayed an Ally." *The Washington Post,* 15 Oct. 2019, https://www.washingtonpost.com/world/national-security/i-cant-even-look-at-the-atrocities-us-troops-say-trumps-syria-withdrawal-betrayed-anally/2019/10/15/4e79b600-eeca-11e9-b648-76-bcf86eb67e_story.html. Accessed 9 Sept. 2021.

Le Feuvre, Stephen. "The Curse of Ham: Getting It Horribly Wrong." *TGC Africa Edition*. The Gospel Coalition, Inc. 3 Mar. 2020. https://africa.thegospelcoalition.org/article/curse-of-ham/. Accessed 10 Sept. 2021.

Lenthang, Marlene. "The Lone Star State's Bloody Shame: How Texas Rangers Murdered Thousands of Mexicans over 10 Years from 1910 and Were Hailed Heroes as State Representative Suggests History is Repeating Itself." *Dailymail.com*, 8 Aug. 2019, https://www.dailymail.co.uk/news/article-7337361/How-Texas-Rangers-murdered-hundreds-Mexicans-border-1915.html. Accessed 1 Oct. 2021.

Lemon, Jason. "More Than 10,000 Christians Call for the Removal of Franklin Graham as Charity's CEO after Prayer Supporting Trump at RNC," *Newsweek.com*, 2 Sept. 2020, https://www.newsweek.com/more-10000-christians-call-removal-franklin-graham-charitys-ceo-after-prayer-supporting-trump-1529241. Accessed 5 Sept. 2020.

Levin, Sam T. "White Supremacists and Militias have Infiltrated Police Across US, Report Says." *The Guardian*, 27 Aug. 2020, https://www.theguardian.com/us-news/2020/aug/27/white-supremacists-militias-infiltrate-us-police-report. Accessed 1 Oct. 2021.

"Liberal." *Dictionary.com*, 2021, https://www.dictionary.com/browse/liberal?s=t. Accessed 13 Oct. 2021.

Library Staff. "Religion and President Johnson." *LBJ Presidential Library*, http://lbjlibrary.net/collections/quick-facts/lyndon-baines-johnson-religion.html. Accessed 8 Nov. 2021.

Lindevaldsen, Rena. "Why We Need Constitutionalist Judges." *Decision: The Evangelical Voice for Today*, Billy Graham Evangelistic Association, 1 Oct. 2019, https://decisionmagazine.com/why-we-need-constitutionalist-judges/. Accessed 31 Oct. 2021.

"List of Nicknames Used by Donald Trump." *Wikipedia*, 2021, https://en.wikipedia.org/wiki/List_of_nicknames_used_by_Donald_Trump. Accessed 4 Nov. 2021.

Little, Becky. "The Most Damaging Myths About Slavery, Debunked," 3 May 2018, https://www.history.com/news/debunking-slavery-myths. Accessed 5 Sept. 2021.

Little, Becky. "Why Bibles Given to Slaves Omitted Most of the Old Testament." *History.com*, A&E Television Networks, LLC, 3 Apr. 2019, https://www.history.com/news/slave-bible-redacted-old-testament. Accessed 6 Sept. 2021.

Loewen, James W. *Lies my Teacher Told Me: Everything Your American History Textbook Got Wrong*. New Press, 2018.

Lovelace, Jr., Berkeley. "White House Threatens to Fire FDA Chief Unless Pfizer Covid Vaccine Approved

Friday, Reports Say." *CNBC*, NBC UNIVERSAL, 11 Dec. 2020, https://www.cnbc.com/2020/12/11/white-house-threatens-to-fire-fda-chief-unless-covid-vaccine-oked-friday-report.html. Accessed 4 Nov. 2021.

Mahbubani, Rhea. "Nooses Spotted as Pro-Trump Rioters Spark Chaos and Lawlessness on Capitol Hill." *Business Insider*, 6 Jan. 2021, https://www.businessinsider.com/nooses-spotted-as-pro-trump-rioters-spark-chaos-on-capitol-2021-1. Accessed 7 Jan. 2021.

Maisel, Sandy L. and Forman, Ira. "U.S. Presidential Elections: Jewish Voting Record." *Jewish Virtual Library*, 19 Oct. 2020, https://www.jewishvirtuallibrary.org/jewish-voting-record-in-u-s-presidential-elections. Accessed 30 Sept. 2021.

Malone, Sandy. "Capitol Police Weren't Prepared for Riot, Outgoing Chief Points Fingers." *Police Tribune*, 12 Jan. 2021, https://policetribune.com/capitol-police-werent-prepared-for-riot-outgoing-chief-points-fingers/. Accessed 15 Jan. 2021.

Maples, Jeff. "Robert Jeffress Has Sold His Soul to the Devil for Worldly Gain." *Reformation Charlotte*, 11 Mar. 2020, https://reformationcharlotte.org/2020/03/11/robert-jeffress-has-sold-his-soul-to-the-devil-for-worldly-gain/. Accessed 31 Jan. 2021.

Margolis, Matt. "FLASHBACK: Joe Biden Praised Former KKK Leader as a 'Mentor' Ten Years Ago Today." *PJ MEDIA*, 2 July 2020, https://pjmedia.com/election/

Works Cited List

matt-margolis/2020/07/02/flashback-joe-biden-praised-former-kkk-leader-as-a-mentor-ten-years-ago-today-n600037. Accessed 14 June 2021.

Markowitz, David. "Trump Is Lying More Than Ever: Just Look at the Data." *Forbes*, 5 May 2020, https://www.forbes.com/sites/davidmarkowitz/2020/05/05/trump-is-lying-more-than-ever-just-look-at-the-data/?sh=535aa66d1e17. Accessed 3 Nov. 2021.

Mazza, Ed. "Mitch McConnell Brags About Blocking Obama for 2 Years, Then Laughs About it." *HuffPost*, BuzzFeed, Inc., 13 Dec. 2019, www.huffpost.com/entry/mitch-mcconnell-blocks-obama-laughs_n_5df32430e4b0deb78b517322. Accessed 2 Nov. 2021.

McFarlan Miller, Emily. "14 Conservative Christians Who Are Not Supporting Trump." *Religion News Service*, 21 June 2016, https://religionnews.com/2016/06/21/7-conservative-christians-who-are-not-supporting-trump. Accessed 2 Nov. 2021.

Medoff, Rafael. "Facing Up to FDR's Racism," *The David S. Wyman Institute for Holocaust Studies*, 2018, http://new.wymaninstitute.org/2019/07/facing-up-to-fdrs-racism/. Accessed 12 Aug. 2021.

Meier, Alex. "Say Their Names: Stories of Black Americans Killed by Police." *ABC.com*, 7 June 2020, https://abc30.com/george-floyd-protest-say-her-name-his/6236298/. Accessed 3 July 2021.

Merritt, Jonathan. "Trump-Loving Christians Owe Bill Clinton an Apology." *The Atlantic*, 10 Aug. 2016, https://www.theatlantic.com/politics/archive/2016/08/evangelical-christians-trump-bill-clinton-apology/495224/. Accessed Sept 19, 2021.

Michael McVicar, "The Religious Right in America," *Oxford Research Encyclopedias,* 26 Feb., 2018, https://oxfordre.com/religion/view/10.1093/acrefore/9780199340378.001.0001/acrefore-9780199340378-e-97. Accessed 7 Sept. 2020.

Miller, Zeke. "Trump Threatens to Fire in Rift with Disease Expert." *AP News,* 2 Nov. 2020, https://apnews.com/article/trump-threatens-fire-fauci-rift-disease-57c804db048aa7f1c99f227b495f52e6. Accessed 14 Jan. 2021.

"Moderate." *Dictionary.com,* 2021, https://www.dictionary.com/browse/moderate?s=t. Accessed 13 Oct. 2021.

Morgan, David and Cornwell, Susan. "McConnell Thwarts Trump Bid for $2,000 Coronavirus Economic Relief Checks." *KSL.com,* 29 Dec. 2020, https://www.ksl.com/article/50074668/trump-blasts-weak-republican-leaders-over-2000-checks-defense-bill. Accessed 31 Dec. 2021.

Nashrulla, Tasneem. "Minneapolis Officer Derick Chauvin Had 17 Complaints Against Him before He Was Charged with Murder for George Floyd's Death." *BuzzFeed.News,* 29 May 2020, https://www.buzzfeednews.com/article/tasneemnashrulla/minneapolis-derek-chauvin-history-of-complaints-george-floyd. Accessed 15 June 2020.

"Nathan Bedford Forrest." *History.com,* A&E Television Networks, LLC, 9 Nov. 2009, www.history.com/topics/american-civil-war/nathan-bedford-forrest. Accessed 7 Sept. 2021.

Naureckas, Jim. "Ronald Reagan's Racism Should Come as No Surprise." *FAIR,* 31 July 2019, https://fair.org/home/ronald-reagans-racism-should-come-as-no-surprise/. Accessed 2 Feb. 2021.

Nelson, Sophia. "White Male and Conservative: Trump's Damaging Legal Legacy." *USA TODAY,* Gannett Satellite Information Network, LLC., 3 July 2020, https://www.usatoday.com/story/opinion/2020/07/03/trump-and-judiciary-lack-diversity-column/5357852002/. Accessed 8 Aug. 2021.

Oast, Jennifer. "'The Worst Kind of Slavery': Slave-Owning Presbyterian Churches in Prince Edward County, Virginia." *The Journal of Southern History* vol. 76, no. 4 (2010): 867-900. http://www.jstor.org/stable/27919282. Accessed Dec. 28, 2020.

Ocasio, Bianca Padro. "Trump said Puerto Rico Is 'dirty' and Its Residents 'Poor,' Says Former DHS Official." *Postguam.com,* 21 Aug. 2020, https://www.postguam.com/the_globe/nation/trump-said-puerto-rico-is-dirty-and-its-residents-poor-says-former-dhs-official/article_c301050e-e295-11ea-a48d-2f446d39eb43.html. Accessed 12 Aug. 2021.

Okun, Tema. "White Supremacy Culture." Showing up for Racial Justice, March 12, 2021, https://

surj.org/resources/white-supremacy-culture-characteristics/. Accessed 8 Aug. 2021.

O'Neil, Tyler. "5 Reasons why Trump Vetoed the Military Spending Bill." *PJ Media*, 23 Dec. 2020, https://pjmedia.com/news-and-politics/tyler-o-neil/2020/12/23/5-reasons-why-trump-vetoed-the-military-spending-bill-n1227597. Accessed 30 Dec. 2020.

O'Leary, Megan. "Ahead of the 2020 Election and Amid Multiple Crises, Trump and Biden Supporters See Different Realities and Futures for the Nation." *PRRI.org*, 19 Oct. 2020, https://www.prri.org/press-release/ahead-of-2020-election-and-amid-multiple-crises-trump-and-biden-supporters-see-different-realities-and-futures-for-the-nation/. Accessed 8 Nov. 2020.

Pace, Julie and Tucker, Eric. "President Trump Fires FBI Director James Comey." *PBS*, 9 May 2017, https://www.pbs.org/newshour/politics/president-trump-fires-fbi-director-james-comey. Accessed 7 June 2020.

"Pageant Contestants Claim Trump Entered Dressing Rooms while they were Half-Naked," *Fox.com*, 12 Oct. 2016, https://www.foxnews.com/entertainment/pageant-contestants-claim-trump-entered-dressing-rooms-while-they-were-half-naked. Accessed 12 Sept. 2020.

Pavlovitz, John. "White Evangelicals, This is Why People are Through with You." *Johnpavlovitz.com*, 24 Jan. 2018, https://johnpavlovitz.com/2018/01/24/white-evangelicals-people/. Accessed 14 May, 2020.

"Patriotism." *Websters Dictionary,* 2020, http://webstersdictionary1828.com/Dictionary/patriotism. Accessed 30 Oct. 2020.

Pinkoski, Nathan. "What is Christian Democracy." *Tocqueville21.com,* 2 Oct. 2020. https://tocqueville21.com/le-club/what-is-christian-democracy/. Accessed 14 Nov. 2021.

"The Preamble." *Constitution Annotated,* Library of Congress, https://constitution.congress.gov/constitution/preamble/. Accessed 31 Oct. 2020.

"President Donald Trump Impeached." *History.com,* A&E Television Networks, LLC., 18 Dec. 2019, https://history.com/this-day-in-history/president-trump-impeached-house-of-representatives. Accessed 2 Jan. 2020.

"Progressive." *Dictionary.com,* 2021, https://www.dictionary.com/browse/progressive?s=t. Accessed 1 Nov. 2021.

Pruitt, Sarah. "When One of George Washington's Enslaved Workers Escaped to Freedom." *History.com,* A&E Television Networks, LLC., 8 Feb. 2018, https://www.history.com/news/george-washington-and-the-slave-who-got-away. Accessed 3 Jan. 2020.

Putterman, Samantha. "Graph on the US Abortion Rate During Different Presidents Based on Real Data, But Needs More Information." *Politifact.com,* 25 Sept. 2020, https://www.politifact.com/factchecks/2020/sep/25/facebook-posts/graph-us-abortion-rate-during-different-presidents/. Accessed 12 Aug. 2021.

"Qualified Immunity." *Law.cornell.edu*, Legal Information Institute, https://www.law.cornell.edu/wex/qualified_immunity. Accessed 12 Sept. 2020.

"Reagan, Nixon and Race." *UVA Miller Center,* 2021, https://millercenter.org/the-presidency/educational-resources/reagan-nixon-and-race. Accessed 12 Sept. 2021.

"Reconstruction: United States History." *Britannica.com,* 2021, https://www. britannica.com/event/Reconstruction-United-States-history. Accessed 30 Oct. 2020.

Religious news service authors. "Contradictions Marked Nixon's Religious Life: Presidency: He Had Both Defenders and Critics Among the Clergy. His Quaker Upbringing Shaped His Personality, Biographers Say, But Necessarily His Actions." *Los Angeles Times,* 30 Apr. 1994, https://www.latimes.com/archives/la-xpm-1994-04-30-me-52214-story.html. Accessed 13 Nov. 2020.

"Repeal of 'Don't Ask, Don't Tell.'" *Human Rights Campaign*, https://www.hrc.org/our-work/stories/repeal-of-dont-ask-dont-tell. Accessed 10 Sept. 2021.

Reuters. "Kentucky Clerk Who Refused Gay Marriage Licenses Can Be Sued." *NBC NEWS*, NBC UNIVERSAL, 26 Aug. 2019, https://www.nbcnews.com/feature/nbc-out/Porvenir-clerk-who-refused-gay-marriage-licenses-can-be-sued-n1046306 Accessed 10 Sept. 2021.

Reyes, Raul A. "'Porvenir, Texas' Details Massacre of Mexican Americans by U.S. Soldiers, Rangers." *NBCNEWS*, NBC

UNIVERSAL, 27 Sept. 2019, https://www.nbcnews.com/news/latino/Porvenir-texas-details-massacre-mexican-americans-u-s-soldiers-rangers-n1059146. Accessed 9 Sept. 2021.

Riley, Ricky. "13 Mainstream Corporations Benefiting from the Prison Industrial Complex." *Atlanta Black Star,* 10 Oct. 2014, https://atlantablackstar.com/2014/10/10/12-mainstream-corporations-benefiting-from-the-prison-industrial-complex/. Accessed 21 Sept. 2021.

"Robert Mueller Appointed Special Counsel." *CBS NEWS,* CBS Interactive Inc., 17 May 2017, https://www.cbsnews.com/news/doj-appoints-special-counsel-in-wake-of-comey-developments/. Accessed 30 Sept. 2020.

Robbins, Dr. Jeffrey W., and Crockett, Clayton, editors. *Doing Theology in the Age of Trump: A Critical Report on Christian Nationalism.* Cascade Books, eBook, 2009.

Robinson, B.A. "Controversial Comments by Leading Fundamentalist Jerry Falwell 1979-2006." 2006, http://www.religioustolerance.org/falwell.htm. Accessed 13 Nov. 2020.

Robinson, Wills. "Trump 'Ordered for Special Counsel Robert Mueller to Be FIRED a Month After He Began Russia Probe - But Backed Down When Chief White House Lawyer Threatened to Quit over Carrying out the Order.'" *Daily Mail,* 25 Jan. 2018, https://www.dailymail.co.uk/news/article-5314671/Trump-wanted-FIRE-special-counsel-Robert-Mueller.html. Accessed 4 Jun. 2020.

Rogers, Jon and Adu, Aletha. "Why did Donald Trump Pull out of the Iran Nuclear Deal and What Sanctions Are the US Reinstating?" *The Sun*, 16 May 2019, https://www.thesun.co.uk/news/6231230/why-donald-trump-out-iran-nuclear-deal/. Accessed 3 Jan. 2020.

The Rogue Fundagelical. "Jerry Falwell Sr., Laying Racist Foundation." *The Rogue Fundagelical*, 9 May 2019, https://rcwilkinson.com/2019/05/09/jerry-falwell-sr-laying-racist-foundations. Accessed 9 Sept. 2020.

Ross, Allen P. "Genesis." *The Bible Knowledge Commentary: An Exposition of the Scriptures,* edited by John F. Walvoord and Roy B. Zuck, vol. 1, Victor Books, 1985, pp. 41. Print.

Ross, Jr., Bobby. "What is Christian Nationalism?" *The Christian Chronicle*, 30 Oct. 2020, https://christianchronicle.org/what-is-christian-nationalism/. Accessed 11 Jan. 2021.

Rossinow, Doug. "It's Time We Face the Fact That Ronald Reagan Was Hostile to Civil Rights." *History News Network,* Columbian College of Arts & Sciences, George Washington University, 20 Apr. 2015, https://historynewsnetwork.org/article/158887#. Accessed 4 Oct. 2020.

Rothstein, Richard. *The Color of Law: A Forgotten History of How Our Government Segregated America.* Liveright, 2017.

Marcotte, Amanda. "Trump's Failure to Grapple with Covid-19 Problem Is Rooted in the Hollow Gospel of 'Individualism.'" *AlterNet*, 14 May 2020, https://www.alternet.org/2020/05/

trumps-failure-to-grapple-with-the-covid-19-problem-is-rooted-in-the-hollow-gospel-of-individualism/. Accessed 9 June 2020.

Samuels, Brett. "Trump Says He Agrees '100 Percent' with 'Lock Her up' Chants about Clinton." *The Hill*, 16 Oct. 2020, https://thehill.com/homenews/administration/521436-trump-says-he-agrees-100-percent-with-lock-her-up-chants-about. Accessed 2 Nov. 2020.

Satlin, Alana Horowitz. "Trump Sides with Putin Over U.S. Intelligence on Election Meddling." *HuffPost*, BuzzFeed, Inc., 11 Nov. 2017, https://www.huffpost.com/entry/trump-putin-election-hacking_n_5a06de14e4b01d21c83ebdf7. Accessed 12 Jan. 2021.

Schallhorn, Kaitlyn. "Trump Travel Ban: Timeline of a Legal Journey." *Fox News*, 26 June 2018, https://www.foxnews.com/politics/trump-travel-ban-timeline-of-a-legal-journey. Accessed 12 Jan. 2021.

Schenck, Reverend Rob. "What's Gone Wrong with Evangelicals? #7 Abortion and its Politicization." *Revbobschenck.com*, 9 Sept. 2020, https://www.revrobschenck.com/blog/2020/9/7/whats-gone-wrong-with-evangelicals-7-abortion-and-its-politicization. Accessed 10 Nov. 2020.

"Sedition." *The Free Dictionary*. 2003, https://legal-dictionary.thefreedictionary.com/sedition. Accessed 1 Dec. 2020.

Seidel, Andrew. *The Founding Myth: Why Christian Nationalism is Un-American.* Sterling Publishers, 2019.

"Selma Bloody Sunday Attack: Civil Rights Movement." *History.com,* A&E Television Networks, LLC, 6 Mar. 2015, https://www.history.com/news/selma-bloody-sunday-attack-civil-rights-movement Accessed 14 Sept. 2021.

Serwer, Adam. "Lyndon Johnson Was a Civil Rights Hero. But Also a Racist." *MSNBC,* NBC UNIVERSAL, 11 Apr. 2014, https://www.msnbc.com/msnbc/lyndon-johnson-civil-rights-racism-msna305591. Accessed 2 June 2020.

Shackford, Scott. "Trump's Latest Round of Pardons Includes George Papadopoulos, GOP Congressmen, Blackwater Guards." *Reason,* Reason Foundation, 22 Dec. 2020, https://reason.com/2020/12/22/trumps-latest-round-of-pardons-include-george-papadopoulos-gop-congressmen-weldon-angelos/. Accessed 30 Dec. 2020.

Shead, Sam. "Parler CEO Says App Will be Offline 'Longer Than Expected' Because of Amazon, Apple and Google." *NBC New York*, NBC UNIVERSAL, 12 Jan. 2021, https://www.nbcnewyork.com/news/business/money-report/parler-ceo-says-app-will-be-offline-longer-than-expected-because-of-amazon-apple-and-google/2823122/. Accessed 15 Jan. 2021.

Works Cited List

Shirley, Betsy. "The Faith of Jimmy Carter." *America the Jesuit Review*, 11 Apr. 2018, https://www.americamagazine.org/arts-culture/2018/04/11/faith-jimmy-carter. Accessed 11 Sept. 2020.

Siemaszko, Corky. "U.S. Abortion Rate Now at Lowest Level It's Been Since *Roe v. Wade*," *NBC NEWS*, NBC UNIVERSAL, 17 Jan. 2017, https://www.nbcnews.com/news/us-news/u-s-abortion-rate-now-lowest-level-it-s-been-n707791. Accessed 3 Mar. 2020.

Smidt, Remy. "Trump Dismisses His 'Grab Them by the Pussy' Comments Once Again." *BuzzFeed News*, 17 Oct. 2017, https://www.buzzfeednews.com/article/remysmidt/trump-again-dismisses-grab-them-by-the-pussy-comments. Accessed 14 Dec. 2020.

Smietana, Bob. "Christian Author Josh McDowell Steps away from Ministry after Comments about Black Minority Families." *Baptist Press*, 23 Sept. 2021, https://www.baptistpress.com/resource-library/news/christian-author-josh-mcdowell-steps-away-from-ministry-after-comments-about-black-minority-families/ Accessed 28 Sept. 2021.

Smith, Morgan. "Pro-Trump Rioters Tear Down American Flag, Replace It with Trump Flag at U.S. Capitol Building." *MSN.com*, 6 Jan. 2021, https://www.msn.com/en-us/news/politics/pro-trump-rioters-tear-down-american-flag-replace-it-with-trump-flag-at-u-s-capitol-building/ar-BB1cx5Qb. Accessed 7 Jan. 2021.

Solender, Andrew. "Federal Watchdog Finds Trump Advisor Peter Navarro Repeatedly Violated Hatch Act." *Forbes.com*, 7 Dec. 2020, https://www.forbes.com/sites/andrewsolender/2020/12/07/federal-watchdog-finds-trump-adviser-peter-navarro-repeatedly-violated-hatch-act. Accessed 30 Dec. 2020.

Sommerfeldt, Chris. "Pro-Trump Rioters Smeared Poop in U.S. Capitol Hallways During Belligerent Attack." *NYDailynews.com*, 7 Jan. 2021, https://www.nydailynews.com/news/politics/ny-trump-capitol-riot-poopers-20210107-prlsqytyabgdhnexushotl4nam-story.html. Accessed 7 Jan. 2021.

Speegle, Trey. "Racist Southern Socialites – United Daughters of the Confederacy – Rewrote Civil War History (& Remain Active Today)." *World of Wonder*, 4 July 2020, https://worldofwonder.net/how-racist-southern-socialites-the-united-daughters-of-the-confederacy-rewrote-civil-war-history/. Accessed 8 Aug. 2020.

Sprunt, Barbara. "The History Behind 'When the Looting Starts, the Shooting Starts.'" *NPR*, 29 May 2020, https://www.npr.org/2020/05/29/864818368/the-history-behind-when-the-looting-starts-the-shooting-starts. Accessed 15 May 2020.

Stack, Liam. "A Brief History of Deadly Attacks on Abortion Providers." *The New York Times*, 29 Nov. 2015, https://www.nytimes.com/interactive/2015/11/29/

us/30abortion-clinic-violence.html. Accessed 12 Oct. 2020.

Sink, Justin. "Trump Downplays Huge Hack Tied to Russia, Suggests China." *Bloomberg*, 19 Dec. 2020, https://www.bloomberg.com/news/articles/2020-12-19/trump-downplays-massive-hack-floats-china-as-possible-culprit. Accessed 2 Jan. 20201.

Straight Dope Staff. "Was Warren Harding Inducted into the KKK while President? A Staff Report From the Straight Dope Science Advisory Board" *The Straight Dope*, 8 Nov. 2005, https://www.straightdope.com/21343365/was-warren-harding-inducted-into-the-kkk-while-president. Accessed 12 Oct 2020.

Stracqualursi, Veronica. "Trump Signs Executive Order that Critics Warn Politicizes Federal Career Civil Service." *CNN Politics*, 23 Oct. 2020, https://www.cnn.com/2020/10/23/politics/trump-executive-order-federal-employees/index.html. Accessed 30 Oct. 2020.

"The Struggle for Civil Rights: Following World War II, African Americans Demanded Equality before the Law." *UVA Miller Center*, 2021, https://millercenter.org/the-presidency/educational-resources/age-of-eisenhower/struggle-civil-rights. Accessed 9 Nov. 2021.

Swasey, Benjamin. "Trump Retweets Video of Apparent Supporter Saying 'White Power.'" *NPR*, 28 June 2020, https://www.npr.org/sections/live-updates-protests-for-racial-justice/2020/06/28/884392576/

trump-retweets-video-of-apparent-supporter-saying-white-power. Accessed 13 July 2020.

Sweetland Edwards, Haley. "How Christine Blasey-Ford's Testimony Changed America." *Time Magazine*, 4 Oct. 2018, https://time.com/5415027/christine-blasey-ford-testimony/. Accessed 4 Aug. 2020.

Swindoll, Chuck. "Amos." *Insight.org*, Insights for Living Ministries, 2021, https://www.insight.org/resources/bible/the-minor-prophets/amos. Accessed 8 Nov. 20201.

Taylor, Justin. "Is Segregation Scriptural? A Radio Address from Bob Jones on Easter of 1960." *The Gospel Coalition*, 26 July 2016, https://www.thegospelcoalition.org/blogs/evangelical-history/is-segregation-scriptural-a-radio-address-from-bob-jones-on-easter-of-1960/. Accessed 13 Dec. 2020.

Tegna, "Former Trump Attorney Michael Cohen Says He's Cooperating on Multiple Trump Investigations." *We Are Iowa*, 8 Jan. 2021, https://www.weareiowa.com/article/news/nation-world/michael-cohen-trump-investigation-cooperation/507-15dd39cb-5a29-41d5-870f-06c9e6b0ecc7. Accessed 12 Jan. 2021.

Thorbecke, Catherine. "Trump Official Merchandise Stores Removed by Shopify." *ABC News*, ABC News Internet Ventures, 7 Jan. 2021, https://abcnews.go.com/Business/trump-official-merchandise-stores-removed-shopify/story?id=75116903. Accessed 9 Jan. 2021.

Works Cited List

"Treason." *The Free Dictionary*. Farlex, 2003-2021, https://legal-dictionary.thefreedictionary.com/treason. Accessed 30 Oct. 2020

"Trump Administration Revokes Obama Rule Protecting Wetlands and Streams." *The Guardian*, 12 Sept. 2019, https://www.theguardian.com/us-news/2019/sep/12/trump-wetlands-streams-environment-obama-rule. Accessed 12 Jan. 2021.

"Trump Migrant Separation Policy: Children in Cages in Texas." *BBC NEWS*, 18 June 2018, https://www.bbc.com/news/world-us-canada-44518942. Accessed 4 Dec. 2020.

"U.S. Charges Dozens of Parents, Coaches in Massive College Admissions Scandal." *NPR.org*, 12 Mar. 2019, https://www.npr.org/2019/03/12/702539140/u-s-accuses-actresses-others-of-fraud-in-wide-college-admissions-scandal. Accessed 5 Dec. 2020.

"U.S. Public Health Service Syphilis Study at Tuskegee." *Centers for Disease Control and Prevention*, U.S. Department of Health & Human Services, 22 Apr. 2021 https://www.cdc.gov/tuskegee/timeline.htm. Accessed 11 Sept. 2021.

"Vote Common Good," *Vote Common Good*, 2021, https://www.votecommongood.com/what-and-why/. Accessed 2 Nov. 2021.

"Voting Rights Act of 1965." *History.com*, A&E Television Networks, LLC, 9 Nov. 2009, https://www.history.com/topics/black-history/voting-rights-act. 11 Oct. 2020.

Walker, Andrew. "Understanding Why Religious Conservatives Would Vote for Trump." *Nationalreview.com,* 10 Feb. 2020, https://www.nationalreview.com/2020/02/2020-election-religious-conservatives-trump-voters/ Accessed 4 Sept. 2020.

Walker, James. "Doug Collins Reminded Trump 'Attacked' Gold Star Families after Democrats Soleimani Comment." *Newsweek,* 9 Jan. 2020, https://www.newsweek.com/doug-collins-trump-attacked-gold-star-families-democrats-soleimani-iran-1481254. Accessed 5 May 2020.

Wallis, Jim. "Racism Quotes." *Spirituality & Practice,* 2006, https://www.spiritualityandpractice.com/explorations/topics/racism/quotes. Accessed 12 Oct. 2021.

Ward, John. "Evangelicals Opposed to Trump Step out of the Shadows with New Groups and Ads." *Yahoo! News,* 16 Oct. 2020, https://news.yahoo.com/evangelicals-opposed-to-trump-step-out-of-the-shadows-with-new-groups-and-ads-152644503.html. Accessed 15 Nov. 2020.

Watson, Denise. "Slavery and Salvation: Modern Churches Reckon with the History in the Trade." *The Virginian-Pilot,* Tribune Publishing, 2 Aug. 2020, https://www.pilotonline.com/history/vp-db-churches-slavery-08022020-20200802-rqzh6moqobgllpe4idpeonpyje-story.html. 4 Oct. 2020.

Weber, Peter. "Lindsey Graham Is Reportedly back in Trump's 'Good Graces' after Breaking Things Off Last Week." *Yahoo!News*, 14 Jan. 2021, https://news.yahoo.com/lindsey-graham-reportedly-back-trumps-132658529.html. Accessed 15 Jan. 2021.

Whack, Errin. "Who was Edmund Pettus?" *Smithsonianmag.com*, 7 Mar. 2015, https://www.smithsonianmag.com/history/who-was-edmund-pettus-180954501/. Accessed 14 Nov. 2021.

"What is the Sandra Bland Act, and How do I Maximize our Compliance?" *Guardian RFID,* 22 July 2018, https://guardianrfid.com/blog/what-is-the-sandra-bland-act-and-how-do-i-maximize-our-compliance. Accessed 1 June 2020.

"White Nationalist," *SPLC Southern Poverty Law Center*, www.splcenter.org/fighting-hate/extremist-files/ideology/white-nationalist. Accessed 8 Aug. 2021.

Wiersbe, Warren W., *The Bible Exposition Commentary,* edited by David C. Cook, vol. 2, Victor Books, 1996, pp. 136–137. Print.

Williams, Pete. "Supreme Court Hears Why a Baker Refused to Make a Wedding Cake for a Gay Couple," *NBC NEWS*, NBC UNIVERSAL, 5 Dec. 2017, https://www.nbcnews.com/politics/supreme-court/supreme-court-hears-why-baker-refused-make-wedding-cake-gay-n826706. Accessed 2 Jan. 2021.

Williams, Reggie L. *Bonhoeffer's Black Jesus: Harlem Renaissance Theology and an Ethic of Resistance.* Baylor University Press, 2014.

Williams, Yohuru. "The Most Damaging Myths About Slavery Debunked." *History.com,* 6 Feb. 2019, A&E Television Networks. LLC., https://www.history.com/news/debunking-slavery-myths. Accessed 5 May 2020.

Williams, Yohuru. "Why Thomas Jefferson's Anti-Slavery Passage Was Removed from the Declaration of Independence." *History.com,* A&E Television Networks. LLC., 29 June 2020. https://www.history.com/news/declaration-of-independence-deleted-anti-slavery-clause-jefferson. Accessed 31 Aug. 2020.

Yancey, Philip. *What's So Amazing About Grace?* Zondervan, 1997.

Young, Neil. "Reconsidering Reagan's Racism: Trump Is the Culmination of the Gipper's GOP." *Religion Dispatches,* 15 Sept. 2020, https://religiondispatches.org/reconsidering-reagans-racism-trump-is-the-culmination-of-the-gippers-gop/. Accessed 30 Sept. 2020.

Young, Stephen. "Robert Jeffress: Christians Who Don't Back Trump Are Morons, Like Christians in Nazi Germany," *Dallas Observer*, 13 Feb. 2019, https://www.dallasobserver.com/news/dallas-pastor-robet-jeffress-says-anti-trump-christians-are-morons-11561290. Accessed 5 May 2020.

Zirin, James. "The Lawsuit that Changed Donald Trump's Life," *Slate,* The Slate Group, a Graham Holdings Company, 24 Sept. 2019, https://slate.com/news-and-politics/2019/09/plaintiff-in-chief-excerpt-donald-trump-first-lawsuit.html. Accessed 30 Aug. 2020.

www.ingramcontent.com/pod-product-compliance
Lightning Source LLC
Chambersburg PA
CBHW032030290426
44110CB00012B/746